THE

GREAT TRIBULATION;

OR,

THINGS COMING ON THE EARTH

BY

THE REV. JOHN CUMMING, D.D., F.R.S.E.

MINISTER OF THE SCOTTISH NATIONAL CHURCH,
CROWN COURT, COVENT GARDEN.

FIRST SERIES.

"A time of trouble, such as never was since there was a nation."—DAN xii. 1.
"There shall be great tribulation."

NEW YORK:
RUDD & CARLETON, 130 GRAND STREET,
LONDON: RICHARD BENTLEY.
M DCCC LX.

CONTENTS.

PREFACE.

It is impossible for the most thoughtless to overlook the impressive and almost unprecedented character of the age in which we live. Events, as rapid in their succession as they are startling in their magnitude, splendour, and consequences, chase each other like waves on the sea, or fall on us like falling stars on earth of a winter evening.

I stated in "Apocalyptic Sketches" that the last vial—that is, the symbol which denotes the source and measure and duration of the "Great Tribulation"—was, in all probability, poured out in 1848, from which time to 1867 we may expect to feel its intensest effects. Subsequent observation, and comparison of facts as they evolve with the "sure word of prophecy" as it is written, have served to strengthen my conviction of the accuracy of this deduction; and in this volume it is my object to show that the prophecies of the Redeemer enunciated on the Mount of Olives, and other predictions referable to the same category and era, are being daily translated into history. It is under the action of the last vial, which, in order to denote the universality of its effects, was poured "into the air," that we discover those abnormal, physical, political, and social conditions, which persons ignorant of, or hostile to all prophetic investigations, allow to have an intensity and universality, to say the least startling.

Disease, during the last ten years, has steadily struck with destructive blight the potato and the vine, men and cattle, with a force and frequency surely unusual; and the only explanation scientific investigation has arrived at is just that stated in prophecy as the effect of the last vial, a morbific taint or influence in "the air." I do not say there never was before cholera, or diphtheria, or miasma destructive of vegetable life; but surely these influences, all of them the subjects of prophecy, have recently been developed with an intensity, a continuity, and to an extent, and with a concurrence at least most unusual.

Diseases of various types, from the consuming fever of Lisbon in 1857 down to less marked degeneracy of physical health, have been noticed and commented on by physicians. Frequently do they remark that some change, probably in the air, or its *ozone*, or its electricity, has taken place, followed by a weakening of the springs of life. So real is this alteration, that the medical treatment which was proper some ten years ago, is not applicable now. It is no solution of all this to say similar events have occurred in previous years. There is at present an area accumulation and intensity of morbific agencies in the air which no previous year has witnessed. This is, I believe, a fulfilment of the effects of the seventh apocalyptic vial; and men who a few years ago sceptically and scornfully treated this solution, begin at length to recognise at least its high probability.

We have regarded the effect of the pouring of the seventh vial into the air as purely physical. This, however, is but one part of its action—a universal influence is the dominant idea. Has any disturbing action been manifested in other departments of social life?

Let us call to mind the Russian war, of which the Crimea was the centre, while all the European nations either looked on or took part. Here we had the social intercourse and bands and links of nations suddenly shattered, and streams of sorrow and suffering and distress transmitted to countless English firesides. These were alike mysterious and unforeseen.

No sooner was the Russian war covered up, if not quenched, than a quarrel with China, followed by a yet more recent one, that may rise to the dimensions of a great national conflict, broke out. Scarcely had the clouds darkened the sky there, when the most terrible shock our empire ever received occurred in our eastern provinces. A hundred thousand trained and disciplined sepoys, the subjects of the Queen, rose simultaneously against our authority in India, and opposed by a mere handful of heroic men, it seemed doubtful if India could be held. Massacres and murders and barbarities have been inflicted on British men and women and children of unparalleled brutality and cruelty. Never did so many families suffer so severely. Never did a more crushing stroke reach the heart of our nation. Thus, from the pine forests of the North to the palm groves of the East, has the social atmosphere become charged with irritant and disturbing elements, which explode in succession.

Nor is the commercial air less convulsed. During 1857 a commercial panic, called in the *Times* newspaper "a commercial earthquake," smote Europe and America, and house after house, alike old and prudent and reliable, fell. Banks exploded one after another. The prince-merchants of yesterday are penniless to-day; and widows and orphans innumerable have been reduced from comparative competence to absolute beggary.

Let us combine all these shocks, and then reflect if there be not enough to vindicate the interpretation we have endeavoured to establish, that a universal derangement of social and national life,—and, if one might enumerate the incessant murders, suicides, and poisonings with which the papers teem,—of moral life also, is the condition of our world at this moment.

The great earthquake that accompanies the pouring out of this vial occurred in 1848, when Europe reeled like a drunken man, and kings were thrown from their thrones, and even the Pope projected by its force from the Vatican. The disturbances in France, Belgium, Spain, Italy, and Austria, constantly recurring, are its vibrations,—or lesser earthquakes in divers places, not unaccompanied with literal ones also,—as in Naples, Dec. 1857, in which were 9000 killed and 5000 mutilated. These convulsions, graphically and briefly stated as the effects of the pouring out of vial seventh, are enumerated in detail in the prophecy of our Lord on the Mount of Olives. In fact, Matthew xxiv. is the evangelic exposition of the apocalyptic prophecy. This great earthquake, of which that at Naples is only a prefiguration and premonition, is expressed in another shape: "I will shake all nations."

What nation is perfectly quiescent at this moment? Is not France rocking from Boulogne to Bordeaux? Is there not expressed by its rulers, and implied in their stringent enactments, a sense of insecurity? The desperate attempt of Orsini did not create the disquiet—it merely revealed what was suspected and feared. Italy heaves with fires worse than volcanic. Naples is on the eve of insurrection. The partisans of the Pope are already contemplating the removal of the Popedom to Jerusalem. Belgium is agitated with intestine differences. Germany is ill at ease. Russia, recovering from one war, is simply sharpening its sword for another Turkey dies quietly—incidental spasms disturbing its deathbed.

Great changes are passing over the aspect of our own country. China is again stirred to its depth, and its disintegration is begun. Persia enjoys a lull. India, recently torn in pieces by a mutiny become rebellion, and the insurrection of an army, almost the revolution of an empire, has felt effects that must last long. Had we no uneasiness of our own, the scenes of the Crimea, and the more recent events in Lucknow and Delhi and Cawnpore have projected their gigantic shadows, and left a chill as of death on many a warm heart.

What throne in Europe has not felt these successive shocks? What nation on the Continent can be named which is not now undergoing organic change? Everywhere we see the loosening of social bands—the rocking and tilting of thrones—the thirst of change—the restlessness of mind—apparently the throes and agonies of nature groaning and travailing with the birth of a new and nobler genesis. Russia, repulsed, as indicated in Ezekiel, is preparing for her next and victorious march over Constantinople and the seven churches of Asia into Palestine, at that time to be the scene of stupendous marvels and judgments. France, the great actor in the prophetic outline, flushed with her Italian conquests, is reposing in her short bivouac, in order to enter on the arena refreshed and strong as a giant to fulfil her destiny. Austria, furious at defeat and disappointment, longs to avenge her wrongs, and tries by sacrifice to conciliate Hungary. Italy is one huge volcano, still, perhaps, making ready to receive into her fiery bosom the papacy, with all its spoils of plundered nations, and injured kingdoms, and violated rights, and all its sins and its crimes inexpiable for ever.

Our own beloved land may soon be girdled with a belt of fire. Her freedom, her faith, her prosperity, her accessible asylum for the refugee and the oppressed, her gigantic power, her outspoken independence, her trea sures, and her triumphs, are the hate of despots, the envy of courts, and the provocatives of hostility on the part of nations that remember her past superiority, and long to measure swords with her once more. No ordinary events are looming up from every point of the European horizon, like strange birds of evil omen. All the ten years that have passed away, and the seven that still remain of the era of the "Great Tribulation," will cover a time of trouble unprecedented since there was a nation. It is the time when there "shall be great distress of nations, with perplexity," political, social, commercial, and moral—the disintegration of political party, the distrust of trade, the dereliction of moral obligations, confusion of principles, and collision of passions, "the sea and the waves roaring." There also shall be fulfilled and felt what is written in St. Luke, "Men's hearts failing them for fear, and for looking after those things which are coming on the earth, for the powers of heaven shall be shaken."

But Christians are not to be alarmed. "When these things begin to come to pass, then look up and lift up your heads, for your redemption draweth nigh." Our brightest and best things are in reversion. A glorious morning will one day break upon the earth; a rich inheritance will take the place of what will soon pass away. The waves of the "Great Tribulation" will all subside into that quiet bay, on which no tempest shall ever beat, and on whose bosom the sweet sunshine shall sleep for ever.

The lull that now exists among the nations of Europe is very much like that of 1851. It is the eve of more terrible disturbance, and the time of preparation for it. Science and art, and national resources, are tasked in all directions, in order to make the most formidable weapons for offensive and defensive war. The discoveries of modern science, as embodied in the iron rail, the ocean-steamer, and the electric telegraph, will lead to such military gatherings, such concentration of troops, such lightning-like rapidity of action, such shocks of armies, as never were equalled in the history of the world. Everything seems to make ready for no common crisis, no ordinary issue. In the words of Daniel, "there shall be a time of trouble, such as never was since there was a nation." In the words of St. Matthew, "there shall be great tribulation, such as was not since the beginning of the world to this time; no, nor ever shall be." On some, we are told, "wrath is come to the uttermost."

But we must not overlook, in the midst of the coming tribulation, those rays of glory stricken through the clouds, which relieve the density of the night, and indicate beyond the sunshine that sleeps unbroken on the everlasting hills of the heavenly Jerusalem. However sure the tribulation, there are those that "come out of it," and stand resplendent "in white robes," who "shall be purified and made white and tried," who shall "rest and stand in their lot at the end of the days." Of these I have not been unmindful in the lectures which make up this volume. These compose that true Church, the age of which no time tells, the magnitude of which no space includes, and the adherents of which no figures can sum up.

If the first portion of the following lectures deals with the nature and the marks of the "Great Tribulation," the last half has respect to the character, and condition, and hopes, and happiness, and destiny of them who, Dan.el tells us, are blessed,—"Blessed is he that waiteth, and cometh to the thousand three hundred and five and thirty days." There will be found in this part much to cheer and animate, and sustain the people of God in circumstances of unprecedented trouble.

I have shown in previous works, and intimated an opinion not unfrequently in this, that the steady decay of Mahometanism in Europe—that desolating Euphratean flood which several centuries ago overflowed Eastern Christendom—was one of the premonitory symptoms of nearing fulfilment of prophecy.

The following description of this is from the *Times*' correspondent in Sept. 1859:

"The alarming state of the Ottoman empire, which country seems going through a succession of financial somersaults, from which, however, somehow or other, it manages to alight with only an additional contusion, renders the accounts from the provinces truly deplorable; extra taxes being levied on the unfortunate populations, to be redeemed by the imports of future years, while hordes of Albanian Irregulars render the provinces bordering on Greece insecure, and expose the poor inhabitants to every species of extortion and injustice. It is not to be wondered that the old feeling of hatred to the Turkish yoke, which dates from the day that Mahomet II. took possession of Byzantium, should be as much alive as ever. The Christians are replacing everywhere in the East, by a constant and unperceived effort, the Mahometans, who are disappearing; and, under these circumstances, those of the Christian elements which offer some guarantee for the future must naturally attract the attention of Europe. Owing to their religion, the Christian populations of the East consider themselves specially placed under the protection of Russia, and the influence of that power with the Greeks has been generally considered all-powerful."

I have also frequently referred elsewhere to the consuming judgment that now wastes the great Roman Apostasy, and foreshows its nearing ruin. On these I do not dwell in this work.

I hope soon to publish a photographic sketch of the Millennial state, as a companion to this volume.

I need not add that, like all my previous volumes on prophecy, this will receive plenty of that style of secular criticism which consist in scoffs, ridicule, and caricature. The world cannot endure the truths of prophecy. Its argument is, "all things continue as they were." Do not disturb our comforts, our gains, and industry. On such the day of our lord cometh as a thief in the night.

But "to them that look for Him, He will appear the second time unto salvation."

Lord Carlisle, in his little work on Daniel viii.,

expresses his belief that we are nearing the close of our present dispensation; a remark he is not likely to make unless under a deep conviction of its truth. Such an observation from his point of view ought to make secular writers suspect that there is ground of investigation, not matter for merriment and invective, in so sacred and interesting subjects of study.

THE

GREAT TRIBULATION;

OR,

THINGS COMING ON THE EARTH.

LECTURE I.

THE GLORIOUS DELIVERANCE.

"*And at that time shall Michael stand up, the great prince which standeth for the children of thy people: and there shall be a time of trouble, such as never was since there was a nation even to that same time: and at that time thy people shall be delivered, every one that shall be found written in the book.*"—DANIEL xii. 1.

I ACCEPT the generally-received opinion of commentators, that Michael, the prince that standeth for the ancient people of God, is not a created angel, but our Lord and Saviour Jesus Christ. The prophecy seems to imply that having long been seated on his throne as Mediator, interceding in behalf of his own, that man's extremity will become his opportunity; and that he will stand up towards the close of this present Christian economy, amid miracles, and stupendous phenomena, and great and startling issues, in behalf of his cast off, but not finally cast-out people, the remnant of the house of Judah and of Israel. It is plain from the language, "thy people," addressed to Daniel, an inspired prophet, and yet an enthusiastic and patriotic Jew, that the interposition of Christ on this occasion will be primarily in behalf of that remarkable race still preserved, often assailed, but never crushed; like their own burning bush, always blazing, and not consumed; and that the time will come when they, so long cast out, shall at length be grafted in, and restored to their own land; for a Deliverer, as quoted by the Apostle in the Epistle to the Romans, shall come out of Sion, and shall turn away ungodliness from all the children of Jacob. "Thy people," therefore, are primarily the Jews. Nobody can read their history without seeing they are the standing miracle of the age; the inexplicable phenomena of Providence, unless beheld in the only light which casts splendour on the past, and a gleaming and brightening glory on the future, the sure word of God's prophecy. The Jews are found in every capital on earth; least at home in their own; having property everywhere, except in that land which is theirs by title-deeds, in comparison of which those of England's proudest and mightiest noble are but of yesterday; and when one sees them on our streets, or, as I have done, joined with them in singing the beautiful Hebrew Psalms of David in their own synagogue, one cannot help seeing even on their faces an air of melancholy, as if it were the shadow of a great ancestral crime, which eighteen hundred years of suffering have been utterly unable to wash away. They speak all tongues; they are found on the banks of the Thames, the Danube, the Rhine, the Tiber, the Mississippi, the Missouri, the Ganges—everywhere; and yet they never seem to be at home; they are what the poet has called them, "the race of the weary foot," running from themselves, as if to get rid of the recollection of some deed of blood that has stained their hands, and left its indelible imprint upon the hearts of even the most benevolent of them all. If we read the treatment they have received, we see how willing man is to fulfil prophecy where he has no business. When the priests of Rome have been asked, Why do you so maltreat the Jews? when some of our ancient kings, who extracted their teeth in order to extort their gold, were questioned why they did so, they devoutly, or rather hypocritically said, Why, God has pronounced a curse upon them, that they shall be a by-word and a scoff among all people. In other words, man's own lusts, and passions, and thirst of gold made him particularly anxious to help God to fulfil his prophecy, but left it very inconvenient for him to obey the precepts of mercy and of loving-kindness.

There is no place upon earth, I believe, where at this moment they are worse treated than in that very city in which sits a personage most uncomfortably situated at the present moment, who calls himself the Vicar of Christ. There the poor Jews are thrust into a wretched, miserable quarter of imperial Rome called the Ghetto; they are made to pay a heavy tax every year in order to be suffered to exist under even the shadow and in the miserable dungeon of that so-called Holy City and capital of Christendom. A maid-servant, who did not know the meaning of the words she uttered, took hold of a young child, Mortara, dropped a little water on his brow, and uttered in Latin, "I baptize thee in the name of the Father, and of the Son, and of the Holy Ghost." The moment that the parents, who were Jews, went to get their child, what were they told? The Inquisitor-General told them that the mark of the Redeemer was upon that child's brow, and that no power upon earth could compel them to give it back. Sir Moses Montefiore, much to his credit, went as a deputation from his own Church to Rome; got an audience from Cardinal Antonelli; asked him if he would interpose, for he is the real Pope; the other one behind the scenes is a poor, helpless, old man. Antonelli told him to call again; put him off—that is the diplomacy of that latitude; he would see about it. Sir Moses had to wait week after week, hoping against hope; at last he asked if he could have an interview with Pio Nono. At once Antonelli told him it could not be given; that the child was a Christian; that it never could be restored to its mother; she may see it through iron bars, or through a window; but she never can indulge the instincts of a mother, and clasp to her bosom the boy that she knows and feels to be her own. Such is the conduct of the Vicar of Christ, so called, in that capital which one would think would be the most illustrious in the world for its justice and its mercy; but in reference to the Jew it seems to be the most cruel, proscriptive, and persecuting of all. We of England are only second better off; for our own prince, the Prince of Wales, nobly thinking that when in Rome English people ought not to be ashamed of being English people—gave a fine contradiction to the wretched sophistry, that when we are in Rome let us do as Rome does, and in Constantinople as Constantinople does—the Prince of Wales, instead of doing as Rome does, went to his English Church. And where is it, do you think? In an old stable outside the walls of Rome; it being thought a pollution to that sacred capital that an English Protestant Church should be suffered within its walls. But this, however, refers to us; we can bear the persecution; the poor Jew cannot so well bear it.

At this period of trouble Christ interposes; having no sympathy with him that assumes to represent Him, and stands up amidst stupendous miracles of mercy and of unobliterated love in behalf of a people persecuted, a by-word, a scoff, and a hissing among all nations; restores them to their land; replaces them in their ancient and illustrious capital; and oh! it is a sight that one would travel from London to Jerusalem to see—a whole nation restored to Palestine, prostrate at the feet of the Prince of Peace; and in their own magnificent tongue—that mother-tongue from which all others are but distant and debilitated progenies—and with their own deep, musical, Oriental voices lifting up, as the voice of many waters, and as the voice of a great thunder, and as the voice of many peoples, those words of the English Liturgy, "Thou art the King of Glory, O Christ. When thou tookest upon thee to deliver mankind, thou didst not abhor the virgin's womb; when thou hadst overcome the sharpness of death, thou didst open the kingdom of heaven to all believers. Thou sittest at the right hand of God the Father. We," children of Israel, "believe that thou wilt come to be our Judge. O Lamb of God, that takest away the sins of the world, take away the sins of thy people Israel;" and where our fathers said "Crucify him!" we shout "Hosannah!" and where they said, in their ignorance, "Away with him!" we will join and lift the anthem peal that will never cease, "Blessed is he that cometh in the name of the Lord. Lo, this is our God; we have waited for him. Hosannah in the highest!" Such will be fact. My expectation is not fancy, but the inference from the soberest, the barest, the most frequently-repeated prophecy.

But when this takes place, there will be a time of great trouble. "At that time there will be a time of such trouble as has not been on the earth since there was a nation;" and which is stated in the New Testament to be a time of such trouble that there never will be any trouble equal to it. We have that time of trouble delineated in St. Matthew, where, after some portraits of the judgments upon Jerusalem, he gives a reference, clear and unmistakeable, to the close of this present economy. The great time of trouble began in 1848: in other words, it synchronises with the pouring out of the seventh vial; at which the first shock of the great European earthquake occurred: its succeeding shocks still steadily occur, year after year. Review at your leisure the events that have transpired since that time. Why, we are no sooner out of one trouble—I mean the world—than we are plunged into another. In 1849, Europe, Asia, America, were desolated by an overwhelming pestilence; in 1850, Rome, anticipating its ruin, made its last spasmodic grasp or clutch at the sceptre of England, if perchance it might retain a last footing before it goes down into the depths of ruin. In 1851, we had a bright glimpse, by way of symbol, earnest, or type of millennial peace. Then, after that, we had the first hint of the complications in the East; then, from 1854, a war which has sent streams of bitterness into many a happy English home, and left cold shadows upon many a once-bounding English heart. The dead that sleep in the distant Crimea will not soon be forgotten; and I trust the memories of the brave that fell there will never come before us without thanks and gratitude for those that so heroically fought, and many of them so hopefully and piously fell. No sooner had the Russian war been closed, than the great Indian storm burst upon Asia; an empire was in peril; and again how many homes have lost their brightest lights in consequence of that cruel, atrocious, and murderous outburst of a deceived, infatuated, and misguided native population! No sooner had that been lulled, by God's blessing on the heroism of our troops, and the sagacious diplomacy of those who had to rule the storm, than, like a thunder-cloud, we saw all Europe mustering to battle; and upon the beautiful plains of Italy half a million of men meet in deadly conflict, and thousands are numbered with the dead. I stated before, what many thought was impossible, that Russia's destiny was the East. We read in some of the papers, on what authority I don't know, but I infer from the quarter it must be right, that Russia now combines with France; and two such powerful autocrats would seem to be a match for the whole world.

I believe that our own land, whatever be the combination that girdles—even as if it should girdle it with fire—is destined to emerge comparatively unscathed from the conflict; and old England's sun will not set till it mingles with the splendours of that sun that shall have no cloud and no western declension. We separated from the great Apostacy at the Reformation, and God has blessed us ever since, and God will bless us still; and I believe, with all our faults—and we dare not deny them, and we would not conceal them—there is in the depth of our nation a piety, a living religion, unprecedented in its history, and with which no other nation in its spiritual condition can for one moment be compared.

What a change has passed upon the nobility, the middle classes, and through the instrumentality of city missions, ragged schools, and all the noble instrumentalities that God in his great goodness has called into play, upon the poorer classes also! All these things are the commencement of a work that neither Russia, Austria, nor France, nor the whole world, will be able to crush; and if ten righteous men in

Sodom could have saved it from the flames, ten times ten thousand in the heart of our country will shield it in the great tribulation that is coming on the nations of the earth. I may mention as a very striking proof of the position we now occupy, that in Rev. xix. there is a picture which I think refers to that very restoration of the Jews, of which I have been speaking. We read first of all that the great corrupter of the earth, the Romish apostacy, is judged; and when her smoke rises up for ever, the nations sing, Alleluia. The Rev. Mr. Elliot observes, that this is the first Hebrew word that occurs in the songs of the Apocalypse, and he thinks from that word being introduced on this occasion and at this date it indicates that the Jew is present with the Gentile praising God for all his mercies and his judgments. And then a voice, we are told, came out of the throne; a recitative, to use a musical expression; a single voice comes out of the throne, addressed to Jew and Gentile: "Praise our God, all ye his servants, and ye that fear him, both small and great." Then hear the grand response: "And I heard as it were the voice of a great multitude," the grandest music of all. To hear ten thousand people sing the 100th Psalm, or even five thousand, or two thousand, is far grander than all the organ stops that were ever let loose; the voice of a great multitude is the grandest and most thrilling music of all. "As the voices of many waters." Did you ever stand upon the beach, even on a summer evening, and listen to that deep under tone of the ocean praising God? Did you ever stand upon the rocks and hear it when it lifts its great waves to the sky, and they like white-robed choristers unite in praising God? "As the voice of many waters, and as the voice of mighty thunderings, saying, Alleluia;" here again the Hebrew word; "for the Lord God omnipotent reigneth." Now at this very time, mark you, when the judgments come upon the great apostacy, where you hear the voice of the Jew clear and unmistakeable in the great anthem peal, you will find at the close of the chapter a picture of the tribulation which Daniel makes synchronous with these two grand events. "I saw heaven opened, and behold a white horse; and he that sat upon him was called Faithful and True, and in righteousness he doth judge and make war. And he was clothed with a vesture dipped in blood:" the language of awful conflict. "And out of his mouth goeth a sharp sword, that with it he should smite the nations; and he shall rule them with a rod of iron; and he treadeth the wine-press of the fierceness and wrath of Almighty God." And then mark what takes place: "And I saw the beast"—the wild beast, the symbol of the great western apostacy—"and the kings of the earth, and their armies, gathered together to make war against him that sat on the horse, and against his army." And what was the issue? "And the beast was taken, and with him the false prophet"—the exponent of his voice, the priesthood—"that wrought miracles before him. These both were cast alive into a lake of fire burning with brimstone." The word *brimstone* is derived from the German, and means simply *burning stone.* "And the remnant were slain with the sword of him that sat upon the horse, which sword proceeded out of his mouth." Now, that chapter seems evidently to synchronise with the verse on which I have now been commenting in Daniel xii. Well, then, "All thy people shall be delivered;" that is, in the midst of the judgments which I have delineated, or rather, which I have read, God's ancient people, if this refers to the Jews, as I think it does, as well as the first clause, "shall be delivered." And the Apostle, speak ing of this very event, makes the striking remark, "If the casting away of the Jews has been the reconciling of the world, what shall the receiving of them be but life from the dead?" All Israel, he says, shall be saved; and God shall turn away ungodliness from Jacob. The branches that were broken off shall be grafted in, and God's goodness as well as severity shall be exhibited in their case.

But if we refer this to God's own people, which I think we may safely do, then "all shall be delivered that are found written in the book." What book? First, the book of life, impenetrable to us; that secret and mysterious record no human eye can see, no finger can touch or turn over. All attempts of men to specify who are the elect of God have always recoiled upon themselves in disappointment and confusion. Secondly, the book of remembrance. Malachi speaks of a book of remembrance. What is written in that book? Every cup of cold water you have given a disciple, every tear you have shed for Christ's sake, every prayer you have offered, every effort you have made, every donation you have given to make the world wiser and happier for your having passed through it. And then, thirdly, the book of revelation. In it you do not find your names; but you find what is far better, your character. If you find yourselves among the meek, among the merciful, among the holy, among the trusting, among the believing, you need not doubt that your name is written in the mysterious book of life.

So then, from the whole of this tribulation the people of God are safe. "Neither life nor death shall be able to separate us from the love of God that is in Christ Jesus." When these things begin to come to pass, when the great tribulation comes, when the earthquake rolls, and dynasties are smitten from their thrones, and scattered as drift-wood upon the streams and currents of time, you are not to be afraid, but lift up your heads, for your redemption draweth nigh. While you listen on the ground, and try to hear in the distance the tramp of approaching conflict, remember that the world's greatest tribulation is the hour of the Christian's most magnificent deliverance. Preparing for that age, lay up in your hearts a capital of sunshine; when dark days come that sunshine will brighten you; and in the darkest night and at eventide it will be light with you. Let us learn that nothing we desire to preserve, or that God has made, will be injured in that great tribulation. Sin will be expunged; who wants to keep it? Sickness will disappear; who desires to retain it? Sorrow will flee away, and hearts that are now broken will then be bounding; who wishes it to be otherwise? All that God has made, from the star in the sky to the flower upon the field, from the ephemeral insect in the sunbeam to the archangel that worships by the throne, all shall be retained; what has gone wrong shall be made right, what Satan has usurped shall be taken from his grasp; and this weary world of ours, that has wept, and groaned, and suffered so long, shall be emancipated from its thraldom, reinstated in more than its pristine magnificence and beauty, and the world close with a paradise vastly more magnificent and beautiful than that with which it began.

LECTURE II.

THE DOOMED CITY.

We read in the inspired Record of the glory and the gloom of the "City of the Great King"—the joy of the whole earth, Jerusalem.

"*Jesus went out, and departed from the temple: and his disciples came to him for to show him the buildings of the temple. And Jesus said unto them, See ye not all these things? verily I say unto you, There shall not be left here one stone upon another, that shall not be thrown down. And as he sat upon the mount of Olives, the disciples came unto him privately, saying, Tell us, when shall these things be?*" *&c.*—MATTHEW xxiv. 1—6.

IT may prove conducive to the comfort and edification of many, if I now direct attention to some of the leading truths of that grand prophecy, spoken under the shadow of the temple by the Great Prophet, seated on the Mount of Olives, and surrounded by his disciples, half instructed in the nature of the kingdom, but not insensible to their need of additional light.

In this prophecy is much relating to scenes long passed away—the fall of Jerusalem, the joy and the beauty of the whole earth; and the destruction of her magnificent temple, not eclipsed by the Parthenon, the glory of ancient Greece. This prophecy consists partly of predictions relating to the ruin of the temple and the city of Jerusalem; and partly of prophecies at this moment passing into history, and partly of predictions of events, near but still future; and closing with that great epoch when the Son of man shall send his angels with a great sound of a trumpet, and gather his elect together from the four winds, from one end of heaven unto the other. It appears to me, that the design of our Lord's discourse is to convince the Jews that the end of their polity was not the end of the world. For this purpose he shows that far more stupendous phenomena will usher in the last great catastrophe of the earth. This is not the common, but it is no less the true explanation. The question of the disciples naturally divides into three parts. In verse third they say, "Tell us, when shall these things be?" What things? What he had stated in the previous chapter, where he says, in the 36th verse, "All these things shall come upon this generation;" while he breaks forth into one of the most tender and touching appeals to the very inmost heart of Jerusalem, that ever fell from divine or human lips. "O Jerusalem, Jerusalem, thou that killest the prophets, and stonest them which are sent unto thee, how often would I have gathered thy children together, even as a hen gathereth her chickens under her wings, and ye would not! Behold, your house is left unto you desolate. For I say unto you, Ye shall not see me henceforth"—implying that they would see him one day—"till ye shall say, Blessed is he that cometh in the name of the Lord." The disciples, having heard the startling announcement, that the glory of Jerusalem should fade, and that the magnificent temple should be laid in ruins, ask three distinct questions:—First, "Tell us, when shall these things be?" secondly, "What shall be the sign of thy advent, and the signal of thy personal presence and appearance?" and thirdly, "What shall be the sign of the end of the world;—the sign of the finishing up together, the ending up together, of this dispensation?" in which we play a part, being preliminary to that dispensation, when the knowledge of the Lord shall cover the whole earth as the waters of the ocean cover the channels of the great deep.

The Great Prophet proceeds to answer these three questions; and a very careful scrutiny of the whole chapter will show where he responds to the one, and where he replies to the other; although sometimes the approaching ruin of the Jewish economy seems to interlace with and to embosom foreshadows of the approaching ruin of the Gentile economy, and the establishment of Christ's kingdom over all the kingdoms of this world. In the first six verses there is sketched the prophetic portrait of the ruin of the temple and city of Jerusalem. Previous to that, "Many shall come, saying, 'I am Messiah,' whom the Jews were looking for; and they shall deceive many. And ye shall hear of wars and rumours of wars; see that ye be not troubled; for all these things must come to pass, but"—referring to the last of the three questions—"the end is not yet." Then he proceeds from the 7th verse to the close of the 14th, to tell them what shall be the fore-signs of the end of the dispensation. He says, before the end of the temple you will hear of wars and rumours of wars, but the end of the world is not yet come. "For," he says,—mark the word, the illative, in the 7th verse—"for," that is, previous to the end of the world, "nation shall rise against nation;"—very different from "wars and rumours of wars;"—"and kingdom against kingdom; and there shall be famines, and pestilences, and earthquakes, in divers places. All these are the beginning of sorrows;" that is, the beginning of tha, travail which the apostle alludes to, when he says, "All creation groans and travails in pain, waiting to be delivered." "Then shall they deliver you up to be afflicted, and shall kill you;" that is—for he is speaking to the Christian disciples, not to the Jews—"they shall kill you; and ye shall be hated of all nations for my name's sake. And then shall many be offended, and shall betray one another, and shall hate one another. And many false prophets shall rise, and shall deceive many. And because iniquity shall abound, the love of many shall wax cold. But," he adds, "he that shall endure unto the end, the same shall be saved." And then he gives what may be called the very alarm-bell that sounds the last epochs of this dispensation; and shows that the last sands that have sparkled so long as the suns of time are about to run out; "This gospel of the kingdom shall be preached in all the world,"—not, and all the world shall be converted; that is not said;—but it shall be preached in all the world "for a witness unto all nations: and then," the moment this is accomplished, "shall the end come." From the 15th verse down to the 20th, he returns to the approaching catastrophe of Jerusalem and the Jewish polity, where he says, "When ye therefore shall see the abomination of desolation, spoken of by Daniel the prophet, stand in the holy place, then let them which be in Judea flee into the mountains; let him which is on the house-top not come down to take anything out of his house; neither let him which is in the field return back to take his clothes. And woe unto them that are with child, and to them that give suck in those days. But pray ye that your flight be not in the winter, neither on the Sabbath day." But he shows that these things are nothing to the great events that shall usher in the last and closing catastrophe; "for *then*," he says, "shall be great tribulation, such as was not since the beginning of the world to this time, no, nor ever shall be. And except those days should be shortened, there should no flesh be saved: but for the elect's sake those days shall be shortened. Then if any man shall say unto you, Lo, here is Christ, or there; believe it not. For there shall arise false Christs, and false prophets, and shall shew great signs and wonders; insomuch that, if it were possible, they shall deceive the very elect. Behold, I have told you before. Wherefore if they shall say unto you, Behold, he is in the desert; go not forth; Behold he is in the secret chambers; believe it not. For," he says, the advent of Christ shall be of this sort, "as the lightning cometh out of the east, and shineth even unto the west; so shall also the coming of the Son of man be. Immediately after the tribulation of those days"—he has given you the beginning of sorrows,—"shall the sun be darkened, and the moon shall not give her light, and the stars shall fall from heaven, and the powers of the heavens shall be shaken; and then shall appear the sign of the Son of man in heaven;"—they asked, "What shall be the sign of thy coming?"—"and then shall all the tribes of the earth mourn, and they shall see the Son of man coming in the clouds of heaven, with power and great glory. And he shall send his angels with a great sound of a trumpet, and they shall gather together his elect from the four winds, from one end of heaven to the other."

After employing a parable in the 25th chapter to illustrate this great event, and showing the practical instruction which the anticipation of it should leave, he refers back, as in the 31st verse, to the 31st verse of the 24th chapter; the interrening passage being altogether an illustration. Passing from the 24th chapter at the 31st verse, to the 25th chapter at the 31st verse, he says, "When the Son of man shall come in his glory, and all the holy angels, then shall he sit upon the throne of his glory; and before him shall be gathered all nations: and he shall separate them one from another, as a shepherd divideth his sheep from the goats; and he shall set the sheep on his right hand, but the goats on the left. Then shall the King say unto them on his right hand, Come, ye blessed of my Father, inherit the kingdom prepared for you from the foundation of the world." Thus we ascertain the three great answers to the three great questions; first, "When shall these things be?" of which I will briefly speak; secondly, "What shall be the sign of the approach of thy presence?" and thirdly, "When shall be the end or the winding-up of that dispensation which thou hast come to introduce into the world, and to reveal to thy church?"

In the following observations I will first illustrate the desolation predicted to overtake Jerusalem and its magnificent temple. That temple was one of the great wonders of the world. Nations came and gazed with admiration on its magnificence. Its roof was covered with plates of burnished gold, reflecting the sun beams with so great splendour and intensity that it was said no bird could light upon it or bear the excess of glory. Some of the stones with which it was built were forty-five yards long, and many of them of the purest and most beautiful marble. Knit together with all the skill of a master-builder, it appeared to the disciples and to the Jews impossible that any force which man could wield, or any undermining that ingenuity could employ, would ever succeed in reducing to ruin so glorious a structure—so gigantic an edifice, strong in its material grandeur, and stronger in the affections of a people that loved and almost worshipped it, and stronger still as they believed—but most mistakenly believed—beneath the everlasting protection of the God of Israel. For our blessed Lord, a man of sorrows—despised by the great ecclesiastical officers, denounced by the Sanhedrim—chief in a group of fishermen and tax-gatherers, to seat himself under the shadow of that ancient and gorgeous fabric, and to launch this prophecy upon the winds—"In forty years not one stone of it, forty-five yards in length they may be, and of weight inconceivable, shall be left upon another that shall not be thrown down"—was either the evidence of fanaticism, or of the words of the mighty God, the Prince of Peace. In forty years we read all that the Saviour said came to pass; the walls of the temple were levelled with the dust; the plough-share was literally drawn with numberless horses through the ruins of the illustrious fabric; and that remarkable race, long forsaken but not yet forgotten, projected by the terrible convulsion in countless fragments over all the world, are at this moment to be found everywhere, disorganized—disintegrated yet distinct—each fragment reflecting unspent rays of a glory that has passed away, but prophetic, also, of a splendour, a glory, and an elevation that eye hath not seen, and tongue hath not told, and heart hath not conceived—their heritage in reversion. The most depressed amid the nations of the earth now, they shall be the glory of all nations, and their city Jerusalem once more the beauty and the joy of the whole earth, and Palestine the most prolific and pre-eminent of all lands. This will be accomplished in the outset, in all probability, by human means, Britain taking a leading part.

Who does not sometimes gather from the teeming years

as they pass presentiments and earnests of the apprcaching deliverance? The war that closed at Sebastopol began about Jerusalem. The supposed sepulchre of the Prince of Peace became the source of a war that convulsed all Europe. If it be true, as prophecy seems to indicate and history to attest, that the great river Euphrates—that is, the Mahometan flood and superstition—is rolling back to its source, and that Turkey in Europe is to be a Christian nation, and the mosque of St. Sophia to ring with the accents of Christ and him crucified, if not glorified—when that dynasty is dissolved, Palestine, which is now the property of the Sultan, will be somebody's; and who has so great a right to it as that princely race who at this moment wait, and long, and pray, and write upon their tablets in their synagogues the prayer that the Messiah would soon come and take Israel home, and make Jerusalem again the city of the Great King?

Without entering upon this tempting subject, I would specify some of the lessons taught by this most remarkable prophecy of the fall of Jerusalem and its Temple. How frail is the greatest fabric that man can build; how sure is the least word that God has spoken! The Parthenon, the glory of Greece, is now a crumbling ruin; the gigantic monuments that the Pharaohs left to be their burial-places are sinking day by day in the sands of the desert; the temple of Jerusalem, that took ages and the wealth of princes to build, retains scarcely a fragment of its magnificence, if we may except, perhaps, one huge stone close by the Mosque of Omar, between thirty and forty yards in length, and demonstrably one of the stones of the ancient temple, worn hollow by the kisses of grey-haired and venerable rabbis, who year after year kneel at it and kiss it, as if to fulfil the prediction of the Psalmist, "Thy saints take pleasure in her stones; her very dust is dear to them." What is thus proved true of material glory is no less true of all social greatness unsanctified by Christian grace. What is Tyre, the princess of the ancient commercial world? A bleak rock for fishermen to bleach their nets on. What is Rome, whose very name made barbarians tremble? To say, "I am a Roman citizen," was to assert immunity and protection everywhere. The seat of a superstitious and fanatical despot priest. What is Athens, once the eye of Greece—the university of the world, the haunt of men of taste, and genius, and scholarship? A mere nest of bandits, that cannot appreciate its magnificent ruins, and would sell them all as readily as Esau his birthright for a mess of pottage. Our own nation has no immortality apart from character. With all its sins and its faults, it has, I think, a brilliant destiny before it. At the Reformation it separated from the ten kingdoms under the papacy; it has been the great protesting country ever since, where freedom finds a foothold, humanity a champion, and religion the holiest and the purest altar. It is a happy hope—God grant that it may be a true one—that the sun of Britain may shine with advancing splendour until its beams mingle with the rays of the millennial sun, and it ceases to be Britain, Great Britain, only because it is absorbed in the greater glory of the Church and the kingdom of Christ.

It is the sins of nations that sap their strength and dim their glory. What ruined the temple? Not Titus and Vespasian, but the sins of them that worshipped by its altar. What laid in ruins Babylon, Tyre, Rome, Athens? The sins of the people that were in them. What overturned the Seven Churches of Asia? What destroyed the once prosperous Church of Africa? what has made the Church of Rome a wreck, a mere miserable wreck? The sins of them that were its rulers and its people? What can ruin us? Not all the Cossacks of the Don; not all the Russians from their steppes; not all France, and Germany, and Austria; not savage Mussulman, and infuriate Sepoy, nor the wide world combined against us. Let us be true to our religion, our Bibles, our responsibilities, our duties, and our God, and our country will flourish in immortal youth.

The whole earth itself is to be involved in a yet greater catastrophe than that which overtook Jerusalem, and Rome, and Athens, and Tyre, and the Seven Churches of Asia. Peter tells us, "The day of the Lord cometh as a thief in the night, in which the heavens shall pass away with a great noise and the elements shall melt with fervent heat, and the works that are therein shall be burned up;" and then he adds that most practical lesson—"Seeing then that all these things must be dissolved, what manner of persons ought ye to be in all holy conversation and godliness?" When the disciples asked, "What shall be the sign of the end of the world?" our blessed Lord did not say, "That is a curious question that you have no right to ask;" on the contrary, he accepted the question as legitimate, and he proceeded to answer it. The only answer he did not give was the day, the hour, the date; these he did not specify: but the moral signs and prefigurations of the approach of that era he lays down with a minuteness so specific that he that reads may run while he reads. He says, before the destruction of Jerusalem, "Many shall come in my name, saying, I am Christ." Open the page of Josephus, the historian, and you will find it stated that Jerusalem swarmed with pretended Messiahs, all of whose testimony was one—

namely, that if the Jews would only believe in them, they would deliver them from the Romans, and from the impending destruction by Titus and Vespasian. This seems to be a great law of God, that men who reject the truth are given up to believe a lie; men that refuse Christ, the only Messiah, are found to accept the most monstrous absurdities. A grey-haired and aged skeptic, whose wild theories for the regeneration of the world have given him a notoriety not to be envied, after denouncing Christianity in language too severe and unhallowed to be repeated, gave himself up to what he thinks the more rational religion of consulting what is doing in heaven above, and hell beneath, and in the future ages to come by table-rapping and spirit-divining. The men who profess to be so rational that they will not accept the pure and sublime faith of Jesus, become the victims of such irrationality that they believe in old wives' fables, lying legends, and delusions that common sense must reprobate and scorn Our Lord foretold that before the fall of Jerusalem there should be "wars and rumours of wars." These took place, for we read that province rose against province, governor against governor, and internal and internecine quarrels were rapidly depopulating that once populous and magnificent land. But these words, "Nation shall rise against nation, and kingdom against kingdom," were not fulfilled previous to the ruin of the Jewish dynasty. "Rumours of wars" related to the downfall of Jerusalem; but "nation rising against nation, and kingdom against kingdom," did not take place previous to the fall of Jerusalem. Greswell, who writes upon the New Testament with all the skill, the learning, and the sobriety of an accomplished scholar, one of the ablest living divines we have, observes, "There is no instance of any war answering to this description"—namely, "Nation shall rise against nation, and kingdom against kingdom"—"prior to the rupture between the Jews and the Roman government, which ended in the destruction of Jerusalem, and that war happened too late in the period to serve the purpose of a sign, besides being the very event which every sign beforehand enumerated was designed to specify and to forebode." Therefore we are satisfied that nothing occurred previous to the destruction of Jerusalem at all sufficient to exhaust the prophecy, "Nation shall rise against nation."

Our blessed Lord proceeds to another section of the chapter, and tells us what should precede the destruction of Jerusalem, namely, "When ye shall see the abomination of desolation, spoken of by Daniel." This prophecy occurs in Daniel ix. 26, and it might be literally translated thus,—"Upon the battlements shall be the idol of desolation," as, indeed, it is in the margin, which is always the most close and accurate rendering. Now, says our Lord, "the moment you shall see Daniel's idol of desolation upon the battlements of your city, then let them which be in Judea flee into the mountains; let him which is on the house-top not come down to take anything out of his house; neither let him which is in the field turn back to take his clothes. And woe unto them that are with child, and to them that give suck in those days." Now this fact we find literally fulfilled. The Roman eagles were the standards of that people; they were also the idols and the gods that they gave worship and adoration to. Now, we read in heathen and pagan story, that in A.D. 64, the Roman general encompassed Jerusalem, and so far penetrated into the city that he planted the Roman eagles on the very walls adjacent to the Temple itself; that then, owing to some event not explained, he suddenly retreated, after he had planted the eagles upon the walls of Jerusalem; and it was during his retreat and the withdrawal of his army from the siege, that all the Christians then in Jerusalem rushed out, recognising the predicted sign of Daniel, and found shelter in Pella, till the desolation and the tribulation had passed away. This part, therefore, was strictly and literally fulfilled, and relates to Palestine alone. In the parallel passage of the Gospel of Luke—for each Gospel gives us as it were its own peculiar and characteristic account of each transaction—in Luke xxi. 24, we read that "the Jews shall fall;" that is, when Jerusalem falls, "by the edge of the sword, and shall be led away captive into all nations; and Jerusalem shall be trodden down of the Gentiles, until the times of the Gentiles be fulfilled." The moment that Jerusalem fell the Jews were carried away captives; and upon the arch of Titus at Rome, at this moment, well known and frequently alluded to as the triumphal arch, there is the picture of the sacred things of the Jews, raised to commemorate the triumph of Rome over that obstinate and rebellious race, and the utter desolation of all its glory by the removal of its most sacred and solemn symbols. And then "Jerusalem," it says, "shall be trodden under foot." Now what is its condition? Once it was the most fertile land in the world; its wine, its corn, and its oil were all but proverbs everywhere; its mountain sides were arranged into terraces; and the fruits of every clime, from those of our own northern to those of more favoured southern lands, were raised upon its terraces in succession upwards to the skies. Palestine seemed to retain lingering on its bosom the last unshaded beams of Paradise, and to have mingling with its air the very atmosphere of Eden, yet unexhausted and undestroyed. But what is its condition now—speaking from the testimony of others? All its fertility is gone; its terraces that rose up its mountain sides are rent and torn by the lightning and the earthquake; its rocks are exposed and laid bare, and its soil washed away by floods and storms; its early and its latter rain at this moment is literally powder and dust; the plagues of the land that were predicted are realities; its cities are cities of the dead; there is but a thin and a scattered population anywhere; the Arab robber is its actual governor, the Sultan its nominal one. Commerce will not embark its capital in Palestine; emigrants find safety anywhere than there. What a change has passed upon that glorious land since Moses looked upon it from Mount Nebo, and since the spies brought from it the grapes of Eshcol, that struck with admiration those that for the first time beheld them! If we turn to its people, literally, in the words of the prophet, they are plucked off from the face of the whole earth.

Chateaubriand, who visited Palestine, and has written perhaps the most eloquent picture of its present desolation, uses such language as the following respecting it. "If I should live a thousand years I can never forget that desert when Jerusalem first appeared, and which seemed still inspired with the majesty of Jehovah. When the guide exclaimed, 'Behold the holy city—Jerusalem!' I did not at first know what it was. I believed it to be only a mass of shattered rock."

"The flaming monotonous sunshine above, and the rocky wastes beneath realize too faithfully Deut. xxviii. 3. 'Thy heavens over thee shall be as brass, and the earth under thee as iron. The Lord shall make the rain of thy land powder and dust.' No river nor any stream flows by, no fertility surrounds it, no commerce seems able to approach its walls, no thoroughfare of nature finds the way to it. Her palaces are ruins, her hotels dreary convents, and her chief boast and triumph is a tomb."—*The Crescent and the Cross.*

Robinson says, "The houses of Jerusalem are built on mountains of rubbish twenty or fifty feet above the natural level. Nobody seems to make repairs as long as his dwelling does not absolutely refuse him shelter. If one room tumbles about his ears he removes to another, and permits rubbish and vermin to accumulate in deserted halls."

Lamartine says, "Jerusalem is the Queen of the Desert. Every local name retains in it some mystery, every cavern speaks of futurity, each rocky height reverberates the accents of some prophecy. The wasted rivers, the cloven rocks, and the yawning tombs attest the prodigy. The desert seems still stricken dumb with horror, as if it had not yet dared to break the silence which was felt when the voice of the Eternal had been heard."

Such is the portrait of Jerusalem. Now if I were to quote prophecy after prophecy predicting its ruin, and were to translate the prophecy of the future into the history of the past, you would conceive that I was reading an actual account of what some traveller had witnessed in 1859, rather than predictions uttered two or three thousand years ago. The people are a standing miracle. Ever since the glory departed from between the cherubim, and the Temple fell, and Jerusalem was laid in ruins, its people appear truly phenomenal. A race insulated from all the nations of the earth, mingling with them, yet never absorbed into the mass and made one with them. Where is the ancient Greek? As likely in Austria as in Athens. Where is the ancient Roman? He is not represented by the sensual and effeminate Italian of the present day; he is more likely here or in Moldavia than in Italy; at all events, Greek and Roman are merged, and lost, and absorbed, amid the mass of the nations of the world. But in every capital you will hear at morning dawn that deep-toned, rich bass voice, its tone indicating its Oriental origin, and not silent also to a suggestive mind about its future destiny; you will find the Jews princes and pedlers, the usurers and the bankers of the world; and while hated, scorned, mocked at, a byword, yet kings do homage to them, and emperors draw near to them with obsequious bows, and the exchequers of nations depend upon their word for prosperity or the reverse. The lava that spreads around Vesuvius no more indicates the fact of an explosion, the fragments projected from an earthquake no more indicate that earthquake than these Jews projected from Jerusalem amid some dread convulsion, and scattered like drift of a glorious wreck, refer back and tell you that they were once the children of the great King, a royal priesthood, a holy nation, a peculiar people, the very favourites, while now the forsaken, of the Most High. Persecuted always and everywhere, they prosper still. Except the flying fish, which is persecuted in the air and persecuted in the water, there is no other creature that typifies the oppression, the crushing oppression to which the poor Jew is subject. How absurd, I repeat, to hear professing Christian people say, when they insult the Jew, proscribe and maltreat him, spit upon him, and doubt if a Jew feels, "Oh, it is all perfectly right; did not God predict it would be so?" What! It is your duty to do justly, to love mercy, and to do to others as you would be done by. God will take care of his prophecies, do not you trouble yourselves to fulfil them; He fulfils the predictions He has uttered; your duties remain unimpaired—to show mercy, and to love thy brother as thyself. Instead of being honoured by persecuting the Jews, you provoke a curse; for God has specially said that he will bless them that bless Israel, and they that curse them shall be lightly esteemed.

Yet all the persecution they have borne, all the severe pressure they have been the subjects of, has not effaced or expiated that strange memory they feel of a great ancestral crime, nor extinguished them or their hopes. They are found, as we have stated, scattered throughout every land, transacting the business of every capital; breathing the air of east and west and north and south; they drink of the Thames, the Missouri, the Mississippi, the Ganges, the Danube, and the Rhine; they are everywhere increasing in numbers and influence, seizing the colleges of the continent of Europe, becoming the ablest scholars; and by a great peculiarity, their property consists chiefly of what is called floating capital, they have no hereditary lands as a general rule, they carry their capital in their purses. Why so? Why are the Jews the great money-lenders, money-brokers, and capitalists? All their property is floating that they may be ready when the signal is displayed in the skies to depart, and domesticate themelves in their own home, Jerusalem. They are insulated, separated from the nations, because they are reserved for a great and a glorious destiny. Some day we may yet awaken and hear the tidings of a mysterious rush, when those you are trying to invest with dignities at home will laugh at your contemptuous offers, and depart to that better land which is kept by the Mahometan merely as the servant keeps the empty house for the sake of airing it, till the lawful and rightful inhabitant is ready to take possession. And when they return to Jerusalem—and when in those very streets in which they once cried with execrable scorn, "Away with him, away with him; crucify him, crucify him—they shall shout "Hosanna, blessed is he that cometh in the name of the Lord!" surrounding nations, witnessing the strange spectacle, inexplicable upon any of the ordinary laws of human experience, will receive an impression that Paul says will be to the nations of the earth as if it were life from the dead. If God has fulfilled the prophecies that related to these things minutely, let us learn not to hesitate to believe that prophecics yet unfulfilled He will minutely fulfil too. As the pilgrim gazes on Jerusalem, and studies its ruins, let him think not that it was more guilty than all the capitals of the world; but unless we repent we shall all likewise perish. Jerusalem says to us what we would do well to hear—

'My day of grace is sunk in night,
Our time of mercy spent,
For heavy was my children's crime,
And great their punishment."

LECTURE III.

THE GREAT CONVULSION; OR, SHAKING OF NATIONS.

Hosea anticipates the great Apocalyptic Earthquake of the seventh Vial.

"*Thus saith the Lord of hosts; Yet once, it is a little while, and I will shake the heavens, and the earth, and the sea, and the dry land,*" *&c.*—HAGGAI ii. 6—8.

ONE feels a difficulty in supposing that the Mahometan, the Pagan, and the Hindoo, can in any sense be said to desire the presence, or the knowledge, or the glory of Christ. Christ by name, and as revealed in the Gospel, is not desired by all nations; but that desire which lies deep in the heart of humanity—the sense of want, and yearning for satisfaction, nothing in the world can satisfy but Christ. He is the living bread for the hungry; living water for the thirsty; and all in all to them that trust in his blessed name. He only can satisfy, even when men know it not. For instance, an infant wakes from its sleep, cries in its cradle; its desire is nutriment or food: it does not know what it wants; and yet its cry is the evidence of a want its proper nutriment alone can remove. Even so it is with humanity: it does not know what can meet its want. There is a restlessness, an aspiration upwards, and a groping round and downwards in quest of something to satisfy its deep desires, which it even now puts forth. It is the evidence of man's ruin that he seeks to satisfy those wants from fallen nature; it is the evidence of the infinite capacity and greatness of his soul that no created thing in the universe is able to satisfy it.

This promise has sometimes been applied by learned divines, in this instance I think erroneously, to the first advent of our blessed Lord. No one surely can venture to assert that when Christ came, 1859 years ago, all nations were convulsed. The very reverse was the fact. The temple of Janus was shut; there had been a respite from war for years; and amidst the peace of a world not at peace with God, but enjoying a momentary calm, the Prince of Peace was born. But the prediction here is an express declaration that he will shake all nations, that he will shake the heavens and the earth. If we refer to the New Testament, and therefore inspired comment upon this prophecy, we shall find it still remains to be fulfilled. The Apostle Paul says, "Whose voice then shook the earth; but now he hath promised, saying, Yet once more I shake not the earth only, but also heaven." Paul quotes this very prophecy as unfulfilled sixty-four years after the birth of our blessed Lord. If we refer to Peter, we see at once what he alludes to: "The day of the Lord will come, in the which the heavens shall pass away with a great noise, and the elements shall melt with fervent heat. Seeing then that all these things shall be dissolved"—that is, dislocated, convulsed, the heavens and the earth shaken. We read in the Book of Revelation, that at the pouring out of the last vial of judgment, there was a great earthquake, σεισμὸς, shaking of the earth, or shaking of all nations. It is, therefore, evident that this prophecy remains still to be fulfilled, and that such a convulsion as it contemplates will precede that magnificent morn, when the future Paradise, with tenfold the beauty of the last and departed Paradise, shall return to our world, and there shall be high eternal noon; a day without a cloud, and without an end; "a thing of beauty and a joy for ever."

Let us turn our attention for a little to the existing condition of the missionary cause, as indicated in recent reports, as a foretoken of the dawn of the future day; secondly, to the removal of obstructions in the shaking and dislocating of nations, empires, thrones, and principalities; and thirdly, the preparation that seems to be more and more advancing—that preparation expressed in the Apocalypse by the beautiful phrase, the bride making herself ready; that is, the church of Christ making ready for that great epoch when she will lay aside her own garments, and put on her Easter robes; when she will leave behind her her worn and wasted robes of decay, and put on her coronation dress, and be introduced to the King, and heaven and earth proclaim in songs, "the marriage of the Lamb is come, and the bride hath made herself ready."

The British and Foreign Bible Society continues to advance. It is most remarkable in the history of this institution that though there has been a wide-spread commercial convulsion in every nation in Europe, and poverty has overtaken so many, the receipts in 1859 were larger than at any former anniversary. In India its depôts were consumed, and hundreds of thousands of Bibles utterly destroyed; yet it seems to have gathered force from resistance, riches from losses, and to approximate in its action nearer than before to that day when, as its Apocalyptic symbol indicates—the angel holding in his hand the everlasting

Gospel—shall go forth to carry it to all nations. With its increased funds it has instituted a special fund for circulating the word of God throughout the length and breadth of Bengal.

The various missionary societies that have recently held their anniversaries—the City Mission, with its home action among the crowds of city Arabs, as they are called, and convicts, and fallen, and, alas, forsaken and forgotten females in this metropolis; the Church Missionary Society, with its vast organization; that excellent society, first in the missionary field in 1793, the Baptist Missionary Society; the Wesleyan; the London Missionary Society—are more prosperous than usual. They have all come through years of great social and national distress to many; but the gold and the silver are the Lord's, and the gold and the silver have been poured into their coffers more largely and more liberally than at any former year of their history.

Another interesting trait in all great anniversary missionary meetings is a tone of solemnity most refreshing. Sometimes one has been pained at being forced to hear humorous and mirthful declamations when the interests of souls, and the extension of a Saviour's name, were the great subjects. But last May, as if every man felt that the time is short, that the day is far spent, and the night is at hand, every man seemed to speak with a deep sense of solemnity; not sadness or despondency, but solemnity suitable to the subject, and expressive of the deep feelings that Christian men entertain in this momentous crisis in the history of our country and of the world. I was also refreshed by noticing at all the meetings no uncertain sound as to what the Gospel was. There was no sympathy expressed with that misty rationalism which has exhaled from the swamps of a portion of Germany, and floated on the winds into too many English and Scottish pulpits; a system that makes Christ a great feature, his death a grand example, but ignores the distinctive truth of living Christianity—Christ and him crucified, the only foundation of a sinner's hope. And there was as little sympathy expressed with that other system occupying the opposite pole, that borrows from the mint of Rome in order to improve the ecclesiastical currency of England; that mixes up the alloy of the Vatican with the pure gold, the unsearchable riches of Christ. In all the societies there was less rejoicing in the one crotchet that distinguishes the one from the other, and more rejoicing in the ninety-nine essential truths in which all are heartily agreed. There was also apparent in them all a far more hopeful feeling, and less disappointment with results. They seemed to feel that promises, like the blossoms in spring, were ripening into fruit; and that prophecies long forgotten were beginning to pass into performance; and whilst there was nothing boastful, there was everything in their tone that was eminently hopeful. A century ago a Russian Czar set up a post, and inscribed upon the signboard, "The way to Constantinople!" and the heart of Russia has had its polarity in that direction ever since. Eighteen hundred years ago there was set up on a hill in Palestine called Calvary a cross, and on that cross the Son of God was crucified; and over it there was unmistakeably written, "The way to heaven!" and the heart of Christendom feels it deeper, and is sustained by it more at this moment than it ever felt it before.

When you hear of missionaries speaking as if gold could convert the world, or talking as if they were putting off their uniform, instead of putting it on, it is too probable that there is no good there. But when you see a humble reliance on the Spirit of God; when there seems to be worked into their innermost experience the conviction that the victory will be obtained "not by might, nor by power, but by my Spirit, saith the Lord of hosts;" and that the gold and silver are his, and that the work will be prospered by his blessing only, and that blessing to be had by prayer, there is the augury of approaching and rapid success.

Such, then, is a *resumé* or sketch of the more striking incidents noticeable upon the surface of the various missionary meetings recently held in London in the month of May —the missionary month.

Let us turn to the obstructions that are being daily removed in all directions for the action of missions and the spread of the everlasting gospel. The most startling incident of 1858 was the vast revolution that has taken place in India; the disruption of that colossal superstition which has darkened the very sky, and crushed the liberty and oppressed the bodies of thousands—millions, rather, I should say—for so many generations past. It was the Hindoo belief that their system was about to die; they say at Benares there is a pillar of which the Hindoo believes when it sinks into the earth, or becomes reduced to within a foot in height, that their religion will then disappear. In some of the distant parts of India many of them were known to say to missionaries, "Come speedily," believing that their system was at an end, and that Christianity was now to supersede it. The Hindoos recently thought their superstition was rapidly disappearing, and that we, the cause of its disappearance, should be extirpated from that peninsula. The Moslem, cherishing his ancient and unextinguished hate of Christianity, joined with the Hindoo, lashed into mutiny the fanatics of Bengal, and together they kindled that gigantic conflagration which has watered with sorrow many an English hearth, and left traces indelible till the judgment-day. But the result of all this is the subversion of the very system it was designed to prop up; the system itself is utterly disorganized; the nightmare of centuries is lifted up; and now there is hope in the consistent, fair, and upright conduct of our country not establishing Christianity in India, for that would be a very great mistake, but while not disavowing Christianity, leaving it a fair field, and no favour. There is in India at this moment opened up a door for the entrance of missionaries and for the spread of the Gospel unprecedented since it became an appanage to the British crown. When the mutiny first broke out, every paper said, "Lo! that is the effect of the missionaries;" they have lived, however, to recall that, and now it is demonstrable that just where missionary action was most successful, there peace has been least disturbed. The proud Brahmin we petted, and scarcely ventured to convert, not the miserable and degraded caste we were the means of bringing to Christ, has been the real disturber of that empire. There is a shaking and a breaking up throughout India at this moment that will leave a magnificent field for prudent, discreet, spiritually-minded, unpolitical missionaries, who will preach simply the Gospel, and leave the dead of this world to bury their dead in the world. In that spirit, and with these missionaries to enter India and sow the seeds of truth, there is no doubt we shall yet some of us live to see the golden sheaves of a glorious harvest, and thank God that while many a missionary sowed the seed with the tears of weeping eyes, and with the blood of a warm heart, in God's good providence we have entered into their labour, and reaped where they sowed.

We may refer to another great empire which this convulsion, whatever it may prove, has also reached. China was the impenetrable land of past ages: there was no access to it; all inside was wrapped in mystery; a very few missionaries upon its outskirts and sea-board were all that laboured for the regeneration of hundreds of millions of human beings. By what has taken place a door of access has been opened; the missionary may now penetrate heretofore inaccessible fastnesses; we may live to hear of the Gospel sounding even in the streets of Pekin. God grant that no wind may fill the folds of England's flag that does not reverberate with the words of England's Christianity; and that our British ships may never sail further, and that our armies may never penetrate where there shall not be a Bible in the hands of the colporteur, or the Gospel on the lips of the faithful missionary, to show the most benighted of the earth the way to heaven, to happiness, and to God. We used to think China an exception to the rest of the heathen nations; and many people reported they were such a lovely, sentimental, and delightful people, that they were evidence that a nation might be very good and very great, and yet not be Christian. But what is the discovery? That China is not an exception to the Psalmist's statement, "The habitations of the heathen are full of horrid cruelty." This very amiable people, that had so many apologists amid sentimental latitudinarians, is now found out to be as depraved, as cruel, as impure as any Pagan tribe of savages we ever had to do with. We are thankful, not that they are so, but that the entrance of our armies and our ships has revealed what they are. It will only be a stronger incentive to carry into their homes, and their streets, and their temples, and their hearts, that blessed Gospel which possesses the exclusive prerogative of instilling that righteousness that exalteth a nation.

Years ago I stated that the great river Euphrates, the symbol of the Mahometan power in Europe, was soon to be dried up, and that its drying up began under the apocalyptic sixth vial, or about the year, as far as we can ascertain, 1821. Now, what has been its condition since? Read the history of the Moslem in Europe, and you will find that for the last thirty years the symbol in Scripture of the drying up of a river is the exact expression of what is taking place; and, singular enough, every effort to put the "sick man" upon his feet again has been like every prescription of an empiric—it has hastened his decay, and made his death more definite and near. At this moment, as is ascertained by the reports of the American missionaries in Turkey, the Turks are fugitives from Europe, crossing the Bosphorus, and seeking graves in Asia for themselves and their children; the crescent is waning in that sky that begins to brighten with the cross of the Galilean, destined to be the symbol, as it sets forth the only way of salvation for mankind. The Turks are, many of them, appreciating Christianity as they never did before. In Palestine and Turkey, and at the sites of the Seven Churches of Asia, it is not the Mahometan but the Christian who is sunk deepest in superstition. If I had to choose between the Romanism of the Western Church and the superstition of the Russo-Greek Church, I should be tempted to take Mahometanism in preference; for with all the awful errors of the Mahometans they have never yet worshipped idols. It was the universal idolatry of Christendom that provoked God to raise up the Mahometan scourge. When the Mahometans see men bowing before idols, and pictures, and images, they see something they recoil from with all the instincts of their hearts. A Mahometan mosque is much more like what a Christian church should be than the Greek cathedrals, and churches, and chapels. And when the Mahometans saw for the first time the simple worship of the American Presbyterians, who have been the most successful missionaries there, they said, "Oh! but this is not Christianity, this is Protestantism;" they thought it was a totally different religion. Recently when the Church of England resolved, and most nobly resolved, to build a church in Constantinople, it has been laid down as the law of its existence that there must not be a bit of stained glass, nor a painting in a window, nor a picture of anything that can be construed into the likeness of anything in heaven above, or in the earth beneath, or in the waters under the earth.

This is a most wise step, and it is the only way in which you will bring the Mahometans to entertain the subject of Christianity; for as long as it is associated with idolatry, so long they recoil from what is so repugnant to all their deepest feelings. Mahometanism is disappearing, the crescent is waning—the Euphrates drying up, and converts are being daily made. The railway is in Smyrna; missionaries are preaching on its streets the everlasting Gospel at this moment, and all over the East there are those scattered rays that lead many a faithful watchman on the towers of Zion to say, "The morning cometh." If we turn to Western Europe, we find the Papal nations in a state of bewilderment; every nation looks to every other with trepidation, many with dismay, and all seem to see over all the Continent the hopelessness of efforts to patch up and keep things quiet, and prevent the yet more fearful explosion that rends Europe into atoms.

And what is the cause of this? Rebellion and insubordination are always sin; but that which is waking up the mind of nations to a new hope is the dissemination of God's Word. The Bible Society is in one sense, but not an obnoxious sense, the greatest revolutionist in Europe. Christianity is in one respect the greatest revolutionary action among nations; for in proportion as the peoples of Europe become acquainted with the contents of the Word of God, they will see that obedience to rulers, but struggles for truth and for liberty, are the duties of enlightened Christians. Few fail to see that the Papal system has been smitten with a stroke that reverberates throughout the length and breadth of Christendom. Those not remote events—the Papal aggression, the Austrian concordat—were merely the spasmodic clutches of a dying power to avert a doom that is absolutely inevitable. The vicar and representative of Christ has been long shored up by two timbers, and those timbers creaking and cracking the longer that he leaned upon them; and now the certainty of utter desolation and destruction stares the trembling pontiff in the face. In the city of Rome, there is a priest for every seventy people, a teacher of some sort for every thirty people; there are three hundred and sixty-five churches in a city with a population not equal to that of Edinburgh; so that if the people are disloyal it cannot be from want of the means of teaching them the religion of the country, for it is most effectually taught and brought home to every man's bosom and business. In London we have not a teacher of any sort for every ten thousand people; so that if London were the most disloyal and tumultuous city in Christendom you might say it is not the fault of the religion, but the want of means to bring it home to the people of London; yet it is peaceful, celebrating the anniversaries of its great missionary institutions in peace—as a whole, fearing God, and loyal to our beloved Queen. But in Rome the people are restless, watching every moment for a chance to send about his business the vicar of Christ, the infallible teacher of Christendom. There is evidence irresistible that one-third of them are Protestants, that another third of them are disloyal, and that all of them would be thankful to be rid of him who is the centre stone of Papal Christendom, the great ruler of the world, and who professes to speak infallible truths, and to rule with infallible results. The magic of the name is gone—the spell is dissolved; and during the last fifty years, literally nine hundred thousand of the clergy and teachers of the Church of Rome all over Asia, America, and Europe, have fallen away.

How shall we explain what is taking place in India, in Mahometan countries, and all over Papal Europe? How can we explain this vibration of continents, this waking up of millions from the sleep of ages—this upheaving of deep foundations—this unsettled and discontented state which makes men yearn, and long, and cry, some of them in agony, for calm, for consolation, and for peace? Visions of approaching revolution are passing at noon and night through Vatican, Congress, and Divan; the wheels of time seem to revolve with more terrible rapidity—the lines of Providence seem to converge as if approaching some crisis of great intensity.

We Christians know the result and wait patiently: though the earth be removed, though the mountains be carried into the midst of the sea, we will not fear; for we have a river whose streams make glad the city of our God. Sometimes the ocean is stirred by subterranean volcanic action to its very depths; no vessel can approach the scene while the disturbance lasts; we wait a few weeks, and after the convulsion has ceased, a beautiful isle emerges from the water and sleeps on the bosom of the deep: by-and-by it is clothed with verdure and fragrant with flowers, and there is heard in it the hum of a busy capital and the songs of happy Christian men. So will it be when this great seething, this great shaking of the nations of the earth has ceased. There will emerge from it, by a regenesis more magnificent than the genesis of old, a "better country," a "city that hath foundations," that shall never be disturbed by a storm, agitated by a revolution, or torn by the chariot-wheels of war.

Let us notice amid these convulsions the evidence of the Christian Church making herself ready. The Gospel moves over all terrestrial lines with increasing speed. This the reports of Missionary Institutions show, everywhere and always throughout the world. Our religion spreads with a never-retreating and an ever-extending empire. Christianity makes no compromise, and offers no armistice; and yet in sunshine and in shadow, in storm and in calm, it continues to advance; and the record of to-day is Christian converts still added to the Church of such as shall be saved. We see another feature also very interesting, in increased additions to the funds of the Bible and Missionary Institutions of our country. It seems as if Australia and California had been discovered for this purpose: it begins literally to be fulfilled what was said in ancient prophecy, "To Christ shall be given of the gold of Sheba." While there have been such losses, and so severe fiscal and financial convulsions, as we have referred to, missions have maintained more than their usual prosperity, and their progress has been wider and further than before. We see another striking preparation for the universal spread of the Gospel, in the compression of the earth into the dimensions almost of a manageable little kingdom. Edinburgh and Glasgow are as near to London in 1859, as Birmingham was in 1839. New York is nearer London to-day than Inverness was half a century ago. What is this for? It is God dissolving the barrier of distance: it is an approach to the predicted era in the Apocalypse, when there shall be "no more sea;" great continents are becoming neighbours, vast capitals are grouped and clustered together. Wherefore? Not for enriching men, but for saving souls. The mysterious whispering-wire is connecting the most distant capitals of Asia, of America, and I may add Africa, and Europe; may it not be that it also is given in Providence, that it may be sanctified by grace, and made an instrument of good? I delight to look upon the multiplying brilliant discoveries of science, as preparations for a grand issue, as the acts approaching the fifth of a magnificent drama; as the tuning of the instruments preparatory to a grand and glorious jubilee.

Nor is what is now taking place in America, and Ireland also, unsuggestive. Our American brethren, like ourselves, have many peculiarities; some we do not like. We do not prefer their form of government, nor some of their stereotyped courtesies; but still they are a magnificent nation; and one earnestly prays that the two great Protestant nations of the earth—Great Britain and America—may long live and love, sisters in arms, rivals only in renown. Suddenly a wave seems to have swept from one end of the continent of America to the other; and churches, chapels—Presbyterian, Episcopalian, Independent, Baptist, Wesleyan—have been filled every day to overflowing; till halls, and rooms, and even theatres were seized and crowded with people, that met together to pray, and to hear the glorious Gospel

So impressive has been the spectacle presented by America, that the Jews have crowded into Christian temples; and more Jews have been baptized during the last twelve months, than probably for a hundred years before in America. And what is so remarkable, the Roman Catholic papers of America say, what to me is the most striking proof of all, "Whatever these people may be, and whatever may be in this matter, that a tremendous change of great depth and solemnity has passed upon all the population, is manifest and undeniable." What is also remarkable, those petty things about which Christians squabble are all fused or dissipated in the heat and warmth of this—shall I call it?—Pentecostal effusion of the Spirit of God. Episcopalians, and Presbyterians, and Independents, have met and worshipped in the same place, and in each other's churches, forgetting the little things which after all divide us, and rejoicing in the magnificent things which throughout eternity will unite us. Let us, however, recollect, that whenever we see forged money, it proves that there is good coin in existence; there cannot be a forgery unless there preceded a real article also. Whenever there is a work of God, the devil will get up an imitation of it. The goldsmith cannot work gold without alloy; we cannot yet have a perfect work of God upon the earth. What we want is a little charity, to see the predominating goodness in every Christian, and to forgive his little defects, to forget his oddity in his great work; and not to deny it because we see grievous declensions in the midst of it. But, taking it as it stands, what judgment can we form? Men ir New York and in Belfast have left their shops, the market, the counting-house, and gone day after day, during so many hours, to pray; and men that never thought of religion have been overwhelmed by a sense of the startling magnificence of the crisis. God grant that the clouds that have fallen in such sweet showers upon America and Ireland may revisit our country; and that we may have all the excellence that is there, with none of its defects.

I look upon these things, then, as the first shaking of the nations, preparatory to a good issue. Blessed hope; happy expectancy! Pagans that know nothing of the Gospel will soon begin to believe it; deserts that are unbeautified by a single floweret shall soon blossom like the rose; oceans on which is said no prayer, and sung no hymn, shall soon be vocal with the praise of the King of kings. Homes that have no worship, and hearts that have no love, shall not be strangers to it any more; truth shall follow truth, and joy shall multiply upon joy, as star flashes upon star on a clear frosty evening, until the whole heavens are telling forth the glory and the praise of God. For, for the brier shall come up the myrtle-tree, and for the thorn shall come up the fir-tree; and it shall be to the Lord for an everlasting sign, that shall not be cut off. This must one day be; when it shall be, I am no prophet, and cannot predict; but that the signs of the approaching era are thick and multiplied around us is what a reflecting mind cannot deny. But why should we be sorry when it comes? Can you be sorry that you shall be happy; sorry that there shall be no more head-aches, nor heart aches, nor tears, nor crying? Sorry that all the devil's triumphs shall be expunged, sin's havoc put an end to; and that glorious morning dawn when the whole earth shall be covered with the glory of the Lord, as the waters cover the channels of the great deep?

LECTURE IV.

THINGS COMING ON THE EARTH.

The Great Prophet of the Church predicts, as premonitory of the closing days of our present Economy, earthquakes, and famines, and pestilences, and also

"*Because iniquity shall abound, the love of many shall wax cold.*"—MATTHEW xxiv. 12.

EVIDENCES of our approaching the Saturday evening of the world's long week multiply on every side: the shadows of twilight begin to gather from every point of the horizon; and hence the cry should become more imminent, urgent, and emphatic than ever, "The Bridegroom cometh; go ye out to meet him." I dare not speak in the language of dogmatism or rashness, where human frailty has so often foundered, and human imperfection has been so often illustrated. I may, however, refer to the facts as presignificant signs of the beginning of the Great Tribulation. What is all history? Prophecy passing from the past into the present. What are Alison and Macaulay? what are the newspapers that appear every morning? Simply amanuenses in providence, recording what God has predicted in his inspired Word; so that we seeing the prophecy of what shall be, and reading the unconscious record by men who do not think of the prophecy, of what is, are constrained to feel, "O God, thy word is truth." An early sprinkling of this predicted baptism of sorrows is "nation rising against nation, and kingdom against kingdom." It is not difficult to particularize in 1859. Look around—after a peace of forty years, secured by the genius of that great hero whose name has become a household word—dark and sombre shadows began to creep up and the war-clouds to gather and deepen in intensity, and statesmen to prophesy disaster. At length it burst upon the shores of the Euxine, and in the heart of the Crimea, in unprecedented terror and fury; and a war commenced and closed accompanied by horrors personal and physical on earth and ocean, of portentous significance—men's hearts failing for fear. We were no sooner relieved from that war, than news arrived as predicted in Ezekiel xxxviii., xxxix., that Russia is moving eastward as rapidly as it can; at war, its old war, with the Circassians, embroiling us with Persia, and ever seeking and searching a pathway to our Indian possessions; we have no sooner settled in some degree, if settled it can be called, than we find ourselves at war with the colossal empire of China; a war chronic, but no less remarkable and suggestive, when viewed in connection with prophecy. During the last seven years you have heard of that empire dividing into twain, from internal causes; and it is most singular that some of the ablest commentators upon prophecy have the impression that all the ten tribes are in China; that the land of Sin into which they were carried, or the land of China, may contain the ancient Ten Tribes, of whose history and existence we have had no record for the last two thousand years; this may be error. Whether that war was right or wrong, expedient or not, it is not my province to pronounce; I speak of it as a fact; what is the issue of it? The opening of an impenetrable empire to the glorious Gospel, and the approach of the truth to Pekin itself. The rebels in that empire have some way picked up a knowledge of the Gospel perfectly marvellous. While much has occurred that some may deplore, much may have taken place that some may differ from; yet I have not the least doubt that, as in olden times, the sword is the dread pioneer of the olive-tree. That kingdom must be convulsed by war before it overflow with those rivers that make glad the city of our God; and see erected in its bosom that kingdom which is righteousness, and peace, and joy, in the Holy Ghost.

What an awful, and piercing, and heartrending fulfilment of this prophecy has been sweeping over India! What atrocities, what sufferings, what desolating judgments are on the earth! Those that derided the reiterating warnings I have so long given, now recognise the solemnity and awfulness of the year 1857. All Europe watched each act of that Eastern tragedy, itself a seething volcano. Turn next to Italy. A war was kindled, the ultimate limits of which no man can guess. Every nation trembles—there are lulls, but there is no peace,—and all the nations of Europe learn, amid the sprinklings of the last vial, that prophecy has passed into fact, "Nation rising up against nation, and kingdom rising against kingdom." The "Times" observes,—"The chronicles of the last forty-two years are fresh in the minds of all, and how many of those forty-two years have not been mainly illustrated or ensanguined with the military achievements of one nation or another? It has been the fashion to speak of forty years at least of this period as years of peace—but what peace! Now the Spanish and now the Italian Peninsula has been red with the blood of contending armies; now the Turkish fleet has been sunk beneath the quiet waters of Navarin; and now the Russian hordes have perished like flies in the autumn time, as with ever-diminishing strength they staggered on to the diplomatic haven of Adrianople. At one time the cause of 'liberty,' at another that of 'order,' has been effectually vindicated at Paris, as the red gutters of the time could show; at another 'tranquillity,' that Russian idol, was enthroned at Warsaw in a very solemn way. The smoke of the opposing cannon has scarcely yet curled away from off the wide Hungarian swamps. Need we speak of England's share in these peaceful transactions? The North-Western Provinces of India, the banks of the Indus and of the Irrawaddy, have been the witnesses of our military glory. The fleets and armies of this country have already dealt one downright blow at the power of the Tartar dynasty in China, and even now the sword of England is bared, and about to fall in the same quarter with sharper effect. The story of the great contest which was waged in the Crimea may be passed over with but a passing remark, for that is generally admitted to be a stern parenthesis in the loving record of the nineteenth century. The French, however, for twenty-five years of that time have been steadily occupied in pursuing the African hordes from one mountain pass to another, while at the other extremity of that great continent we ourselves have waged two contests of extermination amid the bush of Caffreland. So far of the peaceful history of the Old World. In the New, peace can scarcely be said to have reigned during the piping times of that murderous miser Francia, in Paraguay; nor precisely along the course and at the mouth of the River Plate; nor among the republics on the Pacific sea-board of South

America; nor in Mexico, where of late the sturdy pioneers of the Northern States drove before them the hybrid population of that lovely region, pretty much as of old the steel-clad followers of Cortez swept before them the Indian hosts, as the wind might have swept away the feathers with which they were adorned. It is idle to talk of peace in the past, and a dream to reckon upon it in the future."

We are told also that preliminary to the great period there shall also be "famines in divers places." I will not specify, lest I should be accused of dogmatizing, where positive assertion is so difficult; but is it not fact that during the last ten years, not in one country, but in every country, not even excepting America, famines have prevailed to a very great extent? Ireland was almost desolated by one; our own expenditure and taxation exceedingly increased in consequence. The fairest lands of Europe have recently felt the effects of famine, and failure of the harvest, and deficiency of the crops. India moves from war to famine. The money-market of America was convulsed; there is bread, but no money.

Our own country also felt the storm. There "shall be pestilences in divers places." In 1849 a pestilence burst upon England, travelling from the East through Germany and Austria to our shores; and instead of the average mortality being about a thousand, it rose to three thousand per week. In 1854 it returned, and fell upon some districts of the country with fearful fury; in Golden Square it fell like the blast of the pestilence itself, where men, strong at ten o'clock in the evening, were carried out to be buried at twelve o'clock. And the morbific agencies which originated that pestilence are still in the air. Some unknown and peculiar type of it prevailed on the shores of France last autumn, carrying off whole families at a stroke, and on the shores of our own country creating sad havoc; pestilences smiting the vine, the roots of the earth, the corn in the field, the cattle also, among which they are now talking about the introduction of a new type of disease. It looks like all the plagues of Egypt crowding into the last half of the nineteenth century; giving token that the dread mysterious vial has been poured out into the air, and nations own by their painful experience that God's predictions are truth. Again, it is said there shall also be "earthquakes in divers places." During the last three years there have been more earthquakes than during any twenty-five years during the last eighteen centuries; and some of these attended with such desolating effects that capitals have been swallowed up, whole cities reduced to ruins, thousands of the population destroyed.

From the "Times" of December 30, 1857, I take the following extract:

"Naples, *December* 22.

"The reports which have been received of the damages occasioned by the earthquake since I wrote are of the most alarming and disastrous character. I shall for the present confine myself to the details given by the official journal. The private information—under the circumstances, perhaps, approaching nearer the truth—reports the disasters to be far greater. At Bari the two awful shocks on the night of the 16th had crushed the barracks of gensdarmes and filled the people with terror, who passed the night in the open air. At Ricigliano, a commune of Campagna, ten houses had fallen, five or six persons had been dug out of the ruins, and two persons had been killed. In Caposelle and Senerchia a man and a child had their legs broken in attempting to escape. In many other communes, houses and churches had been split, and the cupola of the church of St. Gregory had fallen in. On Saturday morning two shocks had been felt at six and ten o'clock, A.M., and stair cases had fallen, while many of the houses had fissures in them. Potenza, the capital of Basilicata, however, and the neighbourhood seem to have suffered more than any other part. The shocks there were continuous, and not a single house remains which is habitable. Now Potenza possesses a population of upwards of twelve thousand souls. The palace of the prefecture, the military and civil hospital, the barracks of gensdarmes and of the reserve, the college of Jesuits, the churches, and especially the cathedral, are all rendered useless, and 'no one can, without danger, cross his own doorway.' They were continuing to disinter the numerous victims, the number of whom was unknown. The whole population, who had been in the open air, were beginning to take shelter in wooden barracks erected for the purpose. From other parts of the province very afflicting news had arrived. Tito (a township of near ten thousand souls, near Potenza), Marsico, Nuovo, Laurenzana, and Brienza were almost entirely destroyed. Two-thirds of Vignola had perished. Immense are the disasters in Viggiano, Calvello, Anzi, and Abriola; and more than immense is the terror and desolation of the inhabitants. The pen falls horror-struck from one's hand, so says the Government reporter. With regard to Naples, several lighter shocks had occurred after the severe ones of Wednesday night; but on Saturday, at five and half-past six o'clock P.M., others were felt, which in some parts raised the fearful cry of 'Earthquake! Earthquake!' and again a great number of persons rushed into the streets. The movement appeared to be almost vertical, as the ground swelled beneath my feet, and the table rose and fell. The same scenes might have been witnessed as those I described in my last, and again, for the fourth night, many people spent the night in their carriages in the open squares. On Sunday morning, at ten o'clock, another shock was felt, slight indeed, but sufficient to alarm, and to lead to the idea almost that the earth was in a continual state of vibration. The Government has sent assistance in beds, medicine, lint, food, nurses, and wood for barracks to the site of the disasters, as also engineers, to see what can be done to repair and restore.

"I have been told, however, that one or two of the intendants have come up to say that the orders of the Government to throw open the communal treasuries cannot be obeyed, as in many instances no cash remained ; the drain has been too great for other purposes. I shall give later in my letter any further reports which may arrive.

"I mentioned a short time since that General Sabbatelli had gone through the course of the Puglia railway, as royal commissioner, to enforce the payment of arrears on shares, and to encourage fresh subscriptions. His success is said to have been very considerable.

"Fresh information from the scene of the recent disasters has just arrived. I give it as official, premising by saying that according to general belief the actual amount of destruction has been much greater.

"The ruinous violence of the recent earthquake appears to have been limited to the two provinces of the Principato Suteriore and Basilicata. Up to the 18th, nineteen bodies had been dug up in Potenza, and more were being sought for; three hundred had been dug out of Polla. Montefusco, the corporal of gendarmerie, was taken out alive; so also was the judge of Saponara, but his wife and two children perished beneath the ruins, from which he was dragged smashed and crippled. Lagonegro, on the same night, experienced three shocks in seven hours. None of the inhabitants perished, but almost all the buildings, as well public as private, were cracked, and three are falling, among which are the church of the Capuchins, and the electric station. The shocks continued up to yesterday at this point, though they were slight. The entire population were living in barracks hastily erected in the middle of a great plain. In the commune of Carboni twenty-one have perished, and nineteen have been wounded, not to speak of the damage done to the buildings. In Castelsano, which is nearly levelled with the ground, four hundred persons have perished. The same misfortune has happened to Sarconi, where thirty persons have been killed. The other communes of the district of Lagonegro which have suffered damage in the houses generally, and particularly in the churches, and from which no returns of the dead have been made, are, Maratea, Lauria, Castellucio, Rotonda, Vigianello, Sant' Arcangelo, Calvera, San Martino, Castro Nuovo, and Senise. From the remaining communes of the district no intelligence had as yet been received. It is impossible, therefore, to calculate the number of the dead. The popular voice makes it amount to many thousands. I have heard as many as fifteen thousand, even twenty-two thousand, stated. It is very clear that, according to official information, several thousands must have perished. Commissions have been formed in the suffering localities for the relief of the suffering. Government has sent down fresh supplies of beds, linen, and wood for the construction of barracks. Telegraphic communication had been re-established as far as was possible. Nurses, sisters of charity, and priests had also been sent down, and everything was being done for the comfort of the many thousands who, not only from fear, but from necessity, are now encamped in the open air. Persons who have fled from the awful scenes, and have arrived in the capital, give yet more heartrending details; but the official journal evidently fears the effect of them upon the public mind. No sooner was the shock of last Saturday felt than a horde of thieves and assassins rushed towards the Toledo, but the gensdarmes soon put them down with their drawn swords.

"All is now quiet, and the weather, which has at last taken a turn, inspires people with more hope and courage; still shocks are not unfrequent, and twice since I began this letter have I felt them. It is a feature in the state of things not to be omitted in this painful narrative, that the lottery-offices all last week were placarded with favourite combinations of figures, and that the people rushed eagerly to play. Again, another phase of the national mind was exhibited in the superstitious agony with which all called upon the saints for protection, and, above all, in the reported miracle by their favourite protector, St. Januarius. His blood is said to have boiled, to have been examined by the authorities, and a procession was thereupon formed, in which an image was carried; so I have been told this morning.

"This letter must not leave without my adding, that in these painful circumstances the Government has acted with considerable promptitude in relieving the sufferings of the unfortunate people, and with equal promptness and moderation in preserving public order.

"*December* 23.

"I had no sooner finished my letter of yesterday than many were alarmed by another shock of an earthquake. 'Resina,' says a resident, 'is in a continual state of vibration, and so will be the whole country probably for some time to come.' Some families have left Naples in consequence, and others have been resolving to do so; but such a step appears to me to be one of great folly, for, on the principle that a road is never so safe as after a robbery, so Naples is now doubly assured. This city, too, has never within record suffered any great disasters from earthquakes, though they have desolated the neighbourhood. Vesuvius is doubtless a great protection to us. On the night of the earthquake, and shortly after, a large opening was made at the bottom of the cone, and a great quantity of smoke and stones were ejected; ever since, it has been unusually active.

"I hasten to send you the report which the Government published last night, of intelligence from the scene of ruin. It justifies all that I have said of the indisposition of the Government to tell the whole truth, and as to the probability of private reports being true. 'The mind,' says the official writer, 'shudders to contemplate the details—they surpass beyond measure what has already been published.' 'In Polla alone, two thousand victims had been disinterred, and they were still at work. Pertosa, Atessa, Auletta, entirely destroyed, suffered next after Polla. Then Padula and St. Pietro, and afterwards Sala, Diano, Sassano, Montesanto, S. Arsenio, and Sapri. In all these places the number of dead as yet brought to light is two thousand six hundred! The official journal cannot and will not enter into details, but mentions Melfi, Barile, Avella, Venosa, in the

Basilicata, where houses and churches were thrown down, and people killed and wounded.

"The same of Vallo, Matera, Majori, and Tramonti, in Principato Citeriore. Intelligence had been received from the province of Bari, but not given. Canosa suffered deplorable disasters, but they are not narrated. In Principato Ulteriore, houses were thrown down and people wounded. Abruzzo Ulteriore Secundo suffered less; the same may be said of Capitanata, Molise, and the three Calabrias. I believe the disaster is vastly greater than we have any idea of; but take only the admissions of the 'official journal,' and yet how awful! It was on Sunday last that the reputed miracle in the blood of St. Januarius took place, and that the procession walked."

Naples is not the last sufferer. The slight vibration once or twice touched our own shores, indicating something very like one of the signs of the beginning of sorrows. I know the objection occurs in many minds the moment they read these things. They say, "But there always have been wars; there always have been famines; not a century has passed away without there being 'earthquakes in divers places.'

This proves too much, because it would prove that our Lord's prediction is absurd; if it be not a characteristic sign of the end, then the prediction is altogether impossible, and nothing can ever satisfy you that this prediction has passed into fulfilment, because your constant reply will be, "There have always been earthquakes, there have always been famines, and there have always been wars." Jesus knew these facts and phenomena, as characteristic of every age, just as well as we do; and yet, knowing this, he predicts them as a presignificant sign of the end; pestilences, earthquakes in divers places; the beginning of sorrows. The distinctive peculiarity of the fulfilment of these would seem, therefore, to be that all these shall come in clusters, and in rapid succession, or with simultaneous effects in various parts of the world, and within a very limited period. And as soon, therefore, as these signs come to be concentrated, and exhibited in clusters, and in rapid succession, we are to conclude, not that the end is now come, but that the beginning of sorrows, the birth-pangs of nature are begun, introductory of that birth of a new heaven and a new earth, wherein dwelleth righteousness. I know also that all that can occur will be explained by the man of science as perfectly natural. Men tried to explain the cholera; one said, "It is the want of ozone in the air;" another said, "It is a sort of magnetic influence in the earth;" another said, "It is a severe epidemic borne hither by the wind;" but they were just as wise at the end as they were at the beginning, that is, they knew nothing about it. When an earthquake comes, many will say, "It is only the gaseous element that has become too powerful for the crust of the earth, and has caused an explosion;" and when a famine comes they will show you the insect by the microscope that causes it; but all this is only tracing phenomena a step higher. Who sent this insect? who sent this gas in the earth? who inflicted this pestilence? You do not solve the difficulty, while you only encourage the atheistic feeling which vents itself in the language of St. Peter: "Where is the promise of his coming, for all things continue as they were since the beginning?" and forgetting that as a snare shall it come upon them that dwell upon the face of the earth. These are the presignificant signs of the approaching twilight of this present dispensation; or what our Lord calls, in the eighth verse, "the beginning of sorrows."

Our Lord next states what is one of the great moral pre-significant signs, to which I proceed to call attention, namely, that "iniquity shall abound;" and therefore, as the result of it, "the love of many shall wax cold." Now, can it be said at the present day that iniquity abounds? Before proceeding to answer this question, I must admit that truth abounds, piety abounds, pure and lofty morality abounds. One thanks God for it; and we pray that these things may increase more and more. But the characteristic of the end will be that, with an intenser exhibition of true morality by the Lord's people, there will be an intenser exhibition of degeneracy, and wickedness, and crime. As far as we can understand the age in which we live, does not society seem splitting into two great sections? Tractarianism, Puseyism, Jesuitism, concentrating around Antichrist as their congenial centre; all true religion, whether Church or Dissent, concentrating around Christ Jesus as our living and our glorious Head; men who are truly Christians becoming more intensely so, and men who are thoroughly worldly becoming more intensely so; shams and masks scattered to the winds, and all standing out either as Satan has tempted them or as God's grace has transformed them. If so, we may expect that iniquity will abound. Let us notice some spheres in which it is impossible to deny that iniquity does abound.

Begin first with the visible Church in every branch throughout the United Kingdom: in one section, presentations to benefices are sold to the highest bidder, and advertised in the newspapers; rights the most sacred prostituted to party or personal predilections: in another section, internecine disputes about the appointment of ministers, ending in separation, alienated feeling, envies, jealousies, and all uncharitableness, injurious to practical religion. Here we see the growth of a dark and deadly superstition, there a system of rationalism pervading numbers of preachers, and true religion pining or perishing, or excommunicated from many whose morning promised a brighter and a nobler day. I do not deny that there are signs of the Tractarian system, which was so deadly and so dark, not disappearing, but at least going to its own place; and no one, to whatever section of the Church he belongs, can hesitate to bless God for recent episcopal appointments, as of "light at evening time;" where men are selected for the chief places in the Church of England, not because their antecedents have been noble, nor because they are very learned, nor because they are men that have minded nothing, nor troubled nobody, and good enough to be Bishops, but for their piety and usefulness. But one can see the correlative of this no less forcibly and defined in other parts of the country: we find churches turned into camps, sickles beaten into swords, zeal burning where there should be indifference, and indifference freezing where there should be burning and enthusiastic zeal. I do not like to find fault and fulminate censure; but one can see, with the increase of true religion in every section of the Church, a corresponding increase of superstition, of scepticism, of infidelity, of apathy, sufficient at least to justify the prophecy of iniquity abounding in the Church. If we turn to another department—the State—is there no iniquity there in high places also? How often do we see the ascendancy of party valued more than the ascendancy of great principles; how frequently do we witness patriotism sacrificed to party, and men more anxious who shall rule than what shall rule and dominate? If we pass into the warehouses, the counting-houses, the shops, the markets, the marts of merchandise, what do we witness there? Is not the competition of commercial life at the present day more or less marked by this simple brand, making haste to be rich? Is not the great anxiety in some of our houses of business what shall bring the quickest return, and how they shall obtain the largest profits? Speaking to commercial men, let me ask, in an affectionate spirit of sympathy, would your ledgers and account-books bear to be inspected by God, and judged according to the maxims of the sanctuary, not according to the aphorisms of trade? What your neighbours do never can justify wrongdoing on your parts. No inveteracy of precedent can ever be a warrant for iniquity and injustice. No doubt, there are merchants in our country and tradesmen who are content to be honestly poor rather than to be iniquitously rich; such men are beautiful before God, ornaments and blessings to the market, and indeed to mankind. But when one reads of the scenes that recently appeared, of fearful crimes and dishonesties that burst forth in quarters where they were least expected, shall I be uncharitable if I express my fear that these were incidental ebullitions of a state of things seething and corrupting below, of which other evidences and exponents will appear? If we turn to social life, is there no abounding of iniquity there? Deeds of violence, thought to be the characteristics of barbarous times, are, alas! too characteristic of civilization: murders and appalling crimes are not incidental, but continuous. You cannot look into the east end of this great metropolis without seeing a contrast that shames, and should rebuke, and ought to awaken the sympathies of the west end. Read, as all sometimes, I dare say, do, the wills proved in the courts appropriated for that purpose; read in the newspapers of men dying fabulously rich, possessed of sums one can scarcely realize; and at their very doors, and whilst they have been amassing these vast sums, lie pinching poverty, pining disease, miserable children nursed in the lap of crime, and ripening for the penal colony and for the judgment-seat of God. May not the crimes of the lower classes be retribution on the heads of the higher? May not the deepening sense of the precariousness of property which the crimes of many have generated be a call to those who have neglected the perishing and the destitute to feel more sympathy and to do something to succour and relieve them? You never can wind a chain around the hand of another without winding the opposite end around your own; you never can do wrong without suffering wrong; you never can suffer ignorance, and crime, and iniquity, to grow up like weeds at your door without the atmosphere that you breathe being sooner or later poisoned by them.

It is most melancholy that, while men are fighting about systems of education, thousands, nay, hundreds of thousands, are passing to the judgment-seat of Christ that literally do not know their right hand from their left, and have no fear of God and no reverence of mankind. In the midst of all this—I repeat it again—men die unprecedentedly rich. I should not like to die worth two or three hundred thousand pounds. What an awful thought, to have had so much wealth in a world where so many mouths want bread, and so much poverty and so much ignorance and misery are festering at your very threshold! In vain have we renounced the Pope, in vain have we beaten the Czar, if we are now the victims of Pope Mammon, and the serfs of a Czar more terrible than the Autocrat of all the Russias—imperious and insatiable Self. Iniquity abounds in social life. Avarice grows strong beside pining hunger, and man, apparently thinking that the chief end of man is not, as our good old-fashioned Catechism says, "to glorify God and to enjoy him for ever," but to make a fortune, secondly, to make a will, and leave your money to heirs, however remote. That man is not most to be admired who comes into the world born to riches, or to rank, or to greatness; but he who goes out of the world over whose grave thousands shall stand and say, "He made many a heart happier by his munificence, his liberality, and goodness." An excessive homage is given to wealth in the present day. Is not money made, in the City at least, and I fear in the West-end too, if you would acknowledge it, the test of respectability? Is not the first inquiry about every man, not what he is, but what he has? Do not men often test character not by the creed, not by the moral conduct, but by the balance in the banker's hands? Surely, surely, nothing is more degrading than to admire and respect a man because, not by his own merits, but by the aid of others, he is accidentally rich. There is something chivalrous and noble in showing due reverence to ancient antecedents, to historic greatness, dignity, and descent; but there is nothing but all that is mean and unworthy in worshipping gold, and shouting hosannas to him who is simply the lucky possessor of it. It is not purple, it is not fine linen, but men that fear God, that love their brothers as themselves, that are the strength of cities, the ornaments of the Church, and are entitled to our veneration and esteem. Honour is due to a good man who sweeps a crossing; only pity to a man who is rich in this world's wealth, but poor towards God. Integrity in rags is beautiful; Vice, in purple and fine linen, ought to be execrated with all the execration of hearts that love God and admire the character that reflects his glory.

We see iniquity abounding, too, in those forms which

have been recently exposed where there has been loud profession, vast pretence, ostentatious parade, aid given to every charity connected with religion and beneficence, but all these made to cover designs incompatible with the will of God and inconsistent with the character of a true Christian. How many will rob their employers in order that they may appear in the class of those whose outward appearance seems to indicate their occupying the high and brighter levels of the world! Fashion is the Sinai and the Gerizim of some, the law and gospel of others; and to have equipage, and pomp, and splendour, and retinue, they will be selfish towards the poor, unjust towards their employers, dishonest, and ultimately, as recent events have shown, turn out convicted felons, because they sacrificed their duties towards God to their miserable and contemptible thirst for gaud, and show, and equipage. While I would not needlessly brand our age, one cannot but acknowledge that there is a great deal wrong, that there is much room for prayer for the outpouring of God's Holy Spirit, and for that transforming influence which one day God will give to His Church, when she has cried and sighed because of the abominations that are done in the land.

But if we look abroad to other lands, to Spain, the land of historic greatness, the people that are above the soil seem almost as dead as the people that are below. Italy, long crushed and held down in darkness and the shadow of death, unable to endure longer, lifts up its hands and strikes for freedom. How many of her dungeons still echo with the groans of the crushed and the oppressed! What a state of things where civil liberty is crime, where religious liberty is heresy, and where the circulation of a Bible, or the assertion that you believe it, is visited by the inspection of the police, and probably with imprisonment for years or for life. If we take the picture of France, sketched by one of its bishops the other day, what a terrible state is hers; what ignorance! You speak of France being Roman Catholic; the fact is, it is no such thing. The last statistics show that out of six and-thirty millions inhabiting France, there are only two millions that go to confession and take the sacrament in the Church of Rome. What does that prove? By the laws of the Church of Rome, if any one does not go to confession and take the sacrament once a year, he is *ipso facto* excommunicated; so that upwards of twenty millions are excommunicated by this alone from the Roman Catholic Church. It is not a Roman Catholic country—it is, to a very great extent, I fear, a sceptical country. Austria is the great dungeon of Europe. In Russia, the great mass are slaves, and the few over them tyrants; and scenes are enacted there and deeds done, at which humanity must shudder, and from which religion cannot but recoil. But we are told by an Apostle that all this we are to expect; for, says Paul, "This know, that in the last days perilous times shall come, for men shall be lovers of their own selves, covetous, boasters, proud, blasphemers, disobedient to parents, unthankful, unholy, without natural affection, truce-breakers, false accusers, incontinent, fierce, despisers of those that are good, traitors, heady, high-minded, lovers of pleasures more than lovers of God; having a form of godliness, but denying the power thereof." Such is the dark catalogue of those who are to live in the last days.

Now, what is the result of this upon the Christian Church? That "the love of many shall wax cold." God's people suffering from those that are his enemies discourage those Christian people that are witnesses of the scene. Seeing

Christianity clad in a sackcloth, many a Judas betraying with a kiss, many a Demas forsaking, having loved this present world, true Christians come to be discouraged, and begin like David in the seventy-third Psalm to doubt if there be a God, if there be a Providence, if the ways of righteousness, after all, be ways of pleasantness, and of peace. And then, the last days will load the whole atmosphere with social evil; Christian people breathing that atmosphere will be infected and tainted by it. Who does not know that if you go and live in Paris, or in Vienna, or in some other corrupt capital, insensibly its moral influence contaminates you? You go there resolved to maintain the sacredness of the Sabbath, to keep up your habits of public worship, to read your Bible, to avoid what is sinful, but insensibly and imperceptibly the warmth of your own Christian character evaporates or goes down to the zero of the atmosphere you are obliged to breathe; and you find it literally true that the abundance of social immorality around you makes your love to God in your own heart begin to grow cold. And how does this cooling love exhibit itself? Less sense of the value of Christian truth, of the necessity of pure and scriptural doctrine, and the popular feeling becoming predominant—it does not matter what a man believes if his life only be right: a maxim as scripturally unholy as it is logically untrue and absurd. This cooling love shows itself in less love to the house of God, less desire to listen to the preaching of the Gospel; little things will prevent you occupying the accustomed place, and many things about which you are troubled will deaden and diminish the effects of the great truths that you hear preached and addressed to you.

Another effect of this cooling love will be less given, less done to spread the Gospel, to educate the ignorant, and to do good among all that are about you. • And as prayer is the very breath of the Christian life, there will be less prayer, less sense of the need of it, less frequent and fervent appeal to God that He would pour out his Spirit upon you, and raise your love to the height it once stood at, and make you zealous in all that is holy, and just, and beneficent, and good. Let us then pray, that if iniquity be abounding, our love may be preserved in its morning warmth and purity notwithstanding; let us pray that the Spirit of God would quicken our dead hearts, would warm our cold affections; and would enable us, in this chill, freezing atmosphere of an atheistic world, to maintain that warmth and glow of spiritual life which God will keep burning until it mingle with the splendours and the glories of everlasting day.

What is wanted, therefore, on all sides is intense sympathy with truth, intense love to God, fervent prayer for the pouring out of his Holy Spirit, and the conviction deepening and growing that religion is a reality; that what I am speaking is not fancy, is not fable, but a solemn and an efficacious truth. Do you love God? Is that love shed abroad in your hearts? May we be preserved amid the evil days; may our love burn and glow with ever-brightening flame; and when the evening of this age shall come, should we be spared to see it, may we be among those spoken of by the Apostle, when he says, "We that are alive shall not prevent them that are asleep, for we shall all be changed;" and, unlike the five foolish, we shall be like the five wise virgins, having our loins girt, our lamps burning, and ready to go out and meet the Lord.

LECTURE V.

EVENING CLOUDS.

"*For there shall arise false Christs, and false prophets, and shall show great signs and wonders; insomuch that, if it were possible, they shall deceive the very elect,*"—MATTHEW XXIV. 24.

OUR Lord lays down in these words one of the great characteristics of the approaching close of this economy. We are led to believe, from the words he employs, that before the end of this dispensation all forms of evil will assume an intenser shape, and all systems of error be more fully developed. There shall be seductions, temptations, signs and wonders, charms and fascinations so terrible, so overwhelming, that they would deceive and destroy, were it possible, even the very elect of God.

I do not venture at the present moment to say that there is any system yet, which in intensity and magnitude rises to the height to which this prophecy points; but certainly there are in the present day, looming up at every point of the horizon, strange and portentous forms of error; notions as new as they are strange; doctrines fitted to beguile, confirmed by signs and wonders, so successful, such as they are, that they have beguiled and are beguiling thousands and tens of thousands; and would, if it were possible, deceive the very elect. In the Eastern Church, there is nothing at present to startle. It seems to be dead, its air laden with superstition, its light quenched, its love cold. It is not even galvanized into anything like ecclesiastical activity, if we may except incidental bursts of fanaticism. The churches of Holland, one of the most Protestant lands in former times, are sunk to a fearful extent in rationalistic apathy. The young men of Germany accept the myths, or as they might be called the whims of Strauss, and the still later speculative spirits who have there turned Christianity into caricature, and reasoned everything like fact—if such may be called reasoning at all—out of existence. What is called the Pantheistic system spreads; it has been inaugurated by some master spirits, at the head of whom is Carlyle in our own country, and Emerson, one of the most gifted and eloquent men in America. This system is the reaction of absolute atheism; atheism was the denial of God, pantheism is the very opposite; it is the assertion that everything is God, and everything in nature is part and parcel of God. About this system there is a great charm; it commends itself to abstract and reflective minds; it is adopted by others as evidence of genius. Aspiring and vain young men are more or less tainted with this form of heresy.

In England, there has sprung up what is called the Tractarian error, where certain clergymen have long tried to balance between the Church of Rome and the Protestant Church of England, and have found it impossible. They have left behind them, as a legacy most instructive to future generations, the lesson—that we cannot mix and mingle perfect antagonisms; and that the result of every attempt to assume a half-way position is of necessity either repentance and return, or progression ending in being precipitated into the Church of Rome. One laments to hear of duchesses, and countesses, and nobles, and members of parliament, and nearly two hundred clergymen, passing over in succession to the Church of Rome by the kind offices of the Tractarian system; for in every instance it has been the bridge across the chasm from Protestantism to Rome. There is the Mormon community of Utah adopted into the sisterhood of States; and now under the government of one of the most hardened profligates, one of the most wicked villains that ever reigned, or rather tyrannized over a people—the head and chief priest of the Mormons. It is almost humiliating that Liverpool, Glasgow, London, and Dublin, should furnish thousands of emigrants to this nest of impurity, this scene of abominations, of tyranny and despotism; under a vulgar impostor, if he be not a lunatic. He is illiterate, coarse, sensual, overbearing; and yet at this moment he exercises a power unprecedented in similar circumstances, over a large population that believe in him. This system too spreads, not from its intrinsic claims, but by ministering to all the vile appetites, disease and grovelling passions of the human heart. It acquires power by pandering to crime. It builds a gigantic empire of imposture upon the ruins of morality and social virtue. It is an emanation from beneath. And then as if this cloud were not enough to darken the horizon, I have been shocked at hearing of the accounts of the spread of a system, known as spiritualism, that attempted a lodgment here, and was laughed out of society by every sensible man. It has settled and rooted itself in America, and counts its increasing thousands of followers. It traces its succession most legitimately to the witch of Endor; like her it professes to hold communion with spirits in heaven and in hell; and pretends, blasphemously pretends, to bring down from heaven by knocking on a table, the spirit of any one who has died, from the commencement of the Christian era down to the present moment. It is difficult to believe that such nonsense can flourish out of Bedlam; yet the other day I read in an American paper, that "this spiritualism is spreading over the country; already its adherents are great and respectable in number, above mediocrity in talent, and are found chiefly among the upper classes of America; among men influential in the Church, and in political life, and in literature; many others, like Festus, are half persuaded; and some come Nicodemus-like,"—that is a mistake; it ought to have been Saul-like; for it is for the same reasons that they come. These spiritualists have four or five newspapers of great influence and circulation; the proprietor of one previously a clergyman. They have twenty-five thousand adherents secret or open in Boston alone; more than ten thousand are avowed believers, or, as the orthodox phrase is, professors in spiritualism; they have three places of worship in that city open every Sunday; they have service in different halls, which they have hired throughout the country; their literature is on the increase, some of their books have a large circulation; and a judge upon the bench has adopted it publicly; and some of the preachers of the spiritualist doctrines have congregations and meetings three times a day in connection with this horrid heresy.

How unexpected, how startling, that this system so utterly baseless, so utterly inconsistent with the Word of God, should be taken up by reflecting minds! Does it not suggest to us at least the possibility, shall I say the probability, that these things may be the first sprinklings of the fulfilment of the awful prophecy in my text, that before the end arrive there shall arise false prophets? These false spirits—"They shall shew great signs and wonders." I need not allude to the signs and wonders that those men to whom I have just now referred show; some of them seem startling; but I cannot believe, even with those who have minutely investigated the matter, that there is anything supernatural in spiritualism. I do not believe that they can summon a spirit from heaven or hell; or that Satan would employ so bungling a system to carry out his own purposes and schemes. I have seen no evidence of it. Satan is in it in this sense, that he is in everything that is bad, in everything that would corrupt and contaminate the truth and arrest its progress among mankind, and in this delusion supremely; but in any other sense I cannot believe, notwithstanding all that has been said, that he is there; and still less can I believe that God would send a spirit from its happy home to gratify the itching curiosity of a fool who pretends to have communications with heaven, while he has never sought to have useful communications with his own corrupt and depraved heart. But while it may be nothing as a reality, it may be a presignificant sign, a partial fulfilment of the prophets; and as such alone I regard it. "There shall be false prophets."

Various predictions in the Word of God lead us to suppose that there will be great signs and wonders in behalf of error before the close of the present economy. For instance, in speaking of the great Antichrist, it is said that, "His presence will be with all power, and signs, and lying wonders;" the words "lying wonders" being literally translated not "false wonders," but "wonders that go to prove a falsehood," wonders that are allied to and enlisted on the side of what is falsehood. Then the evangelist John tells us in his Epistle, "Believe not every spirit, because many false prophets are gone into the world;" and he calls upon us to try the spirits, and he lays down the great law and test by which you may know, whatever be their signs, or wonders, or miracles, whether they are or are not from God. In 2 Peter, we are told that many false prophets shall come into the world. And in Rev. xiii. 8, it is predicted very plainly, "And all that dwell upon the earth shall worship him, whose names are not written in the book of life of the Lamb slain from the foundation of the world. And he doeth great wonders, so that he maketh fire come down from heaven on the earth in sight of men." And again, we read in Rev. xvii. a similar prediction. "The beast that thou sawest was, and is not; and shall ascend out of the bottomless pit, and go into perdition; and they that dwell on the earth shall wonder, whose names were not written in the book of life;" "shall wonder," that is, wonder at what he does, at the great and stupendous feats that he accomplishes and performs upon the earth. And thus we have scattered intimations throughout the whole Word of God, that signs, wonders, or miracles, will be done, in our text expressly asserted to be so startling, so striking, that if it were possible, they would deceive the very elect.

Here is our safety, here is what you may fall back on if ever we should be tempted by apparent or real signs and wonders. I need not state that the whole history of the Church of Rome sparkles with miracles; I mean miracles so called. You cannot read the biography of one of its departed saints without seeing that he moves through the world like an electric jar, radiating sparks of light and brilliancy upon the world always and everywhere; his miracles are so profuse that every act is a miracle, and they are miracles wrought on the most fantastic occasions, for the most absurd and fantastic ends, involving, however, their own condemnation by the very objects for which they are supposed or pretended to be wrought. This book is finished and complete; it is now literally and strictly true, "If we or an angel from heaven preach to you any other gospel than that ye have received, let him be anathema."

Every miracle wrought by our Lord, or by the apostles, was wrought to sustain a definite doctrine or a distinct and heavenly mission. On every occasion the miracle was not a freak of power done to startle, but omnipotent power put forth in order to hold up an inspired, a sublime, and a glorious truth. If one suppose that real miracles, as some divines think, have been done in the Church of Rome—and I do not see why we should deny that some supernatural deeds have occurred in it; for if Satan can penetrate the recesses of my heart, and whisper in its depths what is evil without consulting me, it is not supposing more than is reasonable that he may be able to do outward deeds that will startle the senses by their splendour, and indicate, if not a superhuman certainly an infra-natural inspiration and origin. It is not impossible that Satan, who is capable of penetrating man's heart, should be capable of doing deeds marvellous and startling in their brilliancy, and super- or infra-natural in character; and therefore I would not deny that some real supernatural things have been done in the Church of Rome. But suppose its greatest priest, its very pontiff himself, were to come into this capital, and perform what was an indubitable miracle, how should I deal with him and that miracle? I would not turn him out; I would not burn him; I would not persecute him; I would not call him bad names; all of which treatment does no good, and has often done a great deal of harm. But I would bring him and his miracle, the wonder and the wonder worker, to the law and the testimony. Suppose he were to enter the nearest churchyard, and were to speak to the silent dust of some dead saint or Christian that rests beneath the green turf, and were to bid that dead one step forth from the grave after he had lain in it ten, twenty, thirty years; and in obedience to the pontiff's command the dead dust were to come forth,—I am not saying it is probable, I am only supposing it possible; and I am taking the very strongest manifestation of supernatural power in order to illustrate and to enable me to display the test by which we are to try it—I would instantly turn round to Pius IX., and say, "You have done a miracle, confessedly a miracle; you have raised the dead; I cannot deny it. But as every miracle in the New Testament was wrought to prove a definite doctrine, and to attest the divinity of the mission that preached that definite doctrine; let me ask you, what doctrine do you mean to establish by this acknowledged feat of superhuman power?" His answer would probably be, that the Virgin Mary is immaculate, the last dogma that he defined, and the newest discovered doctrine; and secondly, that she ought to be worshipped as she is worshipped in St. Bonaventura's Psalter, where all the Psalms are sung to the Virgin Mary, together with the Litany and the Te Deum; and she is praised and worshipped, and magnified as the Queen of Heaven, and practically the great personage in the upper world. I would instantly ask, Is this doctrine in the Bible? If it be, I accept the miracle as from above, and I regard the doctrine as sealed to be divine. Being a new doctrine, and not being stated in the Bible, of course it would need miracles to attest it; but if it be directly contradicted in the Bible, repudiated clearly and plainly there, no splendour of miracle, no deed of power, no act above the human for one moment would make me accept as from God what the Bible denounces as untrue. I read of Mary that she, Christian and beautiful character as she was, said, "My soul doth magnify," not myself, the Queen of Heaven, but "the Lord, and my spirit hath rejoiced in God my Saviour." Who needs a Saviour? Not a saint, not an innocent, unfallen being, but a sinner. More blessed are they that hear the Word of God and do it, than she who was the mother of the humanity of our blessed Lord.

When I recollect that Scripture so clearly condemns all saint worship, that the mediation of Christ does not need, but utterly rejects it, that Mary herself does not acknowledge herself to be what she is called by the Roman Catholic Church, then I call to mind the man of sin, whose coming is with all signs and lying wonders; then I remember that there shall be false prophets and false Christs, who shall show great signs and wonders, that if it were possible they should deceive the very elect; I should recollect, "If we or an angel from heaven preach to you any other gospel than that ye have received let him be anathema;" and I would instantly turn round to Pius IX., after he had raised the dead, and say to him, "Get thee behind me, Satan; it is written, Thou shalt worship the Lord thy God, and him only shalt thou worship." I at once feel that no splendour of miracle, no stupendous phenomenon, be it supernatural, be it above the level of the human, can ever convince me that a doctrine is true which this book in one single text reprobates and condemns.

We are told that there is one class that will be exempt from the seductive success of all this. They are called the elect. Who are the elect; can we discover them? What are the characteristics of this happy class exempt from all deception, as these characteristics are stated in the Word of God? In every instance in which the doctrine of election is spoken of in the Bible, it is stated, not as in catechisms, confessions of faith, and compendiums of theology, a dry, hard, difficult dogma; but always in connexion with personal character, and practical godliness. Election, in the Scotch Confession of Faith, is like a flower that has been, as you know, by a new process of maceration, stripped of all its vegetable matter, and the skeleton, exquisite in its tracery, very beautiful, but very dry, is all that remains. But election in this holy book is like a thing of life, and of power, and of beauty, embosomed in all that adorns, elevates, and sanctifies the conduct of man. "Chosen of God through sanctification of the Spirit, and belief of the truth;" and "Chosen of God that we should be holy." Mark the distinction; not chosen because you would be holy, but chosen in order that you might be holy; chosen in Christ before the foundation of the world that you might be holy. In the Word of God, election is always embosomed in practical duty. There is no ground, therefore, for asserting that the elect are safe, and borne into everlasting happiness by an irresistible force, do as they like, walk as they may; on the contrary, the route of the elect is through Christ, the road they traverse is paved with holiness; and on either side of that road there grow plants and flowers, full of and giving forth aromatic and delightful fragrance. God, in other words, has chosen the elect in order that they may be holy; and any definition of election, as with ultra-Calvinists—which holds out heaven without character, safety in spite of sin, and says you ought to look into God's secret book to find your name there, instead, as we tell you, of looking into your heart to find

Christian character there—is a caricature and perversion of the doctrine of election altogether. The very nature of the doctrine makes it a holy force. If it be true that God chooses me before I choose him; that my love to him is but the response to his prior love to me; if it be true that he looked upon me in my ruins, and without any claim on my part lifted me by his grace to the hopes of glory, I must be humbled, I must be abased, I must lie in the very dust before him. And who does not know that if humility be not the mother of the Christian graces, certainly iti s the soil in which graces grow and the flowers of Christian character blossom most beautifully?

As matter of history, Churches that have held the doctrine of election have been (it is a strong statement, but it is a true one) the most devoted, the most consistent, the most holy; and Churches that have denied it in name and in substance have been the least holy and vital, vigorous and consistent. Even in the Church of Rome, the Jansenists, who held the Augustinian doctrine, were men of high moral worth; whereas the Jesuits, who hold the ultra-Arminian doctrine, and deny the doctrine of election altogether have been notorious for their diplomacy, equivocation, and practical ungodliness. Election is not fatalism: this is the doctrine of the Koran; this was the belief of the Stoics. On the contrary, it is election through means to a great, a glorious, and a blessed end. But some Christians have great difficulties in understanding how God can act impartially, or the creature be left with any freedom of will at all if election be true. Admit that God does all, and there can be no difficulty in admitting that he decreed long ago to do all that he does. If it be right in God to do a thing to-day, it was right in God to decree tens of thousands of years ago to do that thing. As to the objection, God's decree interferes with my freedom, I answer, it is untrue and impossible. The decree is an abstract thing in the great archives of the past; it does not begin to touch at all till it comes into action; and if the decree that God meant to make you a Christian, and to leave another as he is, not to alter him, has not yet come into operation, you have no right to conclude that it interferes with your freedom or responsibility at all. No decree to save Peter or to pass by Judas exercised the least restriction or coercion upon Judas. In every instance the sin springs from our own will, the election, which is sovereign grace, comes from God. But, you say, is there not at least partiality when God passes by some and selects others? Let me try to explain it. Suppose there be in a prison twelve murderers condemned to death, and justly so, and ordered to be put to death in the course of a few days. The king, or sovereign of the country, opens the gates of every cell, tells them in the most unmistakeable terms that if they will bow down before him and acknowledge their rebellion, and their murders, and their crimes, and seek his royal pardon, every one of them shall be allowed to come out and mingle again with the nation at large. Suppose that the whole twelve spurn the offer, pour contempt upon his proffered royal kindness, upon his tenderness and his mercy—what is to be done? If the whole twelve are executed, there is only done to them what their crime has deserved. Suppose they are perfectly inaccessible to the appeals of mercy, to remonstrances, to entreaties, eloquent and reiterated, and the whole twelve resolve to die on the scaffold rather than own crime and seek pardon, you would say at once, if the whole twelve are put to death, no injustice is done. But suppose that sovereign has the power, which human sovereigns have not, to touch the hearts of six of these, and by an impulse from on high to bring those hearts to melt, and bow, and acknowledge their sin, and seek from him his royal forgiveness, and these six come out and do so, and the six others remain, where is the injustice, where is the partiality? They are all guilty, all deserve to die, and all would die did he not by an act sovereign and gracious touch the hearts of six and bring them to repentance, and restore them. But, you add, is not God partial? does he not respect persons? I answer, does he not do so always and everywhere? One man is born a noble, another is born a commoner: that is in God's providence. One man is born with a sickly and a tender frame, that feels every wind that blows, and suffers under every frost that bites; another man is born with robust health and strength, and is strong, equally strong, in winter and in summer. One man is so prospered in the world that everything he touches almost turns to gold; and another man—and it is a fact that everybody can attest—never succeeds in anything he attempts. One man is gifted with genius from his birth; another man has no genius at all. Now who makes these differences? Unquestionably, God. When you object that in election God is a respecter of persons, you must urge the same objection, if you believe in the existence of a God, irrespective of revelation, for you find the very same respecting of persons, or, if I may use the expression without offence, arbitrary distinctions, in all the varieties of human nature, and in all the scenes of life. I look upon election, therefore, as the interposing of God to prevent the whole world going to destruction; and if God did not choose some in Christ from the foundation of the world, none would be saved.

There is a class of excellent and active Christians who

hold, if I may use the expression, much milder views of the doctrine of election. Many of them do not like the word predestination; they do not like much the word election. But if you come to talk with them, you will find that whilst they disclaim the word, they rejoice in and accept the thing. Ask you that most excellent and venerable patriarch, whose name will not be forgotten in the annals of the Christian Church, Dr. Bunting, "Do you believe that God must touch my heart before I choose, or love, or rejoice in him? Do you believe that God must speak to me before I answer him? that God must draw me before I follow?" His answer would be, "For sixty years I have preached that doctrine, and nothing else." Then you and I need not quarrel; onr difference is about words; you hold predestination only in substance, and I hold it in name and substance both: we are at one, and there need be no strife between us, for we are brethren. In short, a right view of God's sovereign grace—nay more, a right view of God's providential dealings—necessitates belief in election. What brought you first to the house of God where you heard and felt the Gospel? It did not originate from your own heart; it was some touch or impulse from on high, which led you to think first about real religion; it was something external to yourself. In providence we find election; in grace we find election; in fact, God is sovereign, and his sovereignty is election, and election is grace in its sovereign action upon individuals.

If you ask, Can you reconcile this election of God that we should be holy, or this touching the heart of one—which is the same thing—and not touching the heart of another, with the universal overtures of the Gospel of Christ? I answer, I believe both: I believe that no man comes unless

God draw him; that is election: but I believe, at the same time, that there is nothing preventing every individual, the youngest and the oldest, who hears the Gospel, from instant pardon, instant acceptance, instant salvation through the blood of Christ, except what is in that individual's own heart. And when you stand at the judgment-seat of Christ, I remind you again, you will not dare to plead, and there is no record that a single individual has pleaded there, "I was not saved because I was not elect;" and if a lost soul finds itself in hell, this will be its awful and its ceaseless torment, "I am a suicide; I came here because I would; nothing drove me here but my own lusts, and passions, and sins, and wickedness." Now, if you ask me, however, to reconcile the universal overtures of the Gospel with this sovereignty, this election, this grace, I tell you candidly I cannot; and the longer that one lives, the more one learns how many things God has revealed which we believe because revealed, but cannot reconcile one with another. But when I find a fact in nature which I cannot reconcile with a previous classification of phenomena, I do not deny it as a fact, I lay it aside until I get light which will enable me to classify the phenomena properly. So, when I find a text in the Bible, or a doctrine which I cannot reconcile with another text or doctrine, I do not deny that the text is inspired, but I lay it aside in my memory till the time comes when I shall be able to harmonise it. For instance, we all know that there is a sea called the Mediterranean Sea. Into that sea the Nile, the Orontes, the Po, the Rhone, the Ebro constantly flow; the Atlantic itself rushes into it, the Black Sea pours into it through another mouth, or channel; three continents —Europe, Africa, and Asia—are all drained into it. Now, where do all the waters that pour in millions of gallons into that sea go? This was the question that puzzled Europe for centuries. One said there was a subterranean channel, and that the waters went into the very bowels of the earth; another said that there was a contrary current below from what there was above that neutralised the constant flux of water into it; every one had his own theory of an outlet, but nobody thought of denying the fact that this sea received the waters of three continents, though nobody could explain how they escaped. The curious men gave all their own explanation; the cautious and the thoughtful men waited until light should dawn. And at last a chemist in the city of London discovered the solution—that the clouds receive the surplus: evaporation accounts for all. Some such discovery will harmonise those doctrines that we cannot reconcile. You may give a solution now; I may attempt an illustration here; but depend upon it, if these doctrines be here they are everlasting facts; and if they have the inspiration of God, there is harmony, though we see it not, and what we do not know now, let us wait, and we shall know hereafter.

Now, these elect, who are thus characterised by practical godliness, we are told, will never be deceived. Our safety from delusion in all its phases is vital, experimental, heartfelt religion. In other words, if we be Christians—oh, magnificent prospect!—neither life, nor death, nor angels, nor principalities, nor powers, nor height, nor depth, nor any other creature, shall be able to separate us from the love of God that is in Christ Jesus. We may see all systems of error writhing in terrible and intermingling floods, but they shall not touch the soles of our feet; we may see all sorts of signs and wonders wrought to attest and to give splendour and gilding to the most deadly error. But hear, O believer!

however lowly, however humble, hear the glorious promise of Him who is to come like the lightning in the clouds of heaven with power and great glory—"I give unto them eternal life; and none shall pluck them out of my hand."

LECTURE VI.

THE LAST WITNESS.

A very sure but to the world unnoticed token of the arrival of the world's Saturday evening is the fulfilment of the prophecy that—

"*This gospel of the kingdom shall be preached in all the world, for a witness unto all nations; and then shall the end come.*"—MATTHEW xxiv. 14.

TRANSLATING these words literally from the Greek, they read thus: "And there shall be proclaimed as by a herald's voice or trumpet, this the Gospel of the kingdom . . . . in all the habitable globe . . . . for a witness"—that may be accompanied, as the word indicates, with martyrdom—"for a witness to all the nations;" or "unto all the Gentiles," as distinguished from the Jews, "and then the end shall come."

The Greek word for "Gospel," literally rendered "good news," is the same as our English, or rather Saxon word "God-spell;" the word "spell" meaning "news," and "God's-spell" meaning "God's news;" that is, the information that God has to tell us. Every time, therefore, we hear the Gospel, we hear news which God makes known to us. What are these news? If I were to state that there is an El Dorado discovered in Surrey, or a California in Kent, millions would rush from London across all its bridges in order to explore the mine, to collect the gold, and become suddenly rich. I have better news than these; but, unhappily, news not always and everywhere popular. The very fact of our hearts not being thrilled by their announcement is evidence of something cold, dead, insensible to what is the greatest glory, the richest happiness. The best and brightest things that ever vibrated on human ear, or thrilled human hearts, are these. Here is an epitome of the news: that there is for us orphans an everlasting home; for us exiles a country whose beauty and blessedness no tongue can tell, and no heart can conceive; for young men and women, weary in the shops, exhausted in the streets, sorrowful, depressed, dejected, a rest perfect, everlasting, and complete—the rest that remaineth for the people of God. To hundreds it comes as an old story. "Oh, how often," will it be said, "have we heard that!—it has been told us Sunday after Sunday; we have read it in our Bibles; we have been taught it in our schools, and we have committed it to memory from our catechisms."

This insensibility amid light is just the dreadful state of man's heart that we have to deal with. Familiarity with the message takes away its edge, and blunts its impressions. If the lost could only hear that there is a home, and a heaven, and a rest accessible to them; if the poor savages in Africa, and in Labrador, and in Greenland, and in China, could but learn or hear for the first time, and accept the message while they hear it, that this life's close is the commencement of a more glorious one, what a thrill of ecstasy would rush through every heart! Alas! the very exuberance of our blessings makes us insensible to them. This is one of the strangest phenomena, and yet one of the most common, that the more we are familiarized with mercies, the less we appreciate them. Were you a traveller in the distant desert, beneath a burning sky, and on a parched soil, weary, exhausted, scorched, and parched with consuming thirst, oh, with what thankfulness would you welcome one sweet cold spring! you would value it infinitely more than all the wine that the richest and choicest cellars of the greatest and the noblest can furnish. But pure spring water is so common that we do not value it. Fresh air—perhaps in London somewhat corrupted—is so universal that we are insensible to its excellence. Our greatest blessings are scattered on the high road, and because they are so we neither appreciate nor are thankful for them. The greatest mercies, the brightest hopes, the noblest truths, the most thrilling prospects, that ever tongue told or ear heard, are those heard every Sunday; but they are so familiar that they pass from the ear into the air again, as the wind passes through a ruined archway, creating a murmur in its transit, and leaving, instead of an impression, the silence of death. That this world is not the end of us; that this body, with its aches, and its pains, and its fevers, and its sicknesses, and its weaknesses, is not our lasting tabernacle, as it now is; that there remaineth a rest for the people of God, an everlasting home, an inheritance of glory, a crown of joy that fadeth not away—is surely glad tidings. Oh, blessed revelation! oh, bright hope! The ancient heathen hoped that there was an Elysium, but he could not prove it; the Mahometan fancies, on the authority of his Koran, that there is an everlasting harem, where his sensual passions will be gratified to the utmost; but as his conscience becomes pure and his mind enlightened, he grows sick of the sensuous prospect. But we have not to prove the existence of a heaven; it is not a corollary, nor an inference, nor a logical conclusion; it is a revelation from that God who dwells in it, and comes to us in all the certainty of an absolute and an indubitable truth. Has the thought of heaven ever cheered you? Has the prospect of a home ever made your fireside brighter, and your heart bound with joy? Have you sat in the country at eventide, and gazed upon the last rays of the retreating sun, and the emerging stars that begin to sparkle, and the quiet beauty of the moon as she mounts to her midnight throne? Have you ever thought, if not of the words, at least of the sentiments of the poet—

"There is a heaven o'er yonder skies,
A heaven where pleasure never dies;
A heaven I hope and long to see,
Where Christ prepares a place for me."

The amount of hold that truth has on man's conscience, the joy it creates, the impulse it gives, is the measure of your belief and reception of it. Thus, the very first news, good news, is a home beyond the stars, a rest for the weary, when time shall be lost in eternity; a city that hath foundations; a better country, whose sun never sets, whose sky is never covered with a cloud, where the flowers are amaranthine, where the trees never lose their foliage, where all is beauty and blessedness, and the heart has its deepest feelings and its highest longings gratified to the utmost. Is not this good news? But some one says, "We know not the way; how do we get to this heaven?" Hear the good news: there is a way to this heaven. When man sinned, his sin, like a disruptive earthquake, rent this place we call the earth from that grand continent which we call home and heaven. In that tremendous chasm which disruptive sin dug between happy heaven and our poor, lost, stray, sinful earth, a broad, deep, moaning sea rises and beats against each strand continually. How can that chasm be crossed? Ask the infidel, and he will tell you you must take a leap in the dark; if you miss the opposite shore, you must perish. Ask the Romanist; he will tell you the church is the bridge that will carry you across. Ask the New Testament, ask the Son of God; and in his own majestic and emphatic accents, he replies, "I am the way; no man cometh to the Father, but by me." As God, he touches the shores of the great continent of heaven; as man, he touches the opposite shore of the disrupted and broken-off island of time; as God-man, he unites the twain into one; reaching the very heights of God's throne; so that the most depressed, the most forsaken, and most guilty sinner, has but to enter upon that better than Jacob's ladder, which will carry him from the lowest depths to which sin has sunk him to the greatest heights to which God's love can possibly raise him. Is not this good news? And this way is not a new one. It is in one sense the old way; it is in another sense always new. By a new and "living way," says the apostle; that word "new" is applied to all things that never lose their freshness. For instance, of some piece of music you can say, "It is always new;" and yet it was composed by Mozart or by Handel some forty, fifty, or a hundred years ago. You may say of this way, it is a new way; and yet it is an old one. It is old, because it was preached in Paradise; it is new, because it has all the freshness, from the deep interest attached to it, of a first and early discovery. This way has been trodden by many of your fathers, and your children have trod it, and have entered into the everlasting rest. And if you examine it, in one part of the road you will find riches; in another part you will find rank; in another part of it beauty; in another, crowns, and coronets, and purple robes, and great learning, and vast genius, and lofty attainments; in another part, the tear of the weeper not yet dried, the blood of martyrs, as if it only had been shed the other day; all these having cast off the world like a loose garment, and dropped it on the road, that they might tread more unembarrassed the path that leads to God, to glory, and to happiness; in other words, counting all but loss for the "excellency of the knowledge of Christ Jesus our Lord." You have not a way to strike out; no mountains to cleave, no rocks to blast, no vast hills to tunnel through, no deep valleys to raise to a level, no broad oceans to cross. It joins the Pacific of time with the great Atlantic of eternity, without the difficulties of a Panama 'mid the passage, to detain you for single hour. What a blessed way! what good news! what glad tidings, that there is a heaven, a home, an everlasting rest, a joyful retreat. The way to it is so plain that carping scribes may miss it, critical divines may let it go, bitter sectarians may mistake it; but a wayfaring man, that is, an honest man, that wants to find out in the Bible the way to heaven, never can possibly err therein. It is a way, too which has a chart ever directing you, the Spirit of God ever explaining it to you; and so crowded with those that beat it of all classes, ages, complexions, and colours, that no man goes alone to heaven. A great multitude, out of every nation, kindred, people and tongue, whose backs are on the world, and whose faces are Zionward and to God, goes with him.

This good news, this Gospel, is not the discovery of a day: like a sweet stream, it broke forth from the Delectable Mountains in Paradise: it has often been hidden; it is now traceable not by its brawling waters, but by the belt of ver dure which its streams create in their course. At times it is swollen to a majestic river, reflecting the sheen of great capitals, and the splendour of spires and towers that shine in retreating and dawning suns. Oftentimes this stream has been infected by the currents of superstition and of the world; but only that it might eliminate its waters from the impurity of them all. Oftentimes it has been resisted; but the result of all attempts to resist its majestic current has only been to swell its flood, and to carry it on to the infinite and endless main with a more majestic and irresistible career. It is the Gospel that was preached in Paradise, that was believed by Abraham, that was gloried in by Isaiah, preached by Evangelists, written by Apostles, sealed by the blood of Christ, that was loved by Luther, gloried in by Calvin, enunciated with all its first freshness by Knox, and preached by Chalmers, and in thrilling eloquence proclaimed by Whitfield; the everlasting Gospel, the same yesterday, to-day, and for ever. And this Gospel shall spread faster and farther every year. Wherever God's light shines its truth shall be heard; wherever God's heat is felt his love shall glow; wherever the winds of heaven whisper, there God's spirit shall breathe; wherever the flowers blossom, there his grace shall grow; wherever there are sinners wandering through the world, there shall be white-robed saints finding an everlasting home; and whenever death has carried off his victim, there the angel of the resurrection shall sit waiting for the rosy dawn of approaching day, and giving testimony prophetic of its approach, when the trumpet shall sound, and the dead shall be raised, and the living shall be changed; and the green vales of earth shall be covered with imperishable verdure, and the mountain peaks shall burn with rosy sunbeams that never fade; and the islands of the earth shall blossom like Eden, and the continents of the world like heaven; and all height, and depth, and space, and time, shall bless God and be blessed in him Such are the good news—a heaven; such are the good news—a road to it; such are the encouragements to the belief of its universality and its spread. "This Gospel of the kingdom shall be preached." It is not merely a Gospel, good news, but a Gospel of something very specific—of a kingdom. This kingdom is composed first of moral and next of personal elements. "The kingdom of God," says the Apostle Paul, "is not meat nor drink; but righteousness, and peace, and joy." Did all ministers, bishops, priests, and deacons, recollect this, we should quarrel much less. God's kingdom is not meat or drink, is not fasting or feasting; is not keeping Good Friday or not keeping it; is not observing Easter or ignoring it; is not a surplice or a silk gown; is not ceremonial or form; it is something higher, far more precious: it is "righteousness, peace, and joy in the Holy Ghost." Who are the personal subjects of this kingdom? Men of every rank, and every clime; some living under republic, some under despotism, some under limited monarchy; some called Churchmen, some Dissenters, and not a few called Roman Catholics; for we cannot think that every Roman Catholic will be lost. It would be an awful thought. There is a virtue, a vitality in God's eternal truth that penetrates the eclipse of Babylon; and touches and transforms many a humble heart in it, not of it, looking for the kingdom and the glory of the Son of God. There are men of every rank, and class, and degree; of every sect, denomination, and party. Dare I exclude the poor, despised, persecuted, ill-treated, proscribed child of Israel and of Abraham? No, no. Often have I cherished the thought—and if I cannot prove it, I will indulge the thought in itself so sweet—that many a Jew has seen and clung to, and held fast Christ the Saviour, as revealed in Isaiah liii.; while he did not receive him as proclaimed in the New Testament—the Light to lighten the Gentiles, and the glory of his people Israel. It is a delightful thought that the Gospel is not so cramped as we sometimes think. All those petty distinctions that men glory in and erect into shibboleths, depend upon it we may live to be ashamed of in this world; and at the judgment seat of God we shall wonder how we made lines of demarcation where there should have been none; and how we were far quicker to mount the judgment seat and hurl anathemas, than to bow at the throne of grace, and implore grace and lasting blessings.

Now this kingdom, thus composed, shall overflow all kingdoms. Heathendom is gradually dying out over all the world? Livingstone, the indefatigable traveller, and excellent missionary of that noble Society, the London Missionary Society, has penetrated the depths, explored the rivers, and opened new channels of access to hitherto untrodden and unknown lands of Central Africa. Our ships have touched the Pole, and made the North-West Passage. China is every day opening up, it may be amid tears, and bloodshed, and at terrible expense; and God is ruling and overruling, where he does not employ, all means actually contributing to this end. If we look round again upon other forms of error, we shall find that Mahometanism is almost gone; the crescent wanes over all the earth. There is actually a bank established in Constantinople; what is still more remarkable, colonists are courted from France and from England to take up their abodes and residence in Constantinople. The

Gospel may be preached where it could not be preached before; and as if to crown the last proof of the waning crescent—oh, terrible blow to the bigoted Moslem, the Sultan actually gave his arm to the lady of the representative of our sovereign in Constantinople; conducted her either to or from the ball, I forget which; a scene such as was never known in Constantinople or in Turkey for three hundred years. Its outbreak in India will prove its destruction. There is abundant evidence of the waning crescent—the drying up of the waters of the great river Euphrates, that the way of God's ancient people may be prepared. As to Romanism, I have no more belief that it will gain the ascendancy in our country than that Mahometanism will. Its top branches are all withering in the air; its trunk is rotten to its very core; its roots have lost all their vitality; and some morning we may waken and hear like glad music reverberating from earth to heaven, and from heaven to earth, "Babylon the great is fallen, is fallen, is fallen." And shall we be sorry for it? Shall we grieve over it? If we dared to do so unmanly a thing, our sympathies would rush back to the dungeons of Naples, or to the oppressed of Austria, or revisit Smithfield, and the glens and grey moors of Scotland; and witnessing the bloodshed and the martyrdoms perpetrated by it in Christ's injured and desecrated name, they would come back to us armed with indignation, and instead of bidding us deplore the ruin, they would urge us to join with the anthem-peal that rings from heaven to earth: "Rejoice over her ye angels and ye holy saints; for the oppressor of the brethren is gone; and there shall be in it the light of a candle, and the voice of the bridegroom and of the harper no more at all." And then "the kingdom, and the dominion, and the greatness of the kingdom under the whole heaven, shall be given to the people of the Most High, whose kingdom is an everlasting kingdom, and endureth through all generations."

This Gospel—these glad tidings of a kingdom—we are told shall be preached to all the world as a witness. It shall be preached to all nations as a witness; not to convert all nations. Some of our Christian brethren believe that the Millennium is to be the product of the present missionary agency; and that the preaching of the Gospel will end in the conversion of all nations. I do not see this; I believe that it is to bring a people out of the world to God, and to be a witness to all, not the conversion of all.

This prediction is all but fulfilled. The Bible has been translated into every spoken tongue, and the word of God is preached at this moment in earth's countless dialects. I appeal to the Bible Society, where you have a specimen of the Bible in every language spoken under heaven. This glorious Gospel has penetrated the long unvisited Crimea, and awakened accents that will never die on the margin of the Euxine and the Caspian Sea; it has been preached in the Kremlin, and proclaimed upon the steppes of Tartary; it has been heard on the banks of the Don and the Dnieper, by the barbarous and savage inhabitants that are there; on the Caucasus and amid the Ural mountains; over all the North and the North-Eastern nations of Europe. It has penetrated Pekin, it has been heard in Canton; and the roll of cannon and the reverberations of the war-drum, however much we may deplore them, will prove the pioneers of its march and its progress. This Gospel is not unknown in Persia; it has been heard amid the mountains of Afghanistan. The Thames, the Tiber, the Don, the Mississippi, the Euphrates, the Ganges, and the Nile, have reflected its glad sunshine, and re-echoed its grand truths. And perhaps we stand upon the very margin of an age that will witness all these floods and all their populations assembled together, and shouting with a voice that will swell to heaven and never cease on earth, "Hallelujah! the Lord God omnipotent reigneth."

LECTURE VII.

PHENOMENA IN HEAVEN AND EARTH.

"*Immediately after the tribulation of those days shall the sun be darkened, and the moon shall not give her light, and the stars shall fall from heaven, and the powers of the heavens shall be shaken: and then shall appear the sign of the Son of man in heaven: and then shall all the tribes of the earth mourn, and they shall see the Son of man coming in the clouds of heaven with power and great glory. And he shall send his angels with a great sound of a trumpet, and they shall gather together his elect from the four winds, from one end of heaven to the other.*"—MATT. xxiv. 29—31.

IN order that we may be in possession of all the varieties of expression descriptive of this great eclipse, let us turn to other Evangelists; Mark describing it in these words, Mark xiii. 24: "But in those days, after that tribulation, the sun shall be darkened, and the moon shall not give her light, and the stars of heaven shall fall, and the powers that are in heaven shall be shaken. And then shall they see the Son of man coming in the clouds with great power and glory. And then shall he send his angels, and shall gather together his elect from the four winds, from the uttermost part of the earth to the uttermost part of heaven." In Luke xxi. 24, we find these words: "They shall fall by the edge of the sword, and shall be led away captive into all nations; and Jerusalem shall be trodden down of the Gentiles, until the times of the Gentiles be fulfilled. And there shall be signs in the sun, and in the moon, and in the stars; and upon the earth distress of nations, with perplexity; the sea and the waves roaring; men's hearts failing them for fear, and for looking after those things which are coming on the earth: for the powers of heaven shall be shaken. And then shall they see the Son of man coming in a cloud with power and great glory. And when these things begin to come to pass, then look up, and lift up your heads; for your redemption draweth nigh."

Now, whether we are to accept in all their literality the very startling and awful phenomena here predicted, it is extremely difficult to decide. In all probability, judging from predictions already fulfilled, the fulfilment of these will be partly material and literal, partly moral and figurative. Almost all such predictions have a moral and material accomplishment—the latter the shadow of the former—impressing on the senses of mankind the arrival of the predicted judgment. The best way to ascertain the exact meaning of these words will be to compare and collate passages where similar figures are already employed. That these expressions are employed, at least occasionally, in a strictly figurative sense is perfectly clear. For instance, Solomon says, in the book of Ecclesiastes, "Remember now thy Creator in the days of thy youth, while the evil days come not, nor the years draw nigh, when thou shalt say, I have no pleasure in them; while the sun, or the light, or the moon, or the stars be not darkened, nor the clouds return after the rain." Here expressions almost synonymous with those in our Lord's prophecy are employed to denote great distress, feebleness of body, darkness and affliction of mind. We shall also find that the same phrases are employed by the prophets in the Old Testament economy to describe moral, and not merely material phenomena. Isaiah, in his prophecy, uses this very phraseology: "In that day they shall roar against them like the roaring of the sea; and if one look unto the land, behold darkness and sorrow, and the light is darkened in the heavens thereof." In Isaiah xiii. 10, we read, "For the stars of heaven and the constellations thereof shall not give their light: the sun shall be darkened in his going forth, and the moon shall not cause her light to shine." In Ezekiel xxxii. 7, we find similar phraseology used to denote national or wide-spread disaster, where he says, "And when I shall put thee out, I will cover the heaven, and make the stars thereof dark; I will cover the sun with a cloud, and the moon shall not give her light. All the bright lights of heaven will I make dark over thee, and set darkness upon thy land, saith the Lord God." Now, in all these passages, and there are many others that I might quote, unquestionably the impressive figures of the text are employed as the back-ground from which to reflect, with sharper outlines, moral and spiritual retributions. It may therefore be possible that all this expressive and graphic imagery is employed to describe the terrible perplexity, the deep distress, that shall possess the hearts of all nations, when the commercial crisis of America shall be that of all the earth, and the consternation of thousands in 1857 shall be that of millions paralyzed with terror and presentiments of evil. But at the same time it is impossible to deny that they have also a material, and not merely a figurative meaning. Haggai, speaking of the close of this dispensation, says, "Yet once, it is a little while, and I will shake the heavens, and the earth, and the sea, and the dry land: and I will shake all nations, and the desire of all nations shall come:" a prophecy that we are told by the Apostle Paul in his Epistle to the Hebrews, is yet future: "Whose voice then shook the earth: but now he hath promised," writes the Apostle Paul, sixty-four years after the birth of Christ, "now he hath promised, saying, Yet once more I shake not the earth only, but also heaven. And this word, Yet once more, signifieth the removing of those things that are shaken;" that is, material phenomena; "as of things that are made, that those things which cannot be shaken may remain." It would seem, therefore, that we are justified in taking both explanations, that there shall be signs in the sun, obscuration in the stars of heaven, celestial phenomena so startling and unprecedented—so wide-spread and portentous—that the most sober and reflective will feel that we stand on the margin of some great crisis, while Christ's believing and expectant people will recognise in all the warning sign, "Behold, the Bridegroom cometh; the time of your redemption draweth nigh."

At the same time, we shall find that nothing can occur in the shape of material phenomena, however unprecedented or extraordinary, which men will not explain away. I have no doubt that many of the cotemporaries of Noah, while they saw him building the ark, derided his folly, and described Noah and his project in the Charivaris and caricatures of the day as an antediluvian lunatic, while they contemptuously smiled at the stupid old man who dreamed that any force we are acquainted with could raise the ocean from its oozy bed, and cause it to overflow hill and valley, and leave not a living thing over the face of the whole earth. Up to that very morning when the fountains of the great deep burst open, and the windows of heaven poured down water, the philosophers and the astronomers-royal of the age demonstrated with mathematical accuracy that a universal flood was a physical impossibility, and that Noah was, beyond all dispute, a fool and a fanatic, whose requests to the people to enter into the ark ought to be treated with the contempt such counsels deserved. When phenomena shall overtake this world that shall be the divinely-appointed pioneers of the great and final convulsion, demonstrations in leading articles, and letters, and essays, will appear thick as dead leaves in November, showing that all is explicable from electricity, or the polarization of light, or other natural law, and that it is very wrong in Christian ministers to disturb weak nerves, and alarm timid minds; pleading, also, as they did of old, "All things continue as they were from the beginning until now:" not knowing that thousands of signs are pre-signifying the exhaustion of an age in which we play so momentous a part, and the approach of a glorious dispensation, in which I trust and pray that we shall be found heirs of God, and joint-heirs with Jesus Christ.

Immediately after all these things, on which I do not now dwell, there is one prediction that has occasioned not great dispute, but certainly great variety of opinion. It is this: "Then shall appear the sign of the Son of man:" some sign that is to usher in the advent of the Son of man. What is it? All I can do is to let you hear the opinions I have gathered, from the earliest writer, Chrysostom, the Archbishop of Constantinople, down to the most recent interpreter of prophecy. Some say that the sign of the Son of man means simply the advent of the Son of man. But the sign is distinct from the thing signified; and if it be a sign, it surely cannot be what the sign signifies—the advent of the Son of man. Another class of interpreters believe that this sign is to be the appearance of the glorious and radiant resurrection body of our blessed Lord; and the ground on which they say so is, that "To this faithless generation shall be given no other sign than the sign of Jonah the prophet." What was that sign? Christ's resurrection. And as the sign of Jonah was appealed to by him, so the sign set forth and spoken of by the Son of man will be, these interpreters think, the appearance of the glorious and glorified body of the Son of God. But then this, again, seems to me to confound the sign and the substance, or the thing signified, and therefore not a true and natural exposition of it. The third class of opinions was the most common during the earliest ages of the Christian Church. Almost all the Greek Fathers of the fourth ceutury, and one or two of the Latin Fathers,—and their agreement here is singular, whether it be true or superstitious—Chrysostom and his cotemporaries, almost to a man, think that the sign of the Son of man is to be a gigantic luminous cross that will appear in the firmament, covering a space wide as the widest horizon; so brilliant, so overwhelming in its splendour, that no scientific solution, no optical delusion, no resource of astronomy, will be able to explain it or exhaust its meaning.

I do not believe that this is the correct explanation. I merely state it as an almost universal belief in the fourth century of the Christian era. I think it arose in some degree from that incipient superstitious veneration of the cross which has culminated into the rankest idolatry in the Roman Catholic Church. For, after all, the cross, as a material thing, is nothing; it was a Roman instrument of punishment, and that instrument was used because it was the legal and the prescribed one at the time. It is the moral glory of the atonement that is the cross of Christ. That in which Paul gloried was not the wood on which Jesus hung, but the sacrifice which Jesus made and perfected there. Others think that the sign will be the approach of an illuminated cloud, something like the chariot of fire on which the prophet of old ascended into heaven, careering through the sky, and borne on the willing winds, interpenetrated with beams of intense splendour, the sign of the approach of the chariot-wheels of Him who comes to reign, and whose right it is. Other interpreters think it will be the very star that stood over the manger, which, with greater splendour and brilliancy, and subject to a more universal notice, shall stand over that spot on which the feet of the Son of man shall stand, and where Jew and Gentile shall gather together to praise, to adore, and to worship him. A star of almost supernatural brilliancy hung over the Mount of Olives during the summer of 1857. Jew and Gentile were powerfully impressed by its appearance; the former thinking it the sign of the Messiah, and the latter the "sign of the Son of man." Others think that this sign of the Son of man will be the *shechinah;* that which burned between the cherubim in the holy place; that moved like a pillar of bright flame in the desert before the hosts of Israel: and when this glory shall burst upon the world, the light of the sun, and the shining of the moon and the stars will all grow pale in the intensity of that splendour of unearthly brilliancy and glory. It seems to me very doubtful how far these have any foundation in truth. The most probable (for I can only speak of probabilities) interpretation is, that "the sign of the Son of man" will be the accomplishment of all that has preceded. After the Gospel has been preached as a witness to all nations; after there shall come false prophets, deceptive and delusive in their doctrines, captivating, because teaching a lax morality, putting up pretensions to miraculous powers so plausible that, if it were possible, they would deceive the very elect: after the lightning begins to burst from the east in increasing splendour to its lair in the distant west; after all these have come to pass, we shall have the sign, or the assurance, that the coming or approach of the Son of man draweth nigh.

When he comes it will be with power and great glory; and "then shall all the tribes of the earth mourn, and they shall see the Son of man coming in the clouds with power and great glory." Just before he ascended into heaven, he said, "All power is given to me in heaven and in earth;" and so when he comes again he will come armed with that power as a fact which he announced at his ascension as a prerogative and a gift. This power will be felt in the graves of the dead; it will be seen in the gathering and separation of the startled and the agitated living; it will be seen in the paling sun, in the waning moon, in the hiding stars; it shall then not be disputed, but felt as an incontestable fact, that all power in heaven and in earth is his. And he will be accompanied, it is said, with angels. These will constitute his retinue, and form a portion of that great glory with which the Son of man shall come. We have this described in the prophet Daniel five hundred years before these words were pronounced: "I saw in the night visions, and behold, one like the Son of man came with the clouds of heaven, and came to the ancient of days, and they brought him near before him. And there was given him dominion, and glory, and a kingdom, that all people, nations, and languages should serve him. His dominion is an everlasting dominion, which shall not pass away, and his kingdom that which shall not be destroyed." And very beautifully and very exactly it is said in the Acts of the Apostles, "Ye men of Galilee, this same Jesus, who is taken up from you into heaven," that is, in a cloud, "shall so come as ye have seen him go." And in the opening chapter of the Book of Revelation it is said, "Behold, he cometh with clouds; and every eye shall see him, and they also that pierced him; and all kindreds of the earth shall wail because of him." More glorious than on the mount of transfiguration, with more angels than he appeared on Sinai, he cometh to judge the earth.

We have in the next place the accompaniments of his advent. First of all, we are told in 1 Thess. iv. that "The Lord himself shall descend from heaven with a shout;" all going on as it was, the market full of activity, the exchange crowded with intensely interested and anxious men, the sail and the steamer on the ocean, the train rushing along its iron road, the tradesman behind his counter, the merchant in his counting-house, the judge upon the bench, the senator pleading about taxes, about progress, and about reform; at once and without a warning, shall be heard a sound louder than all the parks of all the artillery of earth, or the severe thunders of heaven, whose reverberations shall reach to the highest heaven, and descend to the deepest hell, and cover with their crashing echoes the widest space of God's startled earth and agitated world. When that shout shall be heard, men's blood will grow cold almost at their heart, the pulse of nature for the first time will stand still, and the most sceptical will believe that whatever be the nature or the issues of the scene, a new and startling era has arrived in the arrangements and the providential purposes of God.

On turning to the book of Revelation, we read there that

the angels that accompany our blessed Lord when he comes again in power and great glory, will have each angel his own specific and important mission. One angel, we are told, will cry, lifting up his hand to heaven, and swearing by Him that liveth for ever and ever, that time shall be no longer; all the means of grace have ceased, all opportunities of salvation are gone, grace now must merge into judgment. Another angel will take up a great stone, large as a mill stone, and cast it into the depths of the sea; and thus, with great violence, shall that city Babylon be thrown down, and shall be found no more at all. Another angel will cry with a loud voice, "Thrust in thy sickle and reap the harvest of the earth;" and another will say, "Thrust in thy sharp sickle and reap the clusters of the vine of the earth. And he gathered the vine of the earth, and cast it into the great wine-press of the wrath of Almighty God." At the close of all this, another angel shall be heard, whose voice shall sound louder than the loudest trump, ringing from heaven to earth, and from earth to heaven, "Arise, ye dead, and come to judgment." We can scarcely realize for one moment that solemn, but to a Christian joyous and hopeful scene; when the trumpet shall sound and the dead shall hear. Look at that churchyard; suddenly the green sods begin to heave as if quickened with some strange vitality. Hark again, in that ancient abbey! marble mausolea rend and split, and monuments of bronze seem to crumble before that mysterious breath, almost like spiders' webs. Look again; and the great ocean that has slept so calmly begins to heave and writhe and be convulsed, sending up that deep and moaning cry as of a wounded creature in great pain. Some subterranean earthquake heaves its foundations from their deepest depths. And out of the sea, and out of the green churchyard, and out of the ancient pyramids of Egypt, and out of monuments of bronze, and out of mausolea of marble, myriads of living beings come forth, fresh like Adam from the hands of God, fair as the angels of the sky; and friend recognizes friend, and brother bids welcome to brother; and all congregated together are presented by Christ to himself, a glorious church, without spot, or wrinkle, or blemish, or any such thing.

But this is not all: not only shall that trumpet voice raise the long sleeping and silent dead, but all Christ's people that are living shall instantly be changed. There are some people—no, I do not say there are, but there will be some people—that will never die. We often read the text, "It is appointed unto all men to die;" but it is we that put in the "all;" it is not the Spirit of God. Open your Bibles and turn to the text, and you will find, "It is appointed unto men to die;" it is not appointed unto all men, for a day comes when the whole earth being covered with living men, one half of them shall be changed, lifted up in the cloud, and ushered into heaven; and the other half shall be overwhelmed in the last and crushing catastrophe of a world in flames. When the dead shall be raised, Christ's people that are living shall not die, but be changed. And what a strange and mysterious separation will then take place! Our blessed Lord himself tells us in very solemn and very striking language, "Two women shall be grinding at the mill," one a Christian, the other not, "one shall be taken," changed, lifted into the glorious cloud, "the other shall be left," to perish in the wreck and ruin of all things. And again, he says, "Two shall be in the field," sowing, or reaping, or ploughing, the world going on as it was, "one shall be taken," changed, translated, "the other shall be left," and share in the great catastrophe. In which class shall we be? Among those who will hail the drooping sun, the hiding stars, and the obscured moon; and hear only music in the roll of the last trump, and right joyous words in that great shout that rends heaven and earth; for to us, if we be children of God, will come a voice the sweetest and the most musical that can descend from heaven into waiting and willing hearts, "Come, ye blessed of my Father, inherit the kingdom prepared for you from the foundation of the world."

"Then shall all the tribes of the earth mourn, and they shall see the Son of man." The word "earth" is translated often in the New Testament "the land;" and in many instances unquestionably refers to the land of Judea. The epithet "tribes" is not applied to the Gentiles, it is the distinctive appellation of the Jews. This is the prediction of the fact that the Jews, gathered to their own land, and there attempting to build their temple, and to offer up their sacrifices, shall be converted instantly and in a day by the pouring out of the Spirit of God; and then they shall see Christ, and mourn. Zechariah, speaking of them at this era, and describing great phenomena that are to take place on a day, called "the great day of God," says, "In that day will I make Jerusalem a burdensome stone for all people; all that burden themselves with it shall be cut in pieces, though all the people of the earth be gathered together against it. In that day, saith the Lord, I will smite every house with astonishment." Then in the sixth verse, "In that day I will make the governors of Judah like an hearth of fire among the wood." And in the eighth verse, "In that day shall the Lord defend the inhabitants of Jerusalem; and he that is feeble among them at that day shall be as David; and the house of David shall be as God." And he says in the ninth verse, "And it shall come to pass in that day, that I will seek to destroy all the nations that come against Jerusalem. And I will pour upon the house of David, and upon the inhabitants of Jerusalem, the spirit of grace and of supplications; and they shall look upon me whom they have pierced, and they shall mourn for him, as one mourneth for his only son, and shall be in bitterness for him, as one that is in bitterness for his firstborn. In that day shall there be a great mourning in Jerusalem, as the mourning of Hadadrimmon, in the valley of Megiddon. And the land shall mourn." These words, "every family apart; the family of the house of David apart, and their wives apart; the family of the house of Nathan apart, and their wives apart; the family of the house of Levi apart, and their wives apart; the family of Shimei apart, and their wives apart; all the families that remain, every family apart, and their wives apart," are most significant. What do they show? That the Jews will be replaced in Jerusalem, divided into tribes in their own land, when their repentance occurs, for each tribe is to mourn apart. I believe that splendid prophecy in the last eight chapters of Ezekiel, with its temple, the allocation of the tribes, their distribution throughout the land, will be strictly realized.

A person suggested to me that the whole picture of the temple of Ezekiel in the last eight chapters could be erected only in one spot in the land of Palestine; and that the proportions were so perfect, and their geographical relationships so exact, that a skilful architect might easily draw out a ground plan, and the structure of the edifice itself; and show that it was not a figure to be fulfilled in the bulk, but a literal erection to beautify the coasts and the fields of Palestine. I got a rough sketch prepared by an eminent architect in my congregation. In my schoolroom I asked some one to read the verses of the last eight chapters of Ezekiel in succession, while I pointed with a rod to the picture. Nothing could be more exact than the coincidence between the inspired words and the drawing. This great temple will be raised in Jerusalem, and into it the glory will come in another way than it came into Solomon's temple, when God will pour out his Spirit upon all the tribes settled in various districts of the land; and they shall look upon him whom they have pierced, and they shall discover that Jesus of Nazareth is the Son of God, and they shall mourn, and be in bitterness of heart. Palestine shall have the precedence of all lands, and Jerusalem be in a far higher sense the beautiful metropolis of all the earth.

"He shall gather his elect from the four winds of heaven." In other words, the moment this sign of the Son of man comes—and perhaps the most suggestive and eloquent sign of all will be the return of the Jews to their own land—he will gather his elect people from every end of the earth. Africa, Asia, Europe, and America will pour forth from every point of the world's wide circumference their responsible myriads; all rushing to that great central spot, all with beating hearts, some with broken, others with bounding hearts, to answer for the deeds done in the body, whether they be good or whether they be evil. The Jew shall start from his synagogue, the Arab shall come from his tent, the Moslem emerge from his mosque, the Cossack from his steppes, the wild Indian from his wigwam, the bishop from his cathedral, and the presbyter from his church; all shall hear his voice, and under an attraction that some would not resist if they could, and that others deprecate and would resist if they could, shall appear at the judgment seat of

Christ, there to receive the unalterable sentence of endless, and to some glorious retribution. Such, then, will be the phenomena of that day.

Are we in the number of the elect? Are we washed in that Saviour's precious blood? Are we regenerated by his Holy Spirit? Are we born again? It matters little comparatively what church you prefer, what chapel you worship in, what rites you love, or what sermons you dislike; if you bear the royal signature of Christ, if you are made new creatures. Two eternities are struggling to have you, but one only will embosom you, that eternal joy which is in reversion for all them that love God, and are the called according to his purpose. Happy are the people who are in such a case! On your graves, the bleakest of them all, the heart's-ease may blossom; and on their lintels and on their door-posts the morning of the resurrection already begins to break. It matters little when you die, it matters nothing where you die, or where your dead dust may be laid; this only is the great thing, that you are found in Christ, washed in his precious blood. Come judgment, come tribulation, come the rending earth and the shattered sky; come darkened sun, and clouded stars, and hidden moon; "I," says the Saviour, "give unto such eternal life, and none shall pluck them out of my hand."

LECTURE VIII.

THE LATTER RAIN.

And it shall come to pass afterward, that I will pour out my Spirit upon all flesh;" &c.—JOEL ii. 28—32.

WAS this prophecy exhausted when the Holy Spirit, at the day of Pentecost, was poured out upon the Apostles? I believe not. No phenomena occurred at Pentecost adequate to fulfil the whole prediction. In the 24th chapter of Matthew we find that the phenomena predicted by Joel are also predicted by our Lord to occur when he shall come again, to put the sheep upon his right hand, and the goats upon his left, and apportion each an eternal destiny. It therefore seems that Pentecost was the first sprinkling of a great shower that is destined yet to saturate and refresh all portions of the world's long, bleak, and very thirsty wilderness, the early rain to be followed by the latter During the Christian economy, that is, during the last days, from Christ's birth to Christ's second advent, Joel's prophecy has been fulfilling. The first shower, the April shower as it were, or the early rain, began at Pentecost; there were incidental showers in every succeeding century; but the great and copious baptism that is to prepare a people for the coming of the Lord, or, in the beautiful language of the Apocalypse, to make the bride ready for the bridegroom, remains still to come, and will be the token of that great day when all things shall be made new, and the world shall be restored and regenerated. If this were my peculiar or singular opinion, I should scarcely venture to assert it with such confidence; but Calvin, that acute and able scholar, averse to all that seemed extravagant, says: "Joel views the whole kingdom of Christ, its beginning and its end; and what he predicts is to occur between the first day of Pentecost and the last day of the resurrection of the saints." Howe, the great and eloquent Puritan, whose works are so rich in precious theology, says in his work on the Holy Spirit: "It is plain Peter did not intend that this at Pentecost was the completion of the prophecy." These two divines, and many others I could quote in more recent times, concur in looking at the Pentecostal effusion, eighteen hundred years ago, as only the first and copious shower of what is to occur in the end of the age.

In order to ascertain clearly and plainly what would be the effects of this pouring out of God's Holy Spirit, I think the rational way is to ascertain, first of all, what this Holy Spirit is predicted or asserted to do in individual cases. The Holy Spirit is a person, a divine person. We believe that the Father is God, that the Son is God, that the Holy Spirit is God. If we are asked to explain this, I answer, I cannot; if it be asked do we comprehend it, I answer, No. But there are many more things incomprehensible in our experience than our philosophy will sometimes bow itself to admit. Ten thousand things are about us, and in us, and over us, that we accept as facts, though we cannot comprehend them as mysteries. Now, then, this Holy Spirit being a person, and a divine person, is promised by the Saviour as his substitute, and so far representative, throughout the whole of the Christian economy. Therefore, when we hear of any priest calling himself the vicar of Christ, we feel the thing is monstrous. The Holy Spirit only takes the place of Christ. "I will send you," he says, "another Comforter, that he may abide in you for ever." That Holy Spirit is to abide in the hearts of believers till Christ come, making them meet to welcome to our world their King, their Saviour, and their God. The Holy Spirit's work is delineated in the Gospel of St. John.

By ascertaining what this Holy Spirit is to do in each individual, we shall thereby be able to infer what he will do in the wide world at large. Our Lord says in John xiv., "The Comforter, which is the Holy Ghost, whom the Father will send in my name; he shall teach you all things, and bring all things to your remembrance, whatsoever I have said unto you." Then in the xvth chapter, "But when the Comforter is come, whom I will send unto you from the Father, even the Spirit of truth, which proceedeth from the Father, he shall testify of me." In the xvith chapter, "When the Spirit of truth is come, he will guide you unto all truth; for he shall not speak of himself, but whatsoever he shall hear he will speak; and he will show you things to come." These are the three passages that most expressly and vividly state what the Holy Spirit is to do. He is called the Comforter; but before he assumes that name he is called the "Spirit of truth;" "the Spirit of truth, the Comforter." All true Christian comfort must be based upon truth. There is no comfort in a lie; there may be an opiate, or there may be stupefaction in it; but the truth, the Spirit of truth alone, is the Comforter. As long as he comforts he will tell you the truth; and he will tell you the truth in order to comfort you.

This Spirit of truth is predicted in the first place to guide unto all truth. There is an instinct in our nature that prompts us to ascertain what is truth. What is all literature? Man searching out for truth. What are all the investigations of science? Man wanting to get at the heart and truth of things. We should seek to know religious truth just as we seek to know scientific truth, only that many keep in their hearts lodgers that they will not cast out, and cherish in their practice habits they will not abjure; and therefore do not want, because they do not like the truth to reveal what they are conscious will not bear the light of truth. No man likes to undergo a painful operation; but when he is convinced that the operation is necessary to a cure, he will submit to it. No man likes the truth to come into contact with something which he knows should not be there; but if you are persuaded that to know the worst of the matter is the only way to get at peace and happiness, then you will submit to it. He will teach you all the truth; the truth about God, the truth about yourself; the whole truth about what you were, are, and will be. We do not mean to say that he will flash splendour from the skies, and so fill your souls with supernatural sunshine, or that he will place a tongue of flame upon every head; but that he will make so plain to you God's word, by removing from your mind the dark prejudices that prevent you seeing it clearly, that in his light you shall be able to see all light.

This being the effect of the Holy Spirit's possession of an individual heart, we have only to transfer the personal and the local to the universal, to see what will be the effect of this Spirit poured out upon all flesh. The moment this takes place, all words will be truth, all thoughts will be just, all ways will be straight. Instead of those flickering rays of sunshine that we, in our ignorance, dignify with the name of summer, there shall burst upon the world Eden's own bright, cloudless, lasting noon, and all the earth shall be filled with the glory of God, as the waters cover the channels of the great deep. The crescent that now wanes in the eastern sky shall then give place to the great glory of redemption, Christ, and him crucified. The vast continent of China shall be no longer oppressed by the horrid superstition of Confucius, or stained and marred by crimes that dare not be mentioned; but bask in the sunshine of eternal day. India shall no longer be the victim of Brahmin and Buddhist, and lie beneath a upas tree that spreads death wherever its shadow falls. The years 1857 and 1858 will be recollected one day by millions of that population as the most unhappy and deplorable chapters in their history; and whilst they deplore in tears the past, they will bless God that he has taught them to see their crimes and renounce them, and to rejoice in the blessings and glories of an Indian Pentecost. Austria and Italy, those magnificent lands, will come forth from the grave of a thousand years, their mists cleared away from their eyes, and they shall no longer sit amid the swamps of the Papal superstition, but beneath the shadow of the Rock of Ages and the Tree of Life. Russia, so degraded and debased by a superstition little better than that of Italy, shall open its eyes and see a brighter and a new day. All mysteries to us shall be made plain; the light of the Spirit shall then be in every understanding; the Sun of Righteousness shall then rise with healing under his wings; and all shall be blessed in his light; they shall no more teach every man his brother, saying, "Know the Lord;" for all shall know him, from the least to the greatest.

Such, then, would be the effect of the fulfilling of what God has predicted.

This Holy Spirit, in individual cases, is also represented as the Comforter. This is a very blessed thought—that our religion is not, as some people think it, a creed in one hand and a thunderbolt in the other; or, as some imagine, merely prophesying evil and troubling the camp of Israel; it is a religion of joy; a spring of the highest and most enduring happiness; and if you be not happy, depend upon it it is not your Christianity that makes you unhappy, but the want of it; for as sure as you get the Spirit to teach you the truth, so sure you will get that Holy Spirit to give you comfort, or happiness and joy, in such measure as may be most expedient for you. How delightful it is that we have a Comforter! There are times when we cannot help being depressed; depression however arising not always from spiritual and religious springs, but from those troublesome concerns that we call nerves. Hence many a person searching out a comforting word, would do well to go to a physician and ask him for a prescription. You must not always attribute to religion what is attributable to other and subordinate causes. But when you need consolation, arising from your misapprehension of Divine Truth, how delightful it is that we have One who can comfort us—that we are capable of comfort! The lost in misery are incapable of it; but we are capable of it. We have in the Spirit one who can comfort us. We all know what numbers there are in this world of Job's miserable comforters. You have lost a near and a dear one, perhaps you are sorrowing over some one who has found a soldier's grave amid the burning sands of India. Some person comes to you with a great deal of ostentatious piety, and a very long face, and a voice transposed to the minor key; and tells you, you should not sorrow, you should not weep, you should not feel grieved; it is very sinful of you; it is very wrong of you. How harsh and cold is such advice! Why, Jesus wept; the Son of God had sorrow. To rebuke me for having human nature is to rebuke God for having made me. It is as natural to weep as it is to smile; it is as natural to feel sorrow as it is to feel joy. To go to a sufferer sorrowing in the shadow of a bitter calamity, and to say, "Do not weep; do not be sorrowful; it is sinful to be so," is to aggravate the sorrow, which you had much better let alone. Another comes with some dry, worthless common-place, and says, "It is all very natural; you cannot help it;" and they give this miserable consolation just as a nurse in a sick-room often presents a cup of medicine, she heartily detests, to the poor patient that needs it. But this Comforter presents the right consolation at the right moment; he knows what spring to touch, what note to sound, what word to speak, what leaf from the tree of life to apply to the bleeding heart; and then, "Comfort, comfort ye my people," becomes no more a prophet's vision, but a Christian's deepest and innermost experience. It may be asked now, how does he comfort? Not by bringing a new revelation; nor by adding one chapter to the Bible. It is a great mistake, into which many Christians fall, when they speak of the Spirit's work, as if He takes off some film from the sacred page, or adds some words to the sacred testimony. That is a great error. The Holy Spirit takes of the things that are Christ's and shows them unto us; he brings all things to your remembrance whatsoever Christ has said unto you. In other words, when the Holy Spirit comforts you he does not brighten the truth; but he sweeps away the cobwebs from your minds—the mists, and films, and prejudices from your vision—the distorting and diverging passions from your heart; and thus he enables you to see and draw comfort from that truth which he presents to you.

Who has not felt infinite comfort in sorrow when some long-hidden truth flashed suddenly upon his mind? Who has not felt as if an angel touched him when some unknown but seasonable and consolatory truth came suddenly within the horizon of his mind? Who has not felt as if he had been transported back to Paradise when some flower of Eden, long shrivelled and withered within him, suddenly burst into all its Eden bloom, and shed the very fragrance of heaven over the sorrows and the sufferings of a heavy human heart. Thus the Spirit comforts not by something altogether transcendental and unknown; but by bringing the truth he has inspired into contact with the heart that needs it. This is his peculiar and sovereign power. A preacher can speak to his audience—their ears drink in his words, and their intellects understand them; but many a truth distinctly heard, and many a proposition clearly understood, does not reach the heart or the conscience; it stops short in the head, or lies cold in the memory. The Holy Spirit of God can preach to the inmost heart, just as man preaches to the outward ear; and make the heart feel just as easily as the preacher can make the people hear. Thus he can comfort in a way that man cannot attain.

It is the office of the Holy Spirit also to give life. This gift is eminently the prerogative of Deity. The world can give a new dress, the sovereign can give a new title, the humblest minister can give a new baptism; but the Holy Spirit of God alone can give life to the heart. By life is not meant excitement; excitement is cheap enough; it can be had at a small price anywhere, and on any occasion.

Religious excitement may be fever, which is not health, but the reverse of health. Nor is it outward conformity to outward things; that is not life. The Holy Spirit can quicken the dead heart, stir the stagnant tides in the veins and arteries of that heart, and raise by a mysterious touch the whole temperature of the soul and heart within. There may be no eloquence; there may be no outward, visible, startling phenomena; yet there may be a secret penetrating life flowing through many hearts, and originating in each, not the fever of fanaticism, but the life of true religion. Life is not a violent thing. When a man is extravagant in all his ways, and acts, and deeds, and movements, we set him down as a lunatic; but life makes the footstep firm, the heart beat steadily, all the organization and action of nature healthy; it makes no noise, shows no sign of extravagance; and yet is the mightiest motive force that God vouchsafes to his intelligent creatures. Were each individual throughout our world inspired by this life, what would be the result? Valleys of dry bones would become countless hosts of living men—dead and withered branches would be weighed down with fruit fragrant, beautiful, and ripe. Outward acts would have an elevation, and a purity, and a sublimity that they never had before. Prayer would cease to be a mere form; praise would cease to be a mere song; public worship would cease to be a mere propriety; and while the church would neither be a theatre nor a convent, it would be that floor on which would be transacted interests that stretch into everlasting ages, and stir the spirits that are in heaven with deep and kindling sympathy with what is experienced in this world.

A distinctive characteristic of this Holy Spirit is holiness; that grace whose standard is the law, whose subject is a

Christian, whose authorship is the Spirit of God. Not outward beauty, not ecclesiastical decoration, not gorgeous robes, not resplendent ceremonies; but the simplicity of worship, the purity of truth, the moral grandeur that God the Spirit inspires within and develops without. The drunkard would become sober; the miser would become liberal; evil would flee like a shadow; Satan would be cast out; and Paradise would end the world as Paradise began it; and if trade should be continued, it would be like a liturgy; and if the counting-house should exist, it would be as a sanctuary; and if parliaments were in existence, statesmen would not follow the dictates of expediency but of duty. The priest would give up his breviary; the hypocrite would resign his mask; and whether we eat or drink, or whatsoever we do, we should do all to the glory of God.

If this Spirit were poured out upon the individual, there would be power; for what is he called? He is called "the power of the Holy Ghost?" Why does many a sermon fail to have effect? It may be truth, it may be brilliant, it may be eloquent; but the result is exactly that of the tinkling cymbal and the sounding brass. Why? The power of the Holy Ghost is not in it. Why do we read the Bible very often, and derive very little good from it? The power of the Spirit of God is not sought. Why do Christians quarrel among themselves, and Churchmen hate Dissenters, and Dissenters hate Churchmen? Because they have not the cementing power of the Holy Spirit of God in their hearts. When we see men quarrelling about baskets, we may depend upon it they are not very hungry; when we see ecclesiastics quarrelling about crotchets, we may be very sure they have no very deep conviction of realities. As often as you see men disputing about one little jot on which they differ, and forgetting the ninety-nine magnificent things about which they are at one, they need the Holy Spirit of God to teach them better things. What is wanted in the present day in every sermon, in all our worship, and work, and way, is the power of the Holy Ghost.

How striking is the extraordinary feeling that at this moment spreads all over the United States and the northern parts of Ireland! When I first heard of it I thought it might be spasmodic, or be excited and kindled by those things by which we are sometimes, perhaps, rather unhappily distinguished. I would not say, mark you, that these scenes will not be characterized by many things detracting from their beauty; I do not mean to say that there will not be extravagances. Satan crept into Paradise; Judas went among the Apostles; Peter even denied his Lord; Demas forsook Paul. Wherever there is a work of God the devil gets up a counter work of caricature; this you may expect; that there will be much alloy you may be sure. But now am I pronouncing hastily, am I speaking rashly, when I express my conviction that the calmness of this movement, the subduedness of it, not created by exciting preaching, not even created in the church at all, but among the thousands outside of the church, is something like a wave from on high? May it not be as the first sprinkling of the last shower? And at all events, if there should be much in this that we may not be able to fall in with, is it not a blessed thought that they have lost altogether those unhappy ecclesiastical distinctions that split people asunder; that there is one vast brotherhood that has lasted for months? and we hope it will last long. All that we can pray for is, that all the good of what is taking place in America and Ireland, without any of its alloy or its defects, may visit us too; and that God may hasten that day when he will pour out his Spirit upon all flesh; and not the Church, but the world; not ministers, but the people; not a sect, but the Church universal, shall be refreshed with the dews of God's blessing and with the influences of his Holy Spirit.

LECTURE IX.

EVENING LIGHT.

"*At evening time it shall be light.*"—ZECHARIAH xiv. 7.

IT seems to be implied that our present economy is light and cloud, sunshine and shadow; neither the brilliancy of the perfect day nor the blackness of the absolute night; yet more of darkness than of light; but the promise accompanies the blackest day that at evening-tide there shall flash forth, before the sun sets in his couch in the west, a burst of more than compensatory splendour. At evening-tide it shall be light. Why should God leave us in this economy with so many unsettled questions, unsolved difficulties, or, to use figurative language, with so much darkness intermingling with so much light? Why does he not shed down light upon every problem, give a solution to every difficulty, and enable us to see the past and the present, the infinite and the eternal, in all their unclouded magnificence and glory? The first answer to this is, that it does not arise from any unwillingness in God to show us light, as if he delighted in darkness, or preferred the clouded day to the bright sunshine. His works, in as far as they are not marred by sin, are replete with beauty; his word is light; "God is light; and in him is no darkness at all." The Holy Spirit is the teacher of all light; his people are called the children of light; and light is employed as a figure to denote all that is beautiful, and pure, and holy, in the experience and world of man. There is no evidence, therefore, that God delights in darkness. What does it arise from? We are not ourselves sufficiently prepared at present to know all; for cloud and sunshine, darkness and light, so intermingle and interpenetrate, that we must wait for evening-time to see light cast upon all, and be content at present with a day which is neither light nor darkness, but a mixture of shadow and of sunshine. We can see at once that the reason why we do not comprehend all is, not because God is dark, but because we are unenlightened. He is the Infinite, the Eternal, the Omnipresent; we are the finite, the limited, and the creatures of a day. How shall a finite vessel contain infinite good? How shall the finite grasp and comprehend the infinite, the eternal, the incomprehensible? How shall we, creatures of recent origin, understand even the event that sweeps past before us, when we know that the present event has links with the past, and interpenetrates with the future, and has relations in the height and in the depth that should make the most gifted humble, by teaching how little he really comprehends, and how limited is the horizon of the mightiest genius God gives to mankind? Our difficulty in comprehending and seeing all may arise from the very recency of our existence. The dynasty of man is only six thousand years old. What is this to epochs of which geology gives clear and distinct intimations? We have recently stepped upon a stage where everything is more or less new to us. Hence we are constantly correcting to-day the mistakes of yesterday, and constantly unlearning to-morrow what we learned and acquired to-day, and discovering more and more what even a Sir Isaac Newton needs to learn, what archangels may still learn—the vast chasm that there is between the most gifted of created intelligence and him who is the high and mighty God, who dwelleth in light inaccessible and full of glory. But were our finite capacity the only reason why we do not comprehend all, one would not be so humbled; there is another reason: the heart has lost its true polarity; it is infected by sin; and the understanding has to look through the hazy atmosphere that is around the heart in order to see the light and noon of God's eternal day. How can we expect to see the sun reflected from a muddy pool? How can we hope to read through a lens that has been broken or smoked? How can we see clearly through an atmosphere dim and disturbed; not only dimmed by sin, but disturbed by tempests of passion? How can we see all clearly when, within the compass of our own horizon, there is so much disordered, deranged, and obscured? Well does the Apostle say, "The understanding is darkened." Why? "Because it is alienated from the light of God," and because of "the blindness of the heart;" the blindness of the heart having much to do with the dimness and weakness of the understanding.

In order to show you that this mingled light and darkness is not confined to any one sphere, province, or department of our experience, let me adduce two or three in which it may be illustrated. Let us look into creation. It is really wonderful how little we understand it. The language of the Patriarch upon the plains of Shinar is as fresh and applicable to us in the present day as it was in his own, when he asked, "Who is this that darkeneth counsel by words without knowledge? Gird up now thy loins like a man; for I will demand of thee, and answer thou me. Where wast thou when I laid the foundations of the earth? declare, if thou hast understanding. Whereupon are the foundations thereof fastened? or who laid the corner-stone thereof? Or who shut up the sea with doors, when it brake forth, as if it had issued out of the womb? When I made the cloud the garment thereof, and thick darkness a swaddling-band for it, and brake up for it my decreed place, and set bars and doors; and said, Hitherto shalt thou come, but no further; and here shall thy proud waves be stayed?" Then he says again, "Hast thou entered into the springs of the sea? or hast thou walked in search of the depth? Where is the way where light dwelleth? and as for darkness, where is the place thereof? Wilt thou hunt the prey for the lion? or fill the appetites of the young lions, when they crouch in their dens, and abide in the covert to lie in wait? Who provideth for the raven his food, when his young ones cry unto God?" These are questions we cannot answer; these show that the day of our knowledge of nature alone is darkness and light. We talk of light, and heat, and electricity, and gravity, and chemical attraction; but what are these? Clouds to conceal our ignorance. And when we have reached a great truth in science we have only got a stage deeper into the dense and impenetrable darkness that is beyond; till at last we discover that the more we know in nature the more remains to be unknown; and that the known is merely the illuminated title-page of the unread, unknown. There is not a flower on the way-side, there is not a mineral in the earth, there is not a drop of water, there is not an atom of light, there is not a flash of lightning, there is not a peal of thunder, that are not shrouded in mystery: incidentally the cloud is riven, and a flash bursts through it, to show how little we know, and how thoroughly our ignorance should hide pride from man.

Let us look into providential history; I mean providence as developed in the world at large. Is it not a tangled skein? Do we not often find in it a labyrinth, with no thread equal to guide us through it? What explains the sufferings of good men, and the incidental success of bad men? How is it that often

> "The good die first,
> And they whose hearts are dry as summer dust
> Burn down to the sockets!"

How is it, I ask, that we see sin rampant here, sickness there, pestilence elsewhere? You answer, and you answer very properly, It is sin that explains all. So it does; but this solution only sends us further back. Why is sin? If God be omnipotent, why did he not prevent the intrusion of it? If God be omnipotent now, why does he not crush it? The deeper we think, and the further we penetrate, like Milton's angels, we are the more in wondering mazes lost; till the deepest thinker, like the highest Christian, always sits down the humblest man. We have read two chapters, one in creation, one in providence, where the day is neither night nor day; though in both is the hope that at evening-time it shall be light. Let me narrow the chapter of providence into a paragraph; that paragraph a personal one.

Let any one, however lowly the level that he treads, ask himself, why am I here? How have I come to be what I now am? Who shaped and rough-hewed my history? Who has brought me hitherto? Showers of troubles and bursts of sunshine have fallen upon you in your life's April day, and if any one trouble had been omitted from the shower, or ray from the light, your course had been altogether reversed. Have not what the world calls accidents, but what we may call providential incidents, overtaken you —sometimes overwhelmed you—till you felt as a flower beaten down by the hurricane and the storm? And yet that shower was meted out by God; and it did not come one drop too few, too light, or too short; it had its mission, and that mission was merciful: it had its errand to you, and that errand has left you where you are. There is not an individual who cannot look back at some little eddy in the current of his life, and say, If there had not been that eddy, my whole relationship, character, and course, had been revolutionized. It was the turning of a corner that made you the husband of that wife, the wife of that husband, or has lifted you to prosperity or honour. What explains all? The only explanation is, God superintending all; and though we cannot see the why, the wherefore, or the end, and though we often repine and fret, yet the optimist approaches nearest to the Christian who feels that, whatever comes, God is always in the right: where there is anything wrong, it lies at man's door.

Let us look at another chapter, revelation. Creation is full of inscrutable wonders; providence in its every chapter is replete with impenetrable mysteries. Are there no difficulties in revelation? What is election? what is God's sovereignty? what is the incarnation? what is the resurrection? what is free will? what is grace? what is regeneration of heart? Words that express glimpses of great truths, dimly understood. If you ask me, Has God fixed the current of every individual's life? I say, Yes. Do you ask, then are we Mahometan fatalists? No; your duty is to act as if all depended upon that act; and yet Christians are chosen Christians before they were born. Do we comprehend that? can we explain it? No. It is true, "No mar can come unto me unless the Father draw him?" There is God's sovereignty: is it equally true, "Him that cometh unto me I will in nowise cast out?" Both are equally true. Can you reconcile God's sovereignty with my free will? I answer, No, I cannot, and it is of no use attempting it. Again, we speak of the Trinity. The Father is God, the Son is God, and the Holy Ghost is God; and yet there is but one God. Do you ask me to explain how there can be three, and yet one? I cannot; and the more I look at it the less I comprehend it. But, does that prove that the Bible is wrong? It only shows that it is in harmony with all God's other provinces. Creation is full of impenetrable mysteries; providence is full of impenetrable mysteries; and God's book is full of impenetrable mysteries too. And therefore it is no evidence that the Bible is not true because it has perplexities; it is only true that, like creation and providence, it has depths that we can never sound, and heights that we can never climb. Take the events that sweep past us. If anybody will be at the trouble to go over the history of the last six, or the last ten years, probably the most startling epoch since the beginning of the Christian era, he will find far more than he can comprehend. War breaks out here, peace suddenly closes its wounds there; nations seem as if struck by an electric shock, to become instantly convulsed; and then as if some mighty power laid the influence, they become again composed and quiet. The tempest broods in the East, war-clouds gather in the West; till one leading daily reflector of public opinion says, only forty-eight hours ago, that all Europe is now gazing at the black electric cloud in the skies charged with elements of destruction and ready to burst and overwhelm the earth. Who can explain these things?

Go back some seven or eight years ago, and you hear nothing but prophecies of peace. In 1851, when that fairy vision, that beautiful creation, the Crystal Palace, burst like a gleam of heaven's sunshine upon the earth for a little, every one was congratulating his neighbour. Armies might be disbanded; navies might be burnt; nothing was to reign but peace; nothing to be reciprocated but love and brotherhood. Oh, what miserable prophets we were! How truly have facts contradicted the predictions! At this moment, look abroad on Europe. Let a reflecting mind, that can look below the surface, study it at this moment. God only knows into what tempests it may soon burst, into what quiet bays its troubled waters and its restless surf may ultimately settle; the only thing we know, is that after all, it is but the surface that is troubled; just as in the ocean the heaviest storm that beats upon it, thirty or forty feet down all is calm and untroubled. Come storm, come tempest, come convulsion, come war, come pestilence, come plague, the Lord reigneth; he sitteth above the floods; he holds the reins. Not an atom can fall, not an injury can occur, not a convulsion take place, which he does not permit; and though we cannot see the why of the present troubled state, be still, be patient: at evening time it shall be light.

This leads to the last clause—the prediction of what shall be the issue of all: at evening time it shall be light. What does this prediction teach us? That there is light, though at present we cannot see that light. In other words, the world is not chaos, though it often seems to us to be so; and the instant that the light settles upon what is taking place, we shall see that it was not chaos, nor confusion, but "all things working together for good to them that love God, and are called according to his purpose." There has not been an accident on earth from the days of Adam and Eve in Paradise; and what seem to us accidents are, as they will be seen to have been at the evening time's light, the emissarics and the missionaries of God. In the second place, this idea, "at evening time it shall be light," teaches us, if we apply it to individual life, that it is but a day. The longest life has its morning, its noon, and its night. As long as we are under forty years of age, time feels rather heavy. The schoolboy thinks the holidays will never come; but when he comes to be a youth, he finds that the wheel revolves a little faster; still he thinks it will be a long time before he is settled in the meridian of manhood. But when he has reached forty-five he has reached the top of the hill; he then begins to descend, and he soon discovers how rapid the descent is, till at last, as we look upon month succeeding month, and Christmas following Christmas, we exclaim, "Who could have thought this is 1859?" Our life is but a dream, a tale that is told, a fugitive shadow; the grass that flourisheth and fadeth, or is cut down at noon. But there is an evening time, when it shall be light. Be patient. What God does, you know not now, but hereafter, at evening time, you shall know. Then do not murmur and repine, for there will be an adjustment of all that is wrong, and the explanation of all that is difficult. Rest in the Lord, wait patiently for him; fret not because of evil doers; all things are just as they should be. Our conceptions are often in the wrong; God's works and ways are always in the right.

"At evening time it shall be light" teaches us another lesson, namely, the unexpectedness of God's solution of difficulties, and our extrication out of troubles. When the evening time comes, we expect the sun, to use the common language, to descend more and more, till we see but the mere rim of his disc above the western horizon, and at last he disappears. Then what do you expect? You expect the cool and enveloping, but dark shadow of night to settle on the earth. But instead, to your surprise, at evening time the order of nature seems reversed, and there breaks forth light.

Now, such is the exact expression of what our experience often is. A knock comes to your door; you think it is the hand of poverty: at evening time it is light—it is the hand of one that tells you of a fortune. The postman brings you a letter; your expectation is that it will be sorrowful and sad tidings from the gloomy East—it brings news that your son is promoted, that victory is in the van of your country's armies. A night of weeping overtakes you, and that night of weeping breaks in a morn of joy. You look up into the sky under the shadow of a great calamity; all is cold and dreary within, all is black and ominous without; not a star in your sky, nor a taper in your home, nor warmth on your hearth; you look still, and the great black cloud that was threatening to burst upon you, in the cold shadow of which you pined and were sorrowful, begins to turn out its lining of purple and of beauty and of glory; and if one sun has left you—the sun that shines from the meridian of day—ten thousand suns take his place, as stars in the sky,

> "Ever singing, as they shine,
> The hand that made us is divine;"

and you learn how sinful it is to forebode and distrust; how truly the prophet spoke when he said, "At evening time it shall be light." This is true in the case of each and of all, and in the experience of all. You have lost, perhaps, what was dear and precious to you. God in his providence has taken from you your wealth, your property, your estates; much that made life sunny and the heart happy. Your present construction of it is, "All this is unmingled calamity." You see the cloud only, the dark and shaded day. If you live long enough, you will see there was no chance, but an errand not only of wisdom, but of mercy and love. Many a soul in heaven will bless God through eternal ages that he was confined for years to a sick-bed, or was deprived of the property he made his god; for the loss dimmed the sheen of terrestrial things, made heaven seem nearer and earth appear more worthless, and weaned the heart from a world it was clinging to too closely. The key-note of many a joyous anthem in heaven will be, "It was good for me that I was thus afflicted." Or perhaps you have lost your nearest, dearest, and best beloved. You sit down under the cold shadow of this great calamity, and you see no light; you walk, or rather you sit in darkness; you ponder, you seek direction from God, you look up to him for light, and you find at the evening time of life's saddest and most sorrowful day there breaks forth light; you discover you have got a new grave in which you have an interest on earth, but over it a new mansion, in which you have an interest in heaven. You have lost one tie that knit you to this world, and you have gained another that lifts and attracts you to heaven. Often in our individual, spiritual, and Christian experience, we find the same thing, especially in the evening of life. Youth is the morning, manhood is the noon and the meridian, old age is the evening of life. The shadow becomes longer, the weight becomes heavier; a thousand things begin to show, whether we like to look at it or not, that man is going to his long home. What a happy thing if, as the heart begins to stand still, it ponders more deeply upon better and brighter things! if the grey hair be the reflected light of the better land! When you take a retrospect at that evening time of the past, do you not often discover that your bitterest cup was your best; that your heaviest sorrow was God's greatest mercy; that your protracted illness was wholesome medicine; that your disappointments, aches, and cross winds, the obstructions, the rugged road, and all the difficulties you met in your long journey, were all as wise as they were well; and your evening is so light, because God never forsook you in your morning, or left you to yourself in meridian day? And when we come to that hour that comes to all, when the body shall go the way of all the earth, and the spirit shall go the way of all souls, to be able then in a light that we see for the first time, the evening light, to look back upon the whole of life, and to discover that in the variegated web of life, not one thread in its warp or woof is out of place; that there was not one tear that was not expedient; that there was not one pang that was not of God and from God. Oh, what a blessed and beautiful evening light will that be, when one can say with Paul, "I am now ready to depart; I have fought a good fight, I have finished my course; henceforth there is laid up for me a crown of righteousness; which the Lord, the righteous Judge, will give me at that day!"

And when the evening light of this world shall come—for I believe that as this dispensation draws to its close, the light that will shine upon it will be its brightest—when we shall see the last chapter of its history, and read it in that soft and holy evening light, we shall then find that, after all, right was might, and truth was victory; we shall see no more through a glass darkly, but face to face. Then creation shall be lifted out of its shadow, and we shall understand its mysteries; inexplicable events will be made plain; sore tribulations will be explained; our disappointments will be set in their true light; we shall see that God was always in the right, that our suspicions and murmurings were always in the wrong. Then mistakes will be rectified: we shall miss many a loud professor in that blessed light of whom we were sure that he was going to heaven, and taking many with him; and we shall find many a happy possessor there, who said little, but did much; who also bent the knee in prayer, but as often moved the foot in duty and in obedience to God's word. We shall there, too, discover that many, who thought themselves antagonists, were working in the same harvest-field, and binding up the same sheaf for the Lord of the harvest; and that blows that we thought struck for a party were overruled by God for the good of all mankind. Then we shall see that the worst was well; we shall see why He gave, and why He took away; why that generous man was poor, and could not give; and why that selfish man was rich, and would not give; why the worthless were spared, and the brightest and best were taken. We shall see that under the splendid prosperity we envied, there were abysses we did not know; and that the sorest trials we deprecated were the seals of affection, the tokens of love; and that the heavy storms, and the hard rough road, and all the ills and aches we encountered, were sent of God to quicken our journey home.

Let us learn humility and submission. Our ignorance fails to comprehend, our impatience frets because we cannot do so. We wrangle with Providence; we complain of our position; we dispute about our difficulties; we think the ways of God are wrong. It is our ignorance that is dense;

it is our impatience that is fretful; it is our ways that are crooked. Trust where you cannot comprehend; lean on an Omnipotence that you cannot now grasp. Cease to charge God foolishly. God is ever right, even when He is inscrutable. Never forget God is love to-day; He will be to us love to-morrow; and when we shall see the love that God is to-day in the light of that blessed evening of to-morrow, our greatest grief will be that we ever murmured and complained; and our greatest thankfulness that we could say over the grave that received our dead, "The Lord gave, and the Lord hath taken away; blessed be the name of the Lord:" after the hurricane that swept our homes, what the Patriarch could also say, "Shall we receive good from the Lord, and not evil?" And then we shall see the whole of creation, the whole of providence, the whole of individual life, the whole of Christian life, the whole of revelation, no longer a mystery, no longer light and shadow, but a brilliant transparency, where all is light and love, and we the happy possessors of it for ever and ever.

LECTURE X.

THE STANDING MIRACLE.

There is a great feature which accompanies the procession of the ages to the very end of the age. It is

"*This generation shall not pass, till all these things be fulfilled.*"—MATTHEW xxiv. 34.

WHAT is the generation specified here? We have a key to it in the previous parable of the fig-tree. The fig-tree was used as the symbol of the Jewish nation; as such our Lord blasted it. He found it without fruit, though clothed with magnificent leaves, such as ought to have embosomed fruit; and finding it so he blasted it. Now, he says one of the tokens of the approaching eve of the world's long week will be the budding of the fig-tree. In the buds of spring you have the young prophets of the approaching summer. As soon as you see the shoots begin to peep out from the dark, hard bark, you have a token of the nearness of the sweet sunshine; not of the summer of England, lost in the cold and dreary winter, but of the everlasting summer, whose sunrise shall have no western setting. Who is meant by this fig-tree? The Jews; and therefore it is predicted of them that this race, or generation, shall not pass away till the end. I admit that of this place many critics have taken an opposite view. The common opinion and interpretation is that "this generation" means a race of forty years. γενεα is used occasionally in classic writers in this sense; but it is used also in classic writers, and always in Hellenistic Greek, to mean a race, a nationality, a class. I do not quote passages that every scholar is more or less familiar with.

But the real use of γενεα, here translated "generation," is to be gathered not so much from classic as from scriptural use. The Greek Septuagint and the Greek New Testament are in this matter our proper guides to what is the exact interpretation of the passage. Stier, the most eloquent and evangelical of all the German critics of the present day, asserts that beyond all dispute the γενεα that is not to pass away—the generation that is to outlive all these things—is the Jewish race. I was no less pleased to find that the Dean of Canterbury, Mr. Alford, in his "Critical Commentary," thinks it is beyond critical dispute that γενεα here means the Jewish race, and in no degree the arbitrary interpretation of a race of thirty or forty years, as held by some unripe scholars. Let us see some of the grounds on which we come to this conclusion. We notice, first of all, there is not one previous word about the Jews or Jerusalem when he introduces this verse. If he had at that very moment been speaking of the destruction of Jerusalem, of the dispersion of the Jews, and the fall of the Jewish dynasty, one might refer it to an existing generation; for it is a fact that forty years after these words were spoken, Jerusalem was laid in ruins, and the Jews were dispersed. But the subject he has been speaking of is as follows:—"Immediately after those days shall the sun be darkened; then shall appear the sign of the Son of man; then shall the tribes of the earth mourn; they shall see the Son of man coming in the clouds of heaven with power and great glory. He shall send his angels with a great sound of a trumpet, and they shall gather together his elect from the four winds, from one end of heaven to the other. Now learn a parable of the fig-tree; this generation shall not pass till all these things be fulfilled." If "this generation" means the forty years' race that were living then, what must we infer? That all these things have been fulfilled. Has Christ then come like the lightning? Have the angels gathered his elect from the four winds of heaven? Have all the tribes of the earth mourned? Has the sign of the Son of man been seen? Has the lightning-splendour that heralds the approaching Lord burst upon a world that expected it not? The man would be insane who would assert that all these things have come to pass. But this generation, we are told, is to outlive them all, to be cotemporaneous with all the events that are here described; and only to be absorbed in the collective nationalities of mankind, that is, in the Church of Christ, when all these things have occurred, and the Son of man has come in the clouds of heaven with power and great glory.

Another argument to me conclusive in favour of this interpretation is the thirty-sixth verse: "But of that day and hour knoweth no man, no, not the angels of heaven, but my father only." If you ask many readers of the New Testament, they will quote that text as a reason for not studying the chronology of Scripture prophecy; and they will say, "Of that hour knoweth no man," which is quite true, "except my Eather in heaven." But if this γενεα meant the race then living, who were to live thirty years—the average length of a generation—then, instead of no man knowing the day and the hour, our blessed Lord must have announced it, for he said it would take place in the limits of a generation; and the Jews to whom he spoke these words knew it, for they knew what was the average length of a generation. Our blessed Lord would be represented, if the interpretation be true, as contradicting himself; first saying it will take place within the limits of forty years, and then saying that the day and the hour, meaning the time, no man knoweth, no, not the angels that are in heaven. Therefore I infer that Dean Alford's interpretation is the true one. I may state that Strauss, the infidel German writer, takes γενεα in the sense in which Barnes and Matthew Henry, most excellent men in their way, and most sound in doctrine, though not good critical interpreters of difficult passages of Scripture, have taken it; and he argues, with irresistible effect, that our Lord was contradicted by the facts of the case. Strauss says, Jesus predicted that that generation, which would live thirty years, should not pass away till all these things were fulfilled; but, Strauss says, history proves that all these things have not been fulfilled; that the Son of man is not come like the lightning, that he is not come in the clouds of heaven; that the angels have not gathered together his elect; and his inference, if the interpretation be correct, is most logical—namely, that our blessed Lord here contradicts himself. The last argument I adduce against the common view is this—that long after Jerusalem had sunk in its ruins, and the ploughshare of the Roman had passed through its magnificent remains, the Apostles and the Christians constantly looked and prayed for the second personal coming of our Lord and Saviour Jesus Christ. When did John write the Apocalypse? It was begun in the year 96; but the year 96 was some sixteen years after the destruction of Jerusalem. If, therefore, this referred entirely to the destruction of Jerusalem, and all these things were to transpire then, and Christ was then to come, what does John mean by saying, sixteen years after that event, "He cometh with clouds, and every eye shall see him?" And what does he mean by closing that magnificent Apocalypse, which has all the grandeur and procession of a gorgeous drama, but all the reality of sober and of literal fact, by saying, "Come, Lord Jesus, come quickly," if so be that he had come within the limits of the generation that had already passed away? I cannot quote all the passages illustrating the use of this word, but I may mention one or two where it unquestionably means not a generation of thirty years, but a race of men; or, as we should call it in modern phrase, a nationality. For instance, in Matthew xxiii. 36, he says, "Verily, I say unto you, All these things shall come upon this generation." The Greek word is γενεα. What things were to come upon it?—"Behold I send you prophets, and ye shall kill them, and ye shall scourge them, that upon you may come all the righteous blood shed upon the earth, from the blood of righteous Abel unto the blood of Zacharias, son of Barachias, whom ye slew." That generation did not slay these martyrs; it was the Jewish race that existed from the beginning, and slew these martyrs. And therefore our blessed Lord, in this passage, lays to the charge of that generation the slaughter of Zacharias, and the slaughter of men, from the blood of righteous Abel downwards; showing that he employs the word γενεα, not in the sense of an existing generation, but of a race or nationality of people. In a passage of Psalm xxiv., David speaks of the righteous, "This is the generation of them that seek him, that seek thy face, O God of Jacob."

"This generation" is exactly parallel to another phrase used by Luke, in chapter xxi. 23, where he says, "Woe unto them that are with child, and to them that give suck in those days! for there shall be great distress in the land, and wrath upon this people." Now, here is one evangelist calling "this generation" "this people;" the very commentary that we want; and proving therefore, incontestably, that the generation is the race of the Jews, whose existence shall be coeval with the fulfilment of all the prophecies recorded in this chapter, outlast and outlive them all, till absorbed in the universal church, when Christ and Christian shall be all in all.

Let us look now for the fulfilment of this. First, the Jew exists in every land in all the intensity of his first insulation; his look and countenance demonstrative beyond dispute, of his eastern origin; and that full, deep, rich-toned, thorough-bass voice, so unlike the cracked voices of northern nations, indicating his birth-place also. His thoughts, his hopes, his affinities, his sympathies, have outlived the rush of eighteen hundred years; and the Jew on the streets of London, is strictly and literally the descendant of Abraham, of Isaac, of Jacob, and the patriarchs, and Moses, and Aaron; and there is not a poor ragged Jew in London that cannot boast of an ancestry in comparison of which that of England's proudest nobles is only of yesterday, and scarcely to be spoken of in the same breath. His identity has never been nor can be disputed. The language which he still loves, the language of his prayers, his praises, and his hopes, is that in which the law was thundered, which sounded in the songs sung by the captives in the midst of Babylon, when they hung their harps upon the willows; the language I have heard and joined in in his synagogue, in singing the psalms, with a reference, however, that would to God he had in his heart also—a reference to Him who is the light to lighten the

Gentiles, and the glory of his peop.e Israel. That language was heard in the temple; it gleamed from the stones upon the breast of the high priest; it echoed in the glorious strains of David; it was heard in the synagogue; it was the sacred vehicle of the sublimest thoughts—the most ancient and majestic of human tongues. Who can deny that the Jew upon our streets retains all the identity of his connection with the Jew of eighteen hundred years or two thousand years ago? Let us mark, what is so striking, the contrast he presents to all other races;—the Greek, the Roman, and the Carthaginian are gone; there are more descendants of Cæsar and Regulus probably in London than in Rome at this moment. The wild Albanian is scarcely the descendant of Homer, and Sophocles, and Euripides, and Socrates, and the heroes of Marathon and the conquerors of Thermopylæ. These nations cannot produce one single fragment of genealogy to demonstrate their national succession; or any sheet of parchment or tablet of stone in which they can trace and prove their national family. These streams are merged in the great river of humanity, and are sweeping onward to the boundless and absorbing main. But the Jew is unmistakeably the descendant of those that, alas! crucified the Lord of Glory; but he is also the father of those that will shout, "Hosannah! blessed is he that cometh in the name of the Lord."

In order to show the Lord's prophecy fulfilled in every detail, mark this singular fact—no nation has been so persecuted, so ill-treated, as the Jew. He has been branded with every vile epithet; his name is synonymous in the popular speech with all that is vulgar, avaricious, and mean. If you ask some of these men, Why do you thus treat the Jew? I have heard Christians answer by referring to the predictions about him, It is predicted that he is to be a slave, to be crushed, to have no rest for the soles of his feet, among all lands; and we are only doing what prophecy prescribes. I answer, precepts of charity and loving-kindness belong to us; God, who gives the prophecy, will look to its fulfilment; He does not require our aid to enable him to fulfil his promises. Let us quote commandments for our duties; let us leave predictions of man for the God that inspired them. In poverty, in wealth—under republic and despotism—the Jew has been persecuted. From the Czar of all the Russias to the Republic of America, the Jew has been persecuted. Like the flying-fish that has no peace in any element, the Jew, whether rich or poor, whether under republic, limited monarchy, or despotism, has been equally persecuted and maltreated. The fire and the faggot have been used under royal countenance before now; imprisonment and torture were his common treatment in the middle ages. The only lands where the Jew has been sympathised with in his ruin, though we never doubt that he has inherited a curse that he cannot shake off till the great Curse-Bearer shall take it away—the only lands where he is not persecuted—are those where a pure and Protestant Christianity prevails. And singular enough (I hope you will not think it is taking to one's own country more than belongs to it) the Jew quotes Scotland as the only country in which he has never been maltreated in his past. Singular enough, also, those people that quote the prophecies of his curse, and ill-treat him, seem purposely to omit the prophecies of his restoration, which embosom this, that they that bless him shall be blessed; and that God will bless the man that tries to lighten the load and to mitigate the curse of his suffering, weary-footed, broken-hearted, and sorrowing people Israel. But, strange to say, the treatment that would have extinguished every nation upon earth has only crowded the Jew more intensely to his synagogue and his country; and what has extinguished others and would extinguish us, has, in the case of the Jew, acted like the fire upon his own burning bush; the more it has burned the brighter it has blazed, the greener have been its twigs, unscathed and unscorched even in the depth of the consuming fire. You have in these facts the identity of the Jew still maintained; the existence of the Jewish race in its integrity; there being now eleven millions of Jews more or less insulated throughout the whole world. You have in that the fulfilment of a prophecy stronger than fire, or flood, or force, or persecution; for the least word that God has spoken is more powerful than the mightiest weapons that the greatest dynasties can wield; you have the fulfilment of the prediction, "This generation shall not pass away till all these things be fulfilled." And what shows not only their existence, but that they have prospered even in the depths of persecution, is the extraordinary fact that the Jew is the money-lender of cabinet, of congress, and divan. He is at this moment the great banker of the world. There are some Jewish names that would bring more money in ten minutes than the House of Lords would bring together in ten years. You will find the Jew in Petersburg, in Paris, in Vienna, in Berlin, in every capital, the representative of wealth; in whose presence the very men that have crushed him cringe when they want assistance; and before whom those that in their hearts despise him are constrained, by a mysterious instinct that tells us they are the men of destiny, to bow down and recognize a power stronger than dynasties, mightier than armies, more lasting than the governments of the world.

Now how can you account for all these phenomena? Only by the prediction of God—"This race shall not pass away." They are the only people that have a country, and do not live in it; that have a capital to which their hearts cling as the needle vibrates to the pole, as infants to their mother, as England's most patriotic sons to their home; the Jew's heart's affections cling and cluster around Jerusalem. He still says in his synagogue, with an emphasis that no description of mine can exaggerate, "If I forget thee, O Jerusalem, may my tongue cleave to the roof of my mouth, and my right hand forget its cunning." And that capital shall be theirs again. When the Euphrates shall be dried up—when the crescent shall have waned, as it is waning fast—we shall read some morning of a glorious exodus, far more majestic than that of old; when from all lands, like converging streams and currents, God's ancient people, with their hearts and their hopes in Jerusalem, shall rush together; and every railway and steamer shall make them welcome; and some of us may live to see the Jew again in his own ancient capital; and some of us may hear in Gethsemane, on Calvary, in the garden of Arimathea, voices rich in music, and richer still because the hearts of the singers are in them, singing, "Crown him Lord of all; Hosannah, Hosannah in the highest; lo, this is our God, we have waited for him; blessed is he that cometh in the name of the Lord." Or, in the words of one of the most magnificent anthems in a book which contains so much that is magnificent—the English Prayer-Book, "Thou art the King of Glory, O Christ. We believe that thou wilt come to be our Judge. We therefore pray thee, help thy servants, whom thou hast redeemed with thy precious blood; and number us with thy saints in glory everlasting."

LECTURE XI.

THE FINALLY SAVED.

"*But he that shall endure unto the end, the same shall be saved.*"—MATTHEW xxiv. 13.

THERE has been much to endure in every age, and on every spot of Christendom; there is little to enjoy drawn from this world, and much to endure inseparable from our passage through it. The early Christians passed to heaven amid whirlwinds of persecution; the cross in their heart was the mark the marksmen aimed at; the form of our trials may be altered, but in some shape they remain; and our duty is embosomed in the promise—endure the trials, and thus in the end we shall be saved. It is a fair subject of inquiry, where and from whence do we expect these trials? First of all, from our own heart. If you have a regenerated heart, there is still much in it of alloy, in affinity with the world, with Satan, with temptation, and with sin. If our own heart had its way, it would prefer to be wafted to heaven amid aromatic perfume, and on the wings of gentle gales, and saved the struggle, and the conflict, and the wear and tear of Christian faithfulness. Besides, there is in every man's bosom a diverging influence that tends to draw him aside. Who that knows his own heart best, does not feel it throwing up from its unsounded depths, temptations, thoughts, desires, passions, affinities, longings, lusts, appetites? These things thrust themselves in as foes that the Christian repels. It is the mark of the worldling that he gives them hospitality as friends whom he joyfully welcomes. Now against all these we must be watchful, and watchful continually; we are to endure, that is, bear them, stand them out, pass through them, be conquerors through Him that loved us; and having done all to stand.

We are exposed to the wiles and the machinations of Satan. The existence of the devil is not a myth, nor a romance, nor a metaphor, as the celebrated Strauss would have it; his existence is a mournful experience, his successes are tragedies in high life and in low life; an apostle was not exempt from his action. "Satan hath desired to have thee, that he may sift thee as wheat." What avenue he will select to thy heart, what passion he will fan into burning flame in your heart, what besetting sin he will mount and ride to victory in another's heart, God only knows; he will make the experiment, it is his trade, he is drilled and practised in it; he goeth about a ceaseless traveller, ever seeking whom he may devour; but, blessed thought, he is a coward, he is beaten; resist the devil and he will flee from you; deny him, and he will prevail; mock at him, and he will thank you; pronounce him a myth, and he will cheer you; resist him, and he will flee from you; hear sounding from the skies when the assault is hottest and the trial is bitterest, "He that endureth unto the end, the same shall be saved." In the third place, the world will also assault you: ambition, that tempting and fascinating passion, will spread before the lustful and the envious eye its thrones, its pomp, and its splendour; it will urge you to mount that ladder on which the few have risen to fame, concealing the tens of thousands at its foot who lie there scattered and disjointed wrecks; he will tempt you to seek the bubble reputation even at the cannon's mouth, to sacrifice all that is pure, holy, beautiful and good, in order to grasp so much trash that may be grasped thus, in order to have your name pronounced with *éclat*, to have yourself spoken of as great; not knowing that when you have attained the end—and it is the few that succeed, it is the multitude that are trampled and beaten down—the issue is not worth a tithe of the price. What glittered like a resplendent lake in the distance is only the mirage, the sunbeams reflected from the scorching sand; and like David, who, when seated on a throne, the whole world at his feet, cried, what the human heart will still cry, "Oh, that I had wings like a dove, that I might flee away and be at rest." And the world, in the next place, will assail you in the shape of Mammon, the god of the age, before whose shrine so much faithfulness, so much justice, so much kindness are constantly sacrificed. He will tell you, you must make haste to be rich; thousands are in the race, and you will only succeed by putting forth all your strength, and running at the very top of your speed. Never care, he will tell you, what you trample down; if your competitor falls, just make him a pathway to lift you a little higher, and to help you on a little quicker; do not mind cheating, do not mind lying, do not mind false advertising, do not mind all sorts of deception; in the words of the Latin poet,

> "Rem recte si possis. Si non rem
> Quomodo rem;"

that is, "Money; honestly, if you can get it by honesty; but if not, get money at any sacrifice, and at any price." If you have got money, what is its worth? "What shall it profit a man if"—what is not certain—"if he gain the whole world, and lose his own soul?" It is written upon all the fortunes of the millionaire, it is written upon all the feelings of his own innermost heart, "He that drinketh of this water shall thirst again;" but the poorest widow, that

"Knows no more, her Bible true,"

knows and feels this, and rejoices while she feels it, "But whoso drinketh of the living water that I shall give him shall never thirst; for it shall be in him a well of living water, springing up into everlasting life." It is the proof of the ruin of the soul that it seeks to satisfy itself with the things of this world; it is the proof of its grandeur that all that is in the world together fails to satisfy it. Resist the temptations of ambition, resist the seductions of Mammon; hear in the midst of the struggle and the competitorship of both, "He that endureth to the end, the same shall be saved."

Sin in all its phases, its fascinating aspects, will seek to seduce you. Your ear is open, we know from the fallen nature that is in us, to its siren strains; the eye has not a covenant made with it in every instance, and is open to its vast attractions. We breathe a tainted air, we live in an infected world; we stand, if unwatchful, in jeopardy every moment; we need grace sufficient for us; let us seek that grace, and let us hear the cheering encouragement from Him that gives it, "Be of good cheer, I have overcome the world. He that endureth unto the end, the same shall be saved."

Error will assail you. Truth is an exotic in this world; error is an indigenous plant. At one time error comes in the shape of liberality, latitudinarianism, denying every distinctive truth, and preaching the popular aphorism, "It does not matter what a man believes, if he do what is honest, it will be all right with him." At another time error will come in all the robes of a rigid and exclusive sectarianism, telling you that unless you can pronounce my shibboleth, and repeat my creed, and subscribe my dogmas, you cannot be saved. But by being forewarned you are thereby forearmed. The Bible has no sympathy with latitudinarianism, which makes vital truth or deadly error a matter of indifference; it has no sympathy with the hard and exclusive scepticism which perils one's everlasting prospects on the acceptance of a crotchet; it is liberal in all things that are non-essential, it is strict and uncompromising in all things that are essential; its grand characteristic being unity in things essential, liberality in things that are non-essential, and charity in essential and non-essential together. In holding fast the great truths of the Gospel, in acting out those truths, which is a greater difficulty than holding them fast, you will be met in every sphere and stage of the world with opposition, persecution, resistance, even to the death. The world cannot burn you, but it can deride you; and to some sensitive minds that are not hardened by experience, a gibe, a sneer, is even more intolerable than a blow. The world is so peculiar in its creed, if creed it may be said to have, that the moment you show any feeling to religion above zero, or enthusiasm on subjects of everlasting moment, or a determination to carry out your principles into everyday practice, it will denounce you as a bigot, your religion will be branded as ultra Protestantism, your zeal will be denounced as fanaticism. The world will allow you to be as earnest, as eloquent as you like at the hustings, when you are wanting a place in parliament; and it will say, "What an able man! what a worthy candidate for our borough!" The world will allow you in the House of Commons to speak with all the burning enthusiasm of an indignant patriot, in order to reduce the income-tax from one shilling and ninepence to sevenpence; the world will admire and applaud to the echo the barrister who pleads as if it were a death-struggle for his client; the world admires the merchant who is up at sunrise and goes to bed at sunset, and scarcely takes his meals, in order to catch the market, and to make a larger per centage to-day than he made yesterday. Enthusiasm, earnest and burning enthusiasm, immense earnestness, the world admires and applauds even to the very echo in these things. But show that you believe the awful realities of death, of judgment, of eternity to come; show that you believe the soul is of infinite grandeur, and that its salvation outweighs worlds upon worlds in its value; show that you believe what the Bible says, that you live as the Bible bids, and that you dare do what the Bible commands, and the world that will stand enthusiasm when its own interests are at issue, brands your enthusiasm as fanaticism, your decision as bigotry; and thinks it such a pity that these canting Christians should make such a stir about Sabbaths, and about Bibles, and about sanctuaries, and about all those subjects that trouble and plague the earnest and the great men of the world, who look above these things, and deal with nobler topics, and contemplate far more momentous issues. Be not discouraged; what you can prove to be duty, cleave to; leave for its sake all that man loves, face for its sake all that man fears; count all but loss for the excellency of it; lay down wealth, lay down health, lay down money, lay down estates; concede the largest husk of prejudice, or preference, or prepossession, if it will conciliate a brother; but compromise not the least vital truth if it were to conciliate all mankind. "He that endureth unto the end, the same shall be saved."

But instead of dwelling upon this, the ordinary opposition that you have to meet, let me try to show those forms of religion, those shades and systems of belief, which will not endure, but must collapse in the ordeals to which they will be subjected in a world which tests the real every-day, and rejects all that is pretentious. My argument is, that nothing will endure but vital, evangelical, scriptural Christianity; that nothing will weather what it has to encounter except a heart regenerated by the Spirit of God; a faith that grasps the Saviour; a hope that rides at the anchor sure and stedfast—in other words, real, living, heartfelt religion, that alone will last and endure. But there are various types of religion that seek its place, none of which will endure: to know them is to be warned and guarded against them. There is, for instance, the religion of mere impulse. You hear one day a stirring sermon; it startles you from the lethargy of years; you are roused; you are excited to a very high degree; you think you are now a Christian. Excitement is not conviction: the feelings may be excited, and the heart may remain dead in trespasses and in sins, and as soon as the exciting force is expended the excited feelings will subside; the flame will die from want of fuel, and the cinders and the embers, cold and worthless, will be all that will remain behind. Tears and smiles are like April showers and sunshine; the one do not make religion, and the other are not yet the summer. There is the religion from personal attachment. It seems almost an absurd thing; but he that knows human nature well knows it is a fact, that some persons accept a religion because it is fashionable, or because it is the adoption of some one to whom he or she is deeply attached. You hear a preacher whom you esteem, whose character, whose conduct, whose personal worth you admire, or to whom you are personally, through relationship or friendship, attached; and you look at all he says in the light of the esteem and affection you bear him; and you believe what he says just because you admire and love the man. But this is not religion: the advocate changes, the toy loses its gilding, the relationship is disturbed, an incident upsets your conviction, and you return to the religion that you had, or, rather, to the negative religion that you once cherished: it is not a faith that will endure to the end. There is the religion of sentiment; not the religion of conviction nor of the adoption of the heart, but purely of the imagination. It indulges tender and sentimental emotions; it covers up every awful truth in theology with flowers and with perfume; it turns the most sacred truths into plaintive music for its amusement; it is the sentimentality of piety, extremely beautiful; spends its time in working laces for altar-cloths, in preparing priests' robes, in decorating the altar with flowers, in fitting the sanctuary to all the phases of the varying senses and seasons; it is the religion of painters, of poets, of architects, of ecclesiastical dressmakers and robemakers; it is the piety of Athens and the Academy, not of Jerusalem and the Church of God; it shrinks from the storm; it dreads defiling its delicate Sabbath-day and saint-day robes; it has no martyrs; it scarcely lives; it cannot endure; its advocates, as such, will not be saved in the end. Then there is, in the next place, the religion of intellect; a very striking and, so far, commendable form. The understanding is convinced that Christianity is true; it believes its every dogma from the commencement of the Creed to the Amen at its close; but it is a religion clear in the head, but cold as an icicle at the heart's core; it has no vital force, no warm and sanctifying energy; it is orthodoxy, not regeneration; it is light in the head without love in the heart; it is clear, but cold; it is the religion of the devils, who believe every word of the Creed, and, whilst they do so, tremble. And if your religion is wholly the religion of the intellect, however clear, however tenaciously held, unless it has transformed the heart, it will not endure to the end.

There is, in the next place, a religion which may seem to you at first blush a true and scriptural religion, namely, the religion of conscience. But that religion is not the religion of God, and will not endure. It is a powerful type of religion, and, in its place, a form of it that one must respect: one always must respect the man who is conscientious even when he is wrong. Because a man is conscientious in his adhesion to error, it makes me respect him; but, because it is error that he adheres to, it makes me try to extract him from the meshes of that error, not to accept the error as true. Now, wherever there is the religion of conscience, its whole leverage is terror; it drives to duty, it scares to what is right; it torments you if you neglect to pray, it threatens you if you fail in the least service; it is most repulsive, its duties are drudgery, its service is slavery; it dreads the devil, and fears not God; it is not the religion of Christ; it is a religion that will not endure. There is the religion of the natural affections, than which nothing is more amiable, beautiful, or lovely; and yet it is a religion that will not endure. Its sphere is the home, its shrine is the fireside, every earthly relationship is glorified by it, and yet it is not that religion that will endure to the end. There is the religion of tradition; men believe what their fathers believed; but this religion is not the religion of the Bible; it is not the religion of truth. We build upon the sand, not upon the rock; we believe in our fathers, not in the Apostles; we rest upon a tradition handed down through a century, venerable for years; but if tested by that test before which truth alone can stand, and error must ever fall, it will not endure unto the end. There is another type of religion —the religion of form. It feeds on beautiful pageants, it is charmed with glorious rites; it would not worship in any but a mediæval church; it would not listen to anything short of Mozart's and Handel's choicest pieces. With it the altar occupies the place of God, the sign of the cross Christianity itself; broad phylacteries, and holy places, and beautiful churches, constitute the sum and substance of the religion of form. There is no endurance in it; it collapses the moment it is exposed to trouble. The ear may be engaged, the eye may be gratified, the country may be covered with beautiful cathedrals, but it may be empty of hearts that beat with love to God, and of souls that would die rather than sacrifice vital and essential truth.

What is then the religion that will endure? The religion of the head—its roots in the intellect; the religion of the heart—its roots striking down there also; the religion of the conscience—its law, its atmosphere, its motive power; but all three inspired and taught by the Holy Spirit of God. This religion accepts Christianity because it is true, loves it because it is the manifestation of love, obeys it because it is duty, and ever sings and shouts, and triumphs while it shouts, "I know in whom I have believed, and that he is able to keep that which I have committed to him against that day." This religion is not the mountain torrent fed by the shower, leaving its channel dry when the clouds are emptied of their contents; but it is the stream that moves on through belts of greenness, sprinkles all its banks with odorous flowers, until it mingles and is lost amid the mighty main; it is the oak that waves its branches in the storm, strikes its roots deeper in the tempest, develops itself in the sunshine, and in winter and in summer makes progress towards God, and heaven, and happiness. He that thus believes, that thus lives, and grows, has in him a religion that will overcome the assaults of Satan, that will vanquish all the temptations of Mammon, that will turn aside all the shafts and arrows of ambition, and pride, and pomp, and vain glory; and, enduring to the end, its holy and its happy possessor will be saved.

Pray that this religion may be written on your hearts; pray that God's Holy Spirit may teach your hearts what I can only teach the ear. Never forget, humbling as it is, and it is most humbling, that all the eloquence of Demosthenes, all the argumentative powers of Æschines, all the persuasive language of a Cicero, combined and concentrated in every sermon that you hear, will only be like the tinkling cymbal and the sounding brass, unless the Spirit of God carry it home to your heart, and make it life; to your conscience, and make it law; to your intellect, and make it a conviction; to the whole man, and make you a new creature in Christ Jesus. And while you hold this creed, never forget we are on the winning side. The great majority is, after all, with truth; the minority is on the side of Satan. All the angels in heaven agree with us; all the saints in glory agree with us; the goodly fellowship of the prophets, the noble army of martyrs, the glorious company of the Apostles, agree with us. And not only are we in the majority, but success is as sure as the promises of God; and he that leans, and looks up, and trusts, and perseveres, has a promise that will fail when God's throne is overthrown, and heaven and earth have passed away, and only then; "He that endureth unto the end, the same shall be saved." Great Babylon shall be cast down as a millstone into the depths of the sea; thrones shall be overturned, dynasties shall all be changed; there shall be earthquakes and plagues, and pestilences, and famines, nation rising up against nation, and kingdom against kingdom; and there shall be changes in the sun, and in the moon, and in the stars: and in the hearts of kings perplexity, and distress of nations, men's hearts failing them for fear of the things that are coming on the earth: but he that endureth, he that clings to the Rock of Ages, he that trusts in the living God, has given unto him eternal life; "and none," says he, who never spake but what was truth, "shall pluck him out of my hand." Your trials will only be to you what the fire is to the steel; your afflictions will only be to you what the furnace is to the gold; you will be purified through them and by them; until, reaching the end of the rugged road, and the flinty path, and the thorny way that you have long trod, you appear amid the white-robed group who are welcomed into heaven, not as natives, but as colonists; and of whom one asks, startled by their splendour, struck by the novelty of the scene, and amazed at the overwhelming multitude, "What are these, and whence came they?" Here is the true church, in which there is no sect, nor exclusiveness, nor bigotry, nor latitudinarianism, nor error: "These are they." Who? The Churchman would say, "Who came out of our body;" and probably the Dissenter might say, "Who came out of our body;" and the Church of Rome, to a dead certainty, would say, "Who belong to us;" but Christ's Church is larger, ampler, nobler, more glorious than all this. "These are they," and these are Churchmen indeed, "who have washed their robes and made them white in the blood of the Lamb; therefore are they before the throne of God, and serve him day and night without ceasing."

LECTURE XII.

THE LAST CONFLAGRATION.

A day of no common glory will rise one day on the world. A scene of unprecedented splendour and awe will be reflected from it.

"*For as the lightning cometh out of the east, and shineth even unto the west; so shall also the coming of the Son of man be.*"—MATTHEW xxiv. 27.

To guard God's people against everything like a misapprehension of the true epoch of the advent of Him whose right it is to reign, it is predicted that he shall not be found in the secret places. We are not to listen to any one who says, "Behold, he is in the desert; behold, he is in the secret chamber;" for here is the grand characteristic of his advent—"As the lightning cometh out of the east, and shineth even unto the west; so shall the coming of the Son of man be."

The very first truth taught by this similitude is that Christ's advent shall be sudden; unexpected by the masses; like the flash that leaps from the bosom of the black cloud, sweeps through the sky, and completes its journey in an instant. So shall the coming of the Son of man be. No telegraphic announcement, no roll of drum, no roar of cannon, no clanging of bells will announce His approach. Unexpected by the mass of mankind, there shall burst upon the world one red lightning flash that shall close the age in which we have so deep a stake, and commence that glorious one in which I trust many have so bright and so sure a hope. His advent will also be with intense and vivid splendour. The lightning fills the whole world; leaps from the east, and finds its lair only in the remote and distant west. When not the light, but the searching lightning of that day shall come, it will penetrate the cell of the captive, irradiate with more than the splendours of noon the deepest and the darkest dungeon of the earth; enter cabinet, and congress, and parliament, and divan; search the heart of each individual through all its most sequestered nooks, its most hidden crannies, its supposed impenetrable recesses. It will rush through every cell of the soul—make luminous the page of every memory; till sins we had thought annihilated will start into preternatural freshness, and iniquities we had forgotten will be displayed in all their portentous outlines; and each man's soul shall be as legible to the universe as tree and rock are legible in the dark night in the lightning that leaps with successive and continuous flashes from the east to the distant west. If such shall be the suddenness of our Lord's advent, what an arrest, if it be possible to conceive such a thing, will take place. The world will be going on when Christ comes as it does at this moment. The farmer sowing the seed in spring, or reaping the golden harvests of autumn, in an instant will see that the harvest of the earth is come, and that angels are the reapers. The poet in the midst of his stanza, the painter surveying his unfinished sketch—the judge on the bench, the prisoner in the dock, the jury in the box, the preacher in the pulpit, the tradesman in his shop, the monarch in his palace—will feel instantly arrested, and discover that time has at once plunged into eternity. The ocean steamer will suddenly pause as it ploughs the deep; the railway train at its greatest speed will stand still; the bridal procession will stop midway; the funeral march will cease ere it reach the grave; armies marshalled to battle will lay down their arms, and look and marvel; and the living torrents that rush through every street of this great metropolis, as if struck by some terrible paralysis, will stand still, and find that the day of the final adjustment of all accounts at the great white throne has at length overtaken the earth.

But we have seen that there will be some premonitory signs of the approach of that day, interpreted aright by some. The lightning leaps always from the black bank of cloud. The great cloud careering on the wind, and overspreading the heaven, is therefore the warning that the thunder is about to roll and the lightning to flash forth upon the earth. And will there not be signs, and symptoms, and premonitory warnings, of the approach of that last lightning blaze? On seeing these premonitory signs, some will say, "Your interpretations are ridiculous; the whole thing can be explained on the principles of natural science. To expect that the great black cloud which has risen from the horizon, and overspreads the sky, is charged with divine judgments, and is to burst in scathing lightning upon the earth, is to be fanatical, or superstitious; it is no significant prophetic event; it is only one of the ordinary natural phenomena." When some day men will awaken, and hear that great Babylon has sunk like a millstone in the depths of the ocean, they will say, "It is because Vesuvius and Etna have not burst out as usual; and a new volcanic orifice has taken place." When one day there shall be a rushing crowd of

God's ancient people, seeking rights in Europe, and finding them only in Palestine; when Jerusalem shall be recognised by the earth as its capital and the possession of its own beloved, neither forgotten nor forsaken people, whose it is, and whose property it will be; they will say, "What an enlightened liberal policy, which balances conflicting nationalities, and erects in Jerusalem a dynasty that will resist Russia, keep Turkey in order, and prevent other consequences that might have injured the safety and peace of Europe." When the world shall see unexpected phenomena in the sky—signs in the sun, and in the moon, and in the stars; thousands of telescopes will be directed upward, and every telescope will bring back the intimation, "Oh, it is a meteoric sign, it is an electric phenomenon, it is polar light; it is a mere transient phenomenon; you must not listen to those silly people who believe that there shall be signs in the sun and in the moon. Science has disposed of the miracles of the Bible, and you must take its decisions as alone infallible." And when again there shall be felt perplexity, nation rising up against nation, kingdom against kingdom—France with Russia against Austria, and Prussia and England in mortal struggle; India in revolt, and China at war with us; and commercial convulsions, pestilences and plagues in divers places, they will say, "It is owing to mismanagement, red-tapeism, the want of the right man in the right place. Drain London; attend to sanitary matters, and cholera will disappear and disease die out. Have nothing to do with prophecy. Pay no regard to what are predicted in the word of God." It may be so; but certainly these scientific objectors seem to be the successors, if one would not judge uncharitably, of a class who are a sign of the times, while they say, "Where is the promise of his coming? [illegible] since the fathers fell asleep all things continue as they were from the beginning; and they willingly are ignorant of this, that by the word of God the heavens were of old, and that a thousand years is with the Lord as one day, and one day as a thousand years. And the day of the Lord will come as a thief in the night, in which the heavens shall pass away with a great noise, and the elements shall melt with fervent heat." There is a second class who meet all statements on the subject with "wishes it may not be true" —who may believe that these are symptomatic of some great change, of some looming catastrophe or convulsion coming upon the earth; and justly alarmed, they will deprecate the day, and refuse to speak or think of it. Many a parent will say, as she looks upon the new-born babe, "Oh, let me only live ten—twenty—thirty years, that I may see my child arrive at manhood before all things are ended!" Many a statesman who has spent years in elaborating a most ingenious system of reform in church and state, will feel so grieved that the age will close before his experiment has had a fair trial. The merchant, anticipating a cargo from Australia or California with precious gold, that will enrich him for life, will deplore the impossibility of enjoying himself now. And the poet and the painter, thirsting for immortality, will be grieved and sorry that all their bright visions are gone; for there are men who think that this earth was made simply for their use, and specially for their counting-houses to stand on; its ocean meant to bring cargoes to their warehouses; its rivers intended merely to turn their mill-wheels and to grind their corn; and that anything that stops or arrests the contributions of these is most deeply to be deprecated indeed. But there is another class, God's own people, who will not try to explain phenomena significant of the purposes of God on scientific grounds; and who will not deprecate that day. They will say, "This is the answer to our daily prayer, Thy kingdom come; this is the response to the Church's cry, Come, Lord Jesus; we have been looking for him; and to us he comes the second time without sin unto salvation." They will lift up their heads, for to them draweth nigh redemption.

When that day shall come, what shall be the accompaniments of it? Let us not accept fancies, but hear God's word. Let me read from one part, "To you who are troubled rest with us, when the Lord Jesus shall be revealed from heaven with his mighty angels, in flaming fire, taking vengeance on them that know not God, and that obey not the Gospel of our Lord Jesus Christ." Or take Peter's graphic description of it when he says, "The day of the Lord will come as a thief in the night; in the which the heavens shall pass away with a great noise, and the elements shall melt with fervent heat, the earth also and the works that are therein shall be burned up." Here is no anticipation nor conjecture of man—it is the express and unmistakeable assertion of that Holy Spirit who inspired the Apostles to write these things. At that day when Christ shall come, when the red lightning shall scathe the earth, and set fire to all that is on it, and in it, and about it, we read in his own word that his own people will be caught up in a cloud far above the reach of a burning world; for he says in 1 Thess. iv., "We which are alive and remain at the coming of the Lord, shall be caught up together in the clouds, to meet the Lord in the air; and so shall we ever be with the Lord." We read in the book of Revelation that God's people thus caught up again descend to a new earth and a new heaven, and on the earth they reign with Christ a thousand years; why then caught up in the cloud? To be beyond the reach but not beyond the sight of that last fire which consumes the earth, and burns up all the things that are upon it. I can conceive what a spectacle of awful grandeur will be presented by a burning earth as seen by the happy and safe spectators, from the cloud of glory that floats their beautiful pavilion far above it. Laplace, the astronomer, says he detected ten or twelve orbs in the sky, that first of all burnt with a yellow flame, mixed with smoke; then kindled to an intense white heat; and ultimately they disappeared from their places altogether; so that the telescope has made science acquainted with the phenomenon of a burning, a calcined, and a consumed orb. Now when this world shall be subjected to that last fire, when this lightning flash shall ignite all the elements that wrap it, and all the materials that are in it, and all the things that are upon it, I may, without irreverence, suppose some one, or perhaps many, in the bright cloud in which they have been caught up far above it, to be spectators of the scene; and what will such spectators witness? They will see the crown jewels of England, the iron crown of Charlemagne, the diadem of the last Napoleon, and the sceptre of the Autocrat of all the Russias, seized by the fierce flames, consumed to ashes, and disappear.

I look at another portion of the earth. I see all the cannon of Austerlitz, of Waterloo, of the Crimea, and of Italy; the swords, the bayonets, the fifes, the discordant drums, the tattered colours, the blood-stained banners: all the weapons from every arsenal on earth; all the gunpowder from every magazine of the wide world, seized upon by the red flame, and flashing into one terrible blaze; and the very blaze that consumes all the engines of war revealing legibly in letters that never can be expunged, "The nations shall learn war no more." Look again at that great fire in another division of the world. Therein I see prisons, gaols, gibbets, axes still red even with royal blood; codes of law, ermine, the paraphernalia of courts of justice, and acts of Parliament, laid hold upon and consumed in the blazing fire; and amid the ashes that remain I can read the blessed inscription, "There shall be no more sin!" Therefore there will be no more penalty, nor sorrow, nor tears, nor captivity, nor crime, but everlasting deliverance. Look again to another section of that great fire, ye merchants, ye tradesmen, ye commercial men of the wide world, and what do you see? All the commerce from Threadneedle Street to New York; all the paper in currency, notes of hand, bills not ripe, and bills overdue; ledgers, gold, silver, all that you have been grasping, clutching, hoarding up; over which you have wept, and toiled, and cried; all of it, not one particle of it exempt, is consumed in the blaze, as if to tell high heaven and witnessing earth what trash is that about which men have quarrelled, and by loving which too dearly souls have been destroyed; whilst the illuminating flame will reveal, writ upon the sky, "durable riches" that neither thief nor moth can steal or corrupt, "the unsearchable riches of Christ." I look at another portion of that great fire, and see Magna Charta, the foundation of our freedom, in it; acts of parliament, title-deeds of choicest value, patents of nobility that date to the Norman conquest, charters of venerable age and of great importance, all cast into the flame, and utterly consumed, proving as they are consumed, "The world and all the fashion of it passeth speedily away." I look at another part of the world, and I see from that cloud the impartial flame devour St. Peter's in the metropolis of Italy, while cardinals, and bishops, and priests are saying high mass, with all the pomp and splendour of ecclesiastical circumstance, and the vast cathedral dissolves and disappears like the fabric of a vision, and leaves not a wreck behind. The same flame, fulfilling its mission, seizes on St. Paul's in our own metropolis, and upon the lowliest chapel that stands or sinks under its broad shadow; and vestments, croziers, altars, shrines, images, pictures, monuments, encaustic tiles, and all that men loved, that some almost worshipped, and good taste appreciated, are reduced to ashes in the devouring and the overwhelming fire. I look to another part of the world; I see, what must pain some, the library of our great Museum, the yet more precious library of the Vatican at Rome, reached by the all-devouring and unsparing fire. I see the works of Gibbon, and Voltaire, and Rousseau, and Shelley, and Byron cast into the flame; and as they are consumed they send forth volumes of sulphurous and intolerable smoke. I see the works of Milton, and Shakespeare, and Scott, and the master spirits of every age of our country blazing in the flames, while they shoot up only in brilliant sparks that have all the splendour of the lightning, and all its evanescence too. I see newspapers, monthlies, quarterlies, all cast into the flame, and reduced to tinder. But strange exception! wondrous spectacle! I see one book cast into that devouring, red heap; the flames seem to retreat from it, the red fire seems afraid to touch it. What exceptional book is this? It is the book of God, that has defied flood, and fire, and persecution, and sword, and decay, and now shines with more imperishable lustre in the flame that wraps a world and calcines all besides.

And what is the lesson from all this? "Seeing all these things"—crowns, genius, wealth; all that man venerates, all that man has—"seeing all these things must be dissolved, what manner of persons ought ye to be in all holy conversation and godliness;" and if this be the inference, what ought to be the first anxiety? Is the soul safe? That is the first, the chief, and the last thing. Is it well with thee? is it well with thy soul in the prospect of a judgment-seat, and of that last flame that shall consume the world? To-day is the day of salvation; to-day every soul may be saved. That day, just as you are found, you will be fixed for ever and for ever! If your soul be washed in that Saviour's precious blood, and clad in his perfect righteousness, the lightning flash that spreads from the east to the west will find no conducting medium in you; and amid the fires that calcine the earth, you will be unscathed, as the three Hebrew youths that walked in the midst of the seven-fold heated furnace, and felt it only as if it were paths and beds of roses. Do not set your hearts or affections too much on things that are perfectly lawful in themselves. Men's souls are ruined not so much by indulgence in what is positively sinful as by the excessive love of things in themselves perfectly lawful. Do not embark all your affections upon a transient flower, upon a passing rainbow, upon a fading sunbeam; upon things that now may injure, and that then will be utterly destroyed. Seek to promote things that will survive the last fire. Do not spend your money in building splendid churches, magnificent cathedrals, of fine Gothic architecture, and at great expense; all these things will be consumed like straw huts in the last fire that wraps round a dissolving world. Rather collect living stones; go down to Field Lane, to Brewer's Court; to the depths and subsoil of our debased population; pick out their neglected youths or perishing females; pray for them, instruct them, give your money, which will all be burnt up, in order to secure living stones that shal' last for ever; and thus you will build up, not temples that will perish, but living temples, built of living stones on Christ, the living rock, that will endure for ever. Do not build fine churches; get living churches first, and then raise the dead ones to hold them. What we want, seeing all these things must be dissolved, is living churches. And oh! ten thousand times rather living people worshipping in a shed, or in a cold cellar, than dead ministers, dead worshippers, dead people, dead hearts, under cathedrals whose spires sparkle in rising and in setting suns!

This prospect of a dissolving world is a more practical motive force than the prospect of death. I appeal to you in this matter. Scarcely do we find an instance of an apostle warning and moving by the fear of death. The era I am describing is the apostolic motive power. "I beseech you by the coming of the Lord, and by our gathering together unto him;" "The coming of the Lord draweth near; the judge is at our doors." All these things are constantly set forth in the word of God. But you say, Is not the fear or the prospect of death as fitted to detach our affections from this present world as that prospect of a dissolving earth and an approaching judge? I answer, No; for what do we find men doing now? They are creating a sort of immortality of their own; they are storing up money that they may buy lands, and build houses, and make an estate, and call them by their own names, in order, in the language of the world, to create a family, leave their property behind them, and live along the lines of their successors to many generations. What is inspiring poets, and architects, and painters, and sculptors, ay, and preachers too? The desire of a sort of meagre, mean immortality called posthumous renown; an attempt to create a sort of immortality here; and, in spite of death, to treasure up things that constitute this world's pride, and pomp, and glory. But now when we tell them all these things must be dissolved; that the Judge is at the door; that they must soon appear at the judgment-seat of Christ, we may lead them to lift their thoughts upward instead of sending them forward, and to build for heaven, instead of building for their children and their children's children upon earth.

But some one will say (and people mistake and misapprehend everything), if Christ's coming be so near; if a dissolving world be at hand, and no man knows the day nor the hour, though every man, if a Christian, should study the signs, will not men give up everything? will not some give up their business, or cease to accumulate? I suspect there is very little fear of any one ceasing to accumulate or to toil because of these things. And if any man were to argue, Since it is said that this is the Saturday evening of the world's long week, since these things are almost at our doors, then I will shut my shop; I would tell him, you are contradicting most grossly the command of your blessed Lord, "Occupy till I come." If I were a tradesman, I should be just as happy to be found, when the Saviour comes, dealing justly behind my counter as I should be if found in the pulpit preaching the unsearchable riches of Christ. Our duty is always obligatory. "Occupy till I come" is the order and the marching-order of the great Captain of the faith. We are to go on with our duties, even at the moment that we may see the big black cloud charged with the lightning flash; and each is to seek to be found where Providence has placed him, sanctifying by grace the works and the world, if possible, in which he is engaged. Let me give you an instance of a practical, common-sense illustration. About sixty years ago, there was in America a universal superstition—not an enlightened belief—that the world was about to close. They believed that the world was about to end, because a total eclipse of the sun took place at noonday. There was all the darkness and the gloom of midnight. It happened that the Congress of the United States was assembled at this hour; half the members of the Congress believed that that dense night, caused by a total eclipse of the sun, was really the darkness that preceded the ushering in the judgment and another state and world. They were in great alarm, and two or three of the most agitated got up at once, and moved that the Congress do adjourn. There was a panic. In the midst of the panic, and while some were proposing an adjournment, an old and venerable Puritan, who had learned noble lessons from the Puritans of England, the salt of the country at that time, rose up and said, "Mr. Chairman, we are told that our duties are always imminent, that they are always obligatory. Some in this house are afraid that the last day is come; it may be they are right; I have some suspicion they are so; but as our duties never cease, instead of moving that the house adjourn, as we cannot see in this darkness, I move that the candles be brought in, and that we proceed to the order of the day." That man spoke like a Christian, and he lived like a Christian. And may we be found going on with the orders of the day when the light of the last day shall flash upon this world.

LECTURE XIII.

NEARING DELIVERANCE.

According to the most competent, because inspired judge, the future is to be hailed and prayed for, not deprecated by the Christian, as if it unbosomed only calamity.

"*For now is our salvation nearer than when we believed.*"—
ROMANS xiii. 11.

THE salvation referred to by Paul is unquestionably that large and comprehensive deliverance which is the destiny of all created things, and of all the living rational and responsible beings who have believed in Christ, and are regenerated by his Spirit. Personal salvation is an experience of the present; the salvation alluded to is a fact that lies still in the future. It is not individual safety, but the general salvation of the whole body of the Church, to which Paul refers. It is time to awake, because our salvation, or deliverance, is nearer than when we believed; and the night, which means the whole of this existing economy, is far spent; the day, which means the future, everlasting sunshine, that spreads over all the earth, when Christ takes to him his great power, and sways his sceptre from sea to sea, is near at hand. He speaks of that future deliverance, which he describes in the 8th chapter of Romans, as the manifestation of the sons of God: the redemption of the earth from its groans, its travail, and its expectancy, and that restoration of all things which had been spoken of by the prophets, and is the distinctive feature of that millennial day which approaches faster and nearer as the centuries roll on. Few can fail to be struck, in reading the epistles of St. Paul, with his constant statement of the nearness and the instancy of the advent of our Lord. He says in one passage, "The Lord is at hand;" in another passage, "Looking for that blessed epiphany, the glorious appearing of Jesus Christ, our great God and Saviour." St. James says, "Be patient; the Lord is at hand; the Judge is at the door." Nor can any fair reader of the epistles of St. Paul escape constantly perceiving, not a mere matter of hope, but of fact, that the motive and the hope that he puts before Christians is not the nearness of their death, but the instancy of the approach of their great and blessed hope, our Lord and Saviour Jesus Christ. In other words, the governing hope of the Christian is not his own personal deliverance at death, but the coming of his Lord. His hope in a Saviour that is to come is as entire, intense, and joyous as his trust and faith in a Saviour that has come. The attitude of a Christian is resting by retrospective faith on Christ, bearing his curse, his only atonement, and his looking, prospective hope for that same Saviour to come the second time without sin unto salvation. What salvation? Not the personal safety of the believer, which is secured at his own death; but the universal restoration of heaven and earth, of soul and body, which is the bright hope that, like a star in a dark night, shines in the eye of the believer continually. But when the apostle speaks of Christ being at hand, of his being soon to be revealed, you ask, how could this be?—how could the apostle say so without being deceived, when, as matter of history, we know that eighteen centuries have elapsed since Paul spoke of Christ's advent as at hand? The explanation of some is, that it means no more than the Christian's death, as an equivalent to Christ's coming. But surely that cannot be. When a Christian dies he goes to Christ, it is not Christ who comes to him. But the hope of the Christian is not his going to Christ, but Christ's coming to him. And if language has any definite meaning, we are warranted in translating or interpreting Christ's promised advent the second time without sin unto salvation as the Christian's deliverance from this body of death, and his introduction into the presence of his Lord.

The Church of Christ—meaning by that misunderstood and abused word the whole company of true Christians, of whatever name or denomination; some in Rome, in spite of it, not created by it; some in the Greek Church, equally in spite of it, and in no sense created by it; and some in every denomination upon earth—I say the Church, then, as the company and congregation of all faithful people, of all true Christians, from the days of St. Paul to the present moment, is constantly regarded in the Bible as a unity, which, from the first believer upon earth to the very last believer upon the shores of eternity, constitute in one group what is called in the book of the Apocalypse the bride; and that bride—which means not a section of the Church geographically, nor a portion of the Church chronologically, but the whole body of faithful Christians—is represented as one person, the bride waiting for the Bridegroom, watching the signs of his approach, listening if she can hear the sound of his chariot-wheels, and rejoicing, and cheered with joy unutterable and full of glory, when the sound echoes in her ears, "Behold the Bridegroom cometh;" and, in the language of our blessed Lord, "she goeth out to meet him." If you will carry with you the idea that Christ's Church is one corporate company of all believers, in spite of space and time, elements altogether purposely overlooked in the definition, you will then see that the apostles, in writing to the Thessalonians, the Corinthians, and the Romans, wrote to the Church of Christ then existing, now existing, and that will exist to the end; and therefore that this Church is to be constantly in the attitude of hope—on the tiptoe of expectancy—her lamps burning, her loins girt, and herself ready to meet the Bridegroom, whensoever and wheresoever he shall come. This explains at once the idea which the apostle constantly presses and repeats, the instancy of the advent. It teaches us that we are now to feel what the Christians then felt, and to live under the constant belief that he may be to-morrow, next year, we know not how soon, revealed in flaming fire, taking vengeance upon them that know him not, but to be admired and glorified in all them that believe. If this be the expectation of the Church of Christ, is it not natural—and certainly it is not unscriptural—to watch, and study, and gather up the signs, the tokens of the nearness, or the possible distance of his approach? At all events, is not such conduct in harmony with that of men in all other things? The day and the hour of his advent are uncertain; the fact of his advent is as certain as rising and as setting suns. If you are anxiously watching the return to your home of some one near and dear to you, how hard you will try to catch a familiar sound amid the wind or the pattering rain, or to see the distant shadow in the moonlight! You feel it your instinctive impulse to seek out any sign of the approach of one who is so intimately associated with you.

The watcher on the distant heights looks intently into the east to catch the first beam of the rising sun; the voyager upon a broad and desert sea looks anxiously and often around if he can see some floating weed or some wheeling sea-bird to indicate the nearing land, or the whitening cliffs of his native shore, or the mountain-range within the horizon that tell him that his home is at hand. The Christian, not exempt from the feelings of all, nor forbidden to cherish them, will often look if he can see any signs of that glorious appearing, gilding with its orient beams the distant east. He will often compare sea, and star, and sky, and latitude, and longitude with the revealed and inspired chart which God has given him; a chart that not only lays down the fact that Christ will come, but has spread over it tokens, marks, signs, indications, by which you may gather the high probability that his approach is near.

The Christian, like the voyager on a great sea, may often misinterpret; that is possible, for he is human; and in the difficult path of the unfulfilled to err is common. The mariner may take the piece of drift-wood that he finds upon the sea for a fragment too recently torn from the shore, indicating, therefore, his nearness to land, and it may have been long tossed, or it may be something torn by the storm from the depths of the sea. Or he may take some wing-weary bird for a recent emigrant from the land, when really it has lost its way, has been long at sea, and is sinking with fatigue. Or he may mistake that as the first ray of the rising sun, which is only a phosphorescent meteor. But incidental errors will not make him despair; they will only induce him more carefully to watch and wait, certain that the fact itself will be, and that phenomena indicative of its nearness will multiply as it approaches. So the Christian may err—may seize some startling scene as appearing to him the token of its nearness; or he may interpret some voice in the wilderness as the sound of his chariot-wheels; or he may think that the transient blaze of the meteor is the burst of the morning sun; but if he find that he has fallen into error in so interpreting, he will not therefore despair, or give up his investigation. And far better have the character of him who intently looks, and in his intense longing treats that as a sign which is not, than the sceptic and freezing apathy of the man whose heart is dead, and whose hopes are cold, and who cares for and looks for none of these things. The incidental error of a few cannot shake or shatter the trust of the many; and the error that is made by one watcher for the advent will only lead another, like a buoy upon a wreck in the channel, to avoid the reef on which his predecessor may have suffered.

If this salvation to which the apostle alludes; to which he also refers in Hebrews, when he says, "Christ will come the second time without sin unto salvation;" was spoken of as nearer in the days in which he wrote than it was in the days in which he first believed; we may with greater emphasis say, because we have evidence that the apostle then had not, that this salvation is nearer still. It might be said with some semblance of truth in the days of Paul, "All things continue as they were since the beginning;" but it cannot be said with any semblance of truth that all things continue now as they were from the very beginning. Events predicted by Paul to precede that advent have demonstrably occurred; developments of error, the apostacy, and the decadence of that apostacy, and its nearness to its degradation and destruction, are so palpable now, that being laid down as signs of the nearness of Christ's approach, we can scarcely misinterpret or misunderstand them. During the last ten years event has thundered upon event, and phenomenon trodden upon phenomenon, till the most apathetic, careless, and indifferent, begin to see signs of a supernatural presence, and to read and listen to the explanations of students of prophecy, when they sneered at them or despised them altogether before. We cannot of course expect that all will see this; because, to the very end, thousands will be saying as Peter predicted, "Where is the promise of his coming, for all things continue as they were since the beginning?" And if men ask, as indeed they do, "If only ten or twenty years remain before the coming of Christ;" if our chronology be correct, "Then," some are saying, "what is predicted in the Bible to take place before that event cannot possibly be completed in that time." But in answer so far to this difficulty, who does not know that events are accomplished now in days that used to require years, and in a year that used to require centuries, and in a century that used to require a millennium? Why, nobody in 1854 could have anticipated that events would have occurred which rocked the world with convulsions, and agitated and revolutionised the feelings of Europe during 1855, 1856, and 1859. Nor have succeeding years been less stormy, and who can say that events, as the time gets nearer, may not be more crowded and condensed. The wheel is rolling down the mountain side, and the nearer it approaches the valley below it, becomes more rapid in its revolutions. Every one feels now that time runs at greater speed than it used to do; not that it really does so, but that events are now so many, so stirring, and the excitement of them so great, that months seem days, years seem months, and ages are reduced to years.

But let me notice some of those events which lead us to

anticipate, even more than the apostolic church could, the increasing nearness of these great changes. Can one fail to see all over Europe startling events? If earthquakes in divers places, if famines, if pestilences, and plagues, were to be among the earliest forerunners of a great change; are not these most conspicuous now? Does not every day's news bring accounts of them? Does not every paper reveal in different parts of the world one or more, or many, of these facts and phenomena. I know quite well the objection. "Why, all these things have always been?" So they have: but our Lord knew that as well as you; and yet he says that these things will be forerunners of his second coming unto salvation to all them that believe: this must mean something. I ventured to show the complete fulfilment of the drying up of the Euphrates. If we can identify one fact in history with a specific symbol in the Apocalypse, and if the identification be so exact, complete, and so truly overlapping it that there can scarcely be a mistake, we not only ascertain the fulfilment of a given prophecy, but we ascertain the point of time we occupy in the great calendar of prophecy. Now one of these events that were to take place under the sixth vial, when the unclean spirits were to gather the nations to that great war—not battle, but war—of Armageddon, was, that the great river Euphrates, the symbol of the Turkish power in Europe, from which the Turks started, and to which, as the reflux of a stream, they are going back again, should be dried up, so that the exhaustion of it, or the waning of the crescent, or the drying up of the Mahometan power in Europe, would be the fulfilment of that. This I stated many years ago, and within this present year we have seen the unmistakeable fulfilment of it. And the correspondent of one of the daily papers, writing the other day, speaking of Turkey, says, "Her resources are utterly exhausted." God brings to pass the fulfilment of his own prediction, strangely, indeed, by the very process most justly employed by the western powers to keep up and prevent the evaporation of the great river Euphrates. In the same paper I read, "The admission of the Turkish state into the European system under the counsels and the tutelage of the western powers is now inevitable;" that is, it is no longer to be an independent nationality. Of course it will not be; and I am quoting it simply as a proof of the fulfilment of that statement of the Apocalypse. "The sixth angel poured his vial into the air, and the great river Euphrates was dried up, that the way of the kings from the sunrising," that is, the Jews, "might be prepared." And then what takes place?—and it is for this I quote it. Immediately, during the action of this vial, or before it is completely exhausted—for each vial describes a process, not a fact; the process of the one extending into and interlacing with the process that begins in the succeeding one; during the pouring out of this vial, or just at the exhaustion of that empire, the words are heard, like a startling sound, "Behold I come as a thief." And the constant prediction in the epistle to the Thessalonians is that Christ shall come as a thief in the night; when the great mass shall be saying, "Peace, peace," he shall come instantly as a thief in the night. Or as he himself describes it, "As the lightning cometh out of the east, and shineth even unto the west;" in speed, in startling and overpowering splendour; "such will be the coming of the Son of man." If we be actually, I say, at this epoch in prophecy, the great truth that belongs to the day, the great truth that every Christian should feel, and study, and ponder, is Christ's own saying, "Behold I come as a thief;" just in an hour when you expect not; and at that hour especially when men shall be found most frequently saying, "Peace, peace; all things continue as they were; these prophets are always talking prophecy; there is no meaning or sense in it; it is all nonsense; let us eat, and drink, and be merry; all things continue as they were, and will continue to the end." "Behold I come as a thief," is Christ's own word. Our duty is, "Blessed is he that watcheth;" not miserable, not wretched, but "happy is he that watcheth, and keepeth his garments, lest he walk naked."

Another great event that I have alluded to which shows that our salvation is nearer than when we awoke, or, in other words, that there are tokens of the approach of that great era, is the unequivocal, the irresistible evidence of the decadence and the imminent destruction of that huge sacerdotal tyranny under which Europe has groaned, and which has struck its roots so deep into dynasties, and nations, and governments; I mean the Papal or Western Apostacy. Now this is an event, I may mention, that is one of the most important as a token in the whole Bible. The apostle says that an apostacy, headed by a pope, the man of sin, should begin from Christ's first advent; and that it should be utterly destroyed by his second advent. He says first of all, "Whom the Lord shall consume with the spirit of his mouth;" that is through the preaching of the Gospel; and strike down, at a blow, with the brilliancy, the brightness, of his own personal advent. We read in the Apocalypse, that when the seventh vial is poured out, great Babylon comes into remembrance, to give her the judgment-cup, in drinking which her decay is to be precipitated, her consumption to go on, her sufferings to be increased. And then at the end of it an angel is to cry from heaven, "Babylon the great is fallen;" and her judgments are to come upon her in one day, and she is to sink like a millstone in the great waters. I have always quoted the public press, not its opinions, but its recorded facts, which are modern history, as a striking proof of the fulfilment of prophecy. When I ventured to say a year ago that Romanism was dying, that it was expiring; some thought that that was rash, it was not true; it was merely quiet for a moment. But there do seem to me all the evidences of rapid decay; and that the ascendency of the Pope of Rome, or his proconsul in Westminster, in this country again, is one of the impossibilities of the day, and no more likelihood of it than the ascendency of Mahomet, or any other head of superstition and fanaticism. The Pope trembles in the Vatican. He has a presentiment of the nearness of his doom. What office in Europe would insure his Pontifical life for five years? Now just think what this power was in ancient days: a power that made kings tremble on their thrones; a power that could force a German Emperor to remain doing penance amid the snows in the trenches around the imperial city, till the Pope gave him absolution; a power that could dispose of Britain's crown to whomsoever he pleased; the great power that reigned over the kings of the earth. "How are the mighty now fallen! Is this the man that shook kingdoms, that made the earth to tremble? Is he become as one of us?" And what do recent events indicate? The decadence of the system to the very verge, when like the thief in the night, He comes whose right it is to reign; and the whole is struck down; and that great city is literally swallowed up and destroyed by fire; and the smoke of its torment begins to rise for ever and for ever. I am speaking not of persons, but of the system; and if you knew it as I know it, if you knew what an awful mystery of wickedness it is, instead of being sorrowful, or when you hear of her judgments, letting your sympathies go out with her, and tears begin to be wept over the spectacle; those sympathies of yours would rush back to Smithfield, or travel to the Cottian Alps, or to the dungeons at Rome, or to the Inquisition of Spain; and witnessing the scenes that have been transacted there, they would come back armed with indignation; and instead of weeping over the ruin, you should, as angels bid you, rejoice that great Babylon is fallen—is fallen—is fallen. If this be the recorded state of things, it is another token that our salvation is nearer than when we believed. I do not quote more. I quote these two as prominent and striking foretokens; and the lesson that they all teach is not fear, not alarm, not terror; but, "Prepare, O Israel, to meet thy God. Behold the Bridegroom cometh; go out to meet him."

People say, "What a dreadful thing! But is not death in that sense a very dreadful thing?" As far as you are personally concerned, it is all the same whether your soul goes to him or he comes to you. The real question is, are you justified? are you regenerated? are you sanctified? And if you are, come either, it must be happiness to you. Is it not a very solemn thing, that needs no prophet to predict, that the St. Paul's bell does not strike twice in the hearing of the same persons? the persons that hear it strike twelve hear it not strike one; they that hear it strike one will not hear it strike two. In all probability of those that assemble within the walls of the sanctuary on each Sunday, one drops weary with the march of life, and goes to the judgment-seat. And it is not at all improbable, certainly not impossible, that of all that sit in their pews, looking and listening, one Sun day, several shall be in the course of the next week at the judgment-seat of Christ. Is not that equally terrible? Does not that make you think? And why then should the objection be made to that better event which is happiness to all God's people, and only confusion to them that believe not in Christ and obey not the Gospel? Christians need in these times to be summoned to think and pause, prepare and make ready. We are all too prone to repose at ease, fanned by the gales of worldly prosperity, dreaming of scenes that may never come, and of success that we may never attain; instead of feeling every moment, we know not what a day may bring forth. And if one can only awaken one single soul to pause, to think, to work while it is called to-day; to disentangle the affections from things that perish in the using; to set them not upon things that are beneath, but upon things that are above; to use the world as not abusing it, knowing that the fashion of it passeth away; it will not be in vain that I have called attention to this most important, too much neglected, too frequently forgotten subject. We must, on all these great questions, not ask what the Rabbis say, but try to ascertain what God has revealed in his holy word. Let me ask, if that lightning were to stretch from the east to the west; if the warning voice, "Behold, I come as a thief," told to-day, were to-morrow to be a reality; if the shout were to be heard going from earth to heaven, and from heaven to earth, "Behold, the Bridegroom cometh:" are we ready? are our lamps burning? are our loins girt?—Can we say, "I know in whom I have believed, and that he is able to keep what I have committed to him against that day?" Have I settled the great question of personal acceptance before God through Jesus Christ? If not, we dream upon the edge of a tremendous precipice; we sleep on the margin of the sea on which the flowing tide is rolling inwards with irresistible force. We stand, and eat, and drink, and walk in jeopardy every hour. But if we have accepted the only Saviour; if we have committed soul, body, and spirit, to his keeping; if our ground of trust is, that he was made sin for us, and our conviction be that we are made righteousness by him; if we be justified by faith in his blood, and regenerated by his Holy Spirit; then, whether we are called to the judgment-seat, or Christ comes to us; whether we are taken to him, or he comes to us; it will be equally well, for there is no condemnation to them that are in Christ Jesus. And when we look at scenes in the East and West, thickening, multiplying, ominous of yet future ones, more dreadful and disastrous—we can learn this lesson at least, that that man has no humanity, no philanthropy, and certainly no Christianity, who does not long for that long promised day when earth shall be restored from its thraldom, when the groans of creation shall cease, when all things shall be made new, when Paradise shall return; and Christ the Head shall reign over a happy, a holy, and a peaceful world; and God shall have glory, and we shall praise him day and night, as the monuments of his love, and the purchase of a Saviour's blood, and without ceasing.

Come, Lord Jesus, come quickly. Amen.

LECTURE XIV.

THE DAY AND HOUR.

Many have speculated where they ought to have paused. Dates in the future are not so clear as dates in the past. We cannot read prophecy as we read history: sunshine sleeps on the one; the mists of evening hang on the other.

"*Of that day and hour knoweth no man, no, not the angels of heaven, but my Father only. But as the days of Noe were, so shall also the coming of the Son of man be.*"— MATTHEW xxiv. 36, 37.

HERE we are distinctly informed that the exact chronological day and hour of the advent of our blessed Lord is known to none; but we are also told that there are certain premonitory and significant signs that are meant to be to us evidence of its nearness; and that to these, and not to the day and the hour imagined, calculated, or supposed, we are constantly to attend. Let me first of all notice the practical importance of concealing the day and hour when the Son of man shall come from the knowledge of the Church and of all mankind. Were the day and the hour of the Saviour's advent specifically and unmistakeably stated, it would contradict constantly those passages scattered throughout the whole word of God which say he shall come as a thief in the night; that he will come at the very time when men, so far from expecting the day and the hour, will be congratulating each other on the impossibility of his advent; saying, "Where is the promise of his coming? for all things continue as they were from the beginning until now." If this portion of Scripture says he will come as the lightning bursts from the cloud, and flashes from the east unto the distant west—that he will come with the unexpectedness of a thief that breaks into premises to plunder and to steal; such assertions are utterly incompatible with our knowing the exact day and hour when the Son of man shall come. Were the day and the hour specified by Matthew, but not specified, or rather declared unknown, in the epistle to the Thessalonians, there would be what there is not and cannot be—a contradiction between one portion of the word of God and another. But the very reference employed immediately after—namely, to the days of Noah—shows that while there is no specification of the day or the hour, there will be certain signs, phenomena, and historic visible occurrences, whose approach will be to us pre-significant warnings that the hour and the day at least draweth nigh. For instance, no physician upon earth can specify the day or the hour of a dying man's death; he will tell you he may live weeks or months, but disease is in him that must terminate very shortly in death. That physician does know whether the day of his death be comparatively near or comparatively remote by his pulse, by certain signs and symptoms—by his sufferings, by the ascertained nature of the disease, so much so that he will be able with remarkable accuracy to predict that he cannot live beyond so many days or so many weeks. We may be unable, and are positively unable, chronologically to specify the day and the hour when this dispensation shall end; but we may feel Nature's faltering, hesitating pulse—we may count the wrinkles that gather on her venerable brow, as if to crowd her history into little space—we may detect symptoms of exhaustion in all things that are above, and around, and below; and thus we may be able, with God's inspired chart in our hands, and with the promise of God's Spirit to explain its mystery and its meaning, to say that if the world is to last, as the old Jewish rabbis believed it, a week of seven thousand years, we may calculate approximately whether this be about the Friday, or the Saturday, or the Saturday evening of the world's long week, and thus form a probable estimate of the epoch we live in, of the events that are before us, and of the probable remoteness or nearness of that day when the lightning shall flash from the cloud, and the earth and the things that are therein shall be burned up, and we shall not be destroyed, but transferred to a balmier clime, to a lovelier rest and more beautiful repose, till the earth is made ready; being where Christ is, and where he is there is happiness and everlasting heaven.

After the day of Pentecost the Apostles received information upon this subject which they did not previously possess. No one can read the Gospels without seeing that the Apostles, to the very day that Christ arose from the dead and ascended into heaven, were excessively ignorant of many things, and entertained all kinds of misapprehensions of the truth; so much so that the comparison between Peter before the day of Pentecost and Peter after the day of Pentecost is a comparison between the glow-worm or taper and the brilliancy of a star. If this be so in that specific case, we may be sure it was no less true in all. Hence we read in the Acts of the Apostles that when Christ ascended from the Mount of Olives, and when the disciples asked, "Lord, wilt thou at this time restore again the kingdom of Israel?" he said to them, "It is not for you to know the times or the seasons"—that is the hour and the day—"which the Father hath put in his own power." But mark what follows: "Ye shall receive power, after that the Holy Ghost is come upon you, and ye shall be witnesses unto me both in Jerusalem, and in all Judea, and in Samaria, and unto the uttermost part of the earth. And when he had spoken these things, while they beheld, he was taken up; and a cloud received him out of their sight. And while they looked steadfastly towards heaven as he went up, behold, two men stood by them in white apparel, which also said, Ye men of Galilee, why stand ye gazing up into heaven? this same Jesus, which is taken up from you into heaven, shall so come in like manner as ye have seen him go."

The Apostle Paul, speaking to his Thessalonian converts, says, "Of the times and the seasons"—that is, the hour and the day—"ye have no need that I write unto you; for yourselves know perfectly that the day of the Lord so cometh as a thief in the night; for when they shall say, Peace and safety, sudden destruction shall come upon them. But ye, brethren, are not in darkness; that that day should overtake you as a thief;" as if some clear intimation were given to the apostles subsequent to the Day of Pentecost, which enabled them to form and communicate some idea of nearness to or remoteness from the coming of our Lord. When sailing on the ocean, we come to large pieces of driftwood, we instantly suppose we must be approaching some land—or when we discover quantities of floating weeds, as Columbus did on the very point of despair of finding the great western continent—we take heart and say, "The continent of glory is near, for we see the drift detached from the shore, which must indicate we are approaching land." As the men that watch upon the mountain crags catch the first beams of the rising sun before he comes above the horizon, whilst the people in the glens and valleys below are involved in complete darkness, so the students of the signs of the times, diligently comparing what history records with what the Apocalypse predicts, may form a proximate estimate whether they are distant from or near to that great continent of glory to which earth, this broken-off island, shall be united, in order that heaven and earth may be one again and for ever.

It would be altogether morally without practical good results, and incompatible with other portions of Scripture, if God were to tell us the precise day and the hour. What would be the practical use of telling us either? None would be so wretched as the man who should be told that next year, or ten years hence, and on a certain day, and in a certain month, he shall die. But you may depend upon it that as this book contributes all that is really contributory to our happiness, and if that information had been an element of it, it would have specified that also. But it leaves the day of death undefined, that we may be always ready to obey when the summons comes: in the same manner it leaves the day and the hour of our Lord's advent indefinite, that we may not be in a hurry to make preparation a few days before; but that we may always hear and everywhere act upon the cry that sounds from heaven, "Watch, be ye ready, for in such an hour as ye think not the Son of man cometh." Were that day made known to us, it would be gratifying a very worthless curiosity. But if there be one feature in this book more striking than another, it is its utter refusal to gratify the curiosity of man. To the least or the deepest want of the humblest believer it ministers infinite fulness; but to the most anxious and curious inquiry of the most inquisitive mind it answers literally nothing. The silence of Scripture is often its most eloquent credential. I know not from which to infer most the inspiration of the writers—the pure and transparent eloquence with which they speak on all that is essential, or the deep, unbroken silence that they maintain on all that merely gratifies an itching and a curious inquiry. Suppose that this day and hour had been made known, there is no proof that it would be believed by the unconverted masses of mankind. If the masses refuse to believe the Gospel, surely they would never be persuaded to believe that at a certain day and hour Christ would come like the lightning, and finish this dispensation. If the unconverted and unsanctified multitude believed it, it would do incalculable mischief. We all know that in the days of Noah, when he told them, on the authority of the living God, that in a hundred and twenty years the whole population would be swept away, they laughed at him, not one believed it. And if we were to tell the multitude now, proclaim it in every newspaper, proclaim it from every pulpit that on a certain day and in a certain year Christ would come, not one would believe it; and if any did believe it, what would be the effect on them? What the effect was in Jerusalem—when the people were warned that the ploughshare of Titus would soon overturn their ancient and magnificent temple, they indulged in all sorts of intoxication, excess, and crime.

I have read somewhere that when a shipwreck is inevitable, a godless crew will instantly lay hold upon the stores; and so infatuated do men become in the prospect of certain destruction that some will load themselves with gold and silver; others will get drunk; and most of them, instead of being solemnized and impressed by the certainty of a watery grave, will become maddened and furious, and lose their very senses in the terrible prospect of the crisis. It is therefore on all these grounds well and expedient that we do not know the day or the hour. But, on the other hand, it is most profitable and most improving that we should study the predicted signs; nay, our Lord condemned the men of his day, because while they could predict wet weather and fine weather, from the sky at evening and at morn, they were not acquainted with the moral signs of the age in which they lived. The Scripture in every page is most explicit in giving us tokens and signs by which we are to infer either that the time is near, or that it is remote. This leads me to the great sign given here, instead of the day and the hour—the sign of Noah. Our Lord says that "As it was in the days of Noah, so shall the coming of the Son of man be"—in those days before the flood they were "eating and drinking, marrying and giving in marriage, and knew not until the flood came and took them all away. So shall it be at the coming of the Son of man."

Before I illustrate this more fully, let me notice that there is here a distinct recognition of Noah as a historic person, of the flood as a literal fact. Most have heard that certain German philosophers, who try to be wise, not only above what is written, but against what is written, maintain that the whole of Genesis is a myth. But our blessed Lord here refers to a historic fact in the past to illustrate a real historic event that is approaching from the future; and the very reference that he makes proves that he regarded Noah as a real person, the deluge as a real fact, and used them as the solid background from which to throw up in more brilliant relief the features of a great approaching era. I cannot but notice also in referring to this fact, that the impression produced upon one's mind on reading the account of the deluge, or our Lord's allusion to it, is that this deluge was universal. Certain geologists, men of great talent, power, and research, and many of them pious men, hold the notion that the deluge was local, that it merely swept over a certain portion of the continent of Asia, where the cradle or birthplace of the human family was; and that all the rest of the world was left untouched. I do not enter upon the evidence or disproof of this, but this I do say, that on the face of the narrative in Genesis, on the Apostle Paul's allusion to it in Hebrews, and in our Lord's allusion to it here, the inference seems to me rational and just, that the flood was universal; that the whole of our planet was submerged, and that it covered all the earth, and rose above the tops of the highest mountains, even the mount of Ararat, which is some eight thousand feet, if I mistake not, above the level of the sea, and it must, therefore, have overflowed the population of the globe. We learn another lesson from this reference—history is never obsolete. Past history is very much the reflection of the future, and present and future history is very much the repetition of the past. A great statesman and gifted orator, still alive, though arrived at a great age, said one day in scorn, when replying to the statement of an opponent, "History! what is history? It is simply an old almanack." He meant it in scorn, but there is great force in what he said; it is an old almanack. What is the difference in successive almanacks? The tides are the same, the rising and the setting suns are the same, the characters are substantially the same. Wherein lies the real difference? Simply in the date. The old almanack of the year 1800 is not very much different from the new almanack of 1859; man is still upon the same stage, repeating substantially the same acts, using the same expressions, falling into the same sins, indulging the same reveries, cherishing the same hopes. Human nature repeats itself, history moves in circles, and all the future is the reflection of the past.

I cannot but notice here also this interesting fact—that human nature is substantially the same in the days of Napoleon and of Queen Victoria, that it was in the days of Noah and the patriarchs before the flood. There is no real or great revolution in the heart of man. We may be more civilised; we may travel at a greater speed, and enjoy much greater and more numerous luxuries; we may have made greater progress in acquaintance with the secrets of nature; but substantially human nature now is what it was then; the primeval granite crops up still, the changes are on the surface, and those changes of no material value or depth.

The antediluvians, or those that were in the days of Noah, when the flood came, were eating and drinking, marrying and giving in marriage. This is not stated as a sin; there is no sin in eating, only in eating to excess; there is no sin in drinking, it is only in drinking to excess; there is no sin in marrying, on the contrary, but obedience to a command; there is no sin in giving in marriage. Then where lay the sin? In this: these things were their all; they did not look above them; their whole hearts, and sympathies, and hopes, were confined to this present scene, and beyond the interests of the present they had no stirring and joyous hope for the future.

In the Gospel, where our Lord represents the blessings that he purchased under a feast, those that were invited refused; but the ground they assigned was not any one sinful act. One said, "I have bought oxen," that was quite right, "and I go to prove them;" that was right. Another said, "I have purchased a field, and I go to measure it;" and another said, "I have married a wife, and I cannot come." There was no sin in buying oxen, or in buying a field, or in marrying a wife; but the sin lay in being so absorbed about these things that no nook was left in the heart, and no day set apart in the year, for loftier, holier, and more important things. Often we sin by the excessive love of what is lawful more than in the guilty practice of what is positively forbidden. Where then was the sin of the antediluvians? They married, they gave in marriage, they ate, they drank, they enjoyed themselves; but "they knew not till the flood came." Why did they not know? Noah warned them, entreated them to come into the ark; told them that they would be destroyed unless they came; but still it came upon them one vast and unexpected catastrophe, which they never anticipated or believed, simply because they were given up to an evil heart of unbelief that would not accept any testimony of God, any one fact in the past, or any one possible, or contingent, or predicted phenomenon in the future. When Noah began to build his ark, in which he was engaged one hundred and twenty years; and when he stood at its door and told the people ere it was finished, that in that ark alone there was safety from the approaching flood; and that unless they came into the ark, in which there would be found room for all that would, they would be overwhelmed in a desolating ocean that would cover the very highest, and not spare the very humblest,—I have no doubt they laughed outright in his face; and that one would say to another over his wine, and after they had been eating and drinking, and marrying and giving in marriage, "Have you heard what that old fanatic Noah begins to talk about? The old man is so sunk in dotage that he actually says this world is coming to an end; that there will be no more eating, no more drinking, no more marrying and giving in marriage. Well, if the old fanatic be right, let us eat and drink; there will soon be an end to it. But as to the possibility of the world coming to an end, the thing is so improbable, so impossible, that we cannot believe it." And I have not the least doubt that others said, "Why, look at Noah, he seems as busy as if the world were to last for ever; and he seems to be laying up for his children, Ham, Shem, and Japheth, as if it could have no end; and we do not think he really believes his own doctrine."

The scientific men of that day, I have no doubt, said there is not so much water in the basin of the ocean as would cover the whole earth; and secondly, unless the earth should change the angle of its axis towards the sun, or should revolve with some extraordinary speed, it would be utterly impossible that water should rise high enough to drown the whole world. I have no doubt that others said, Suppose there is to be a flood, I would not trust a dog in that ark which Noah is building. It is one of the most blundering pieces of naval architecture I ever saw. My yacht would carry me through the heaviest sea and under the pressure of a hurricane; and while Noah and his miserable craft would founder, my fine ship would bring me safely through, and land me on some place better than Noah's Ararat. Such, probably, were some of the calculations and conversations of many who would not believe that a flood was approaching; or if they determined that it was within the realm of possibility, they would not believe that the crazy craft that the old man was building could ever stand the sea for six hours. Noah, too, must have met with many difficulties. The apostle says, in the Epistle to the Hebrews, it was by faith that he built an ark to the saving of his soul. Noah, probably, when told to build the ark and prepare for the flood, said, Lord, I believe that thy word is truth; I believe in the approaching terrible catastrophe. But, Lord, thou biddest me build an ark; I am no ship architect, I never built a ship in my life. And even if I should succeed in building a ship, and setting her afloat, I have no compass, I have not a stitch of canvas to stretch to the wind; I never in my life touched the tiller of a rudder or helm of any sort or shape, I can neither hoist nor reef sails. And besides, if I were to take two of each of the animals in this ark, how could I keep order in such a menagerie? The larger animals would devour the lesser, and I should not be surprised if they were to fall upon me, and devour me and my family; and therefore the thing seems to me so impossible that I would rather not attempt it. But the answer is, Noah cared not for the impossibility that stared him in the face; God said, "Do it;" and by faith, believing that He that gave the command was competent to give the skill, the strength, and the genius to execute it, in the language of the apostle in his Epistle to the Hebrews, he built an ark to the saving of his own soul, and of all them that were his. But the rest of the world, as we have seen, believed not. And at last, when the windows of heaven were opened, and poured down their roaring cataracts; and when the great ocean, as if agitated by some subterranean earthquake, threw up its waters in their fury to the very tops of some of the mountains; and when one antediluvian, who laughed at the fanatic for his prophecy, began to feel that the fanatic was right, and that the prophet of one hundred years ago was now the witness to the truth in the hour in which he lived; and when one rushed to his yacht, and another to his great ship, and another to his boat, and found them sink like shells in the rushing and remorseless surges; and when others fled to the hills, and found the water creep up like advancing tides with irresistible force, and bury and overwhelm all; and when palatial residences crumbled away like clay in the waters, and castles that had defied all foes, and weathered all storms, and stood every siege, and laughed at every assailant, were swept away like sand-ridges before the advancing sea; and when one cried to Noah, "Come towards us; land on this side; come near to us, and save and deliver us; only take us in, we will give you any money; we will give you all our estates if you will only take us and ours in,"—the despised prophet of yesterday became the idol of to-day. Noah felt that he had no helm to direct his course, no canvas to stretch, and that he was dependent for every inch of his course upon that mysterious and unseen but not unknown Power that gave him the commission to build the ark; and he was constrained to tell many a one, swimming in his agony, and many others, signalling him from every height which the waves had not yet reached, only to come and take them in—"I warned you of the approaching judgment; I told you on the authority of the living God; you despised my testimony, you have defied the word and the judgments of heaven; the harvest is past, the summer is ended, your sun is set, grace is merged in judgment; there is no hope for you, and no help in me."

"So shall it be when the Son of man cometh."

This is not a mere history; but also a solemn prophecy. Thousands will be just as incredulous when the lightning strikes, and preternatural signs are portrayed in the sky; when the earth begins to groan, and crack, and heave as if with yearning expectancy of deliverance; when all things indicate that this great drama is to be wound up; the world will be as incredulous as ever; and like the five foolish virgins, they will ask oil for their lamps when it is too late to buy it, and they have none to spare; and theirs must be the blackness of darkness for ever.

Just as the ark was the only safety in the days of Noah, so the only safety for us this very day is Christ, the living, the glorious, the indestructible ark. There is none other name, however magnificent, or brilliant from its historic associations, in which or by which we can be saved from the coming judgments of heaven, except the name of the Lord Jesus Christ. His precious blood alone can cleanse us from all our sins; his glorious righteousness will so shelter and so cover us at that dread day, that the fires that consume the round globe will reverently abstain from touching us; and as the three Hebrew youths walked the burning floor of the sevenfold-heated fiery furnace, and had not even the hair of their heads, or the wool of their garments singed; so that happy man who believes in the Saviour, rests upon his precious sacrifice, pleads at that day the password of his name, will feel fulfilled in his happy experience the promise of the prophet, "When thou passest through the waters, I will be with thee; and through the rivers, they shall not overflow thee; when thou walkest through the fire, thou shalt not be burned, neither shall the flames kindle upon thee." Are you trusting to this ark? are you cleaving to the Saviour? Now there is salvation for the worst and the guiltiest; but at that day, when grace shall depart like a vision, when the last fire shall cover the round globe with its piercing and its searching flames, not one cry will be heard, not one appeal for mercy will be regarded, not one sin will be forgiven. The very glory of the Gospel is its simplicity: "Look and live;" "Believe, and thou shalt be saved." When Noah asked the people to come into the ark, they had simply to believe the word he preached, that the ark was suitable for its purpose, enter into it, and make the experiment. What would have been the use of their saying, Are its timbers strong enough? is the planking thick enough? is the caulking good? is there tar enough to keep out the water? will she break her back upon the waves? Noah's answer was, God says there is safety here; God says there is no safety elsewhere; do not believe appearances; mind only what God says. What he says to us this day is, Christ is the deliverer. You ask, can any good thing come out of Nazareth? How is it possible that one that died eighteen hundred years ago can do me any good? Will not my own upright life be a nobler plea than that Jesus died for sinners? I answer, Whatever appearances may be; whatever your reasoning may prompt; believe God's testimony concerning his Son. That testimony is clear, absolute, without any modification: "He that believeth on the Son of God hath everlasting life; he that believeth not, shall not see life; but the wrath of God abideth upon him."

Have you, dear readers, fled to this ark? Are you in the happy group who met in the ark of old, and meet and are meeting to-day in a better ark still? For that ark of Noah carried its inmates across the surging waves, landed them upon the barren heights of Ararat, thence to go forth upon a world dismantled and depopulated; renewing their pilgrimage of tears, and struggles, and toils, and sickness, and death.

But this glorious ark, built in heaven, having capacities for all, and a welcome for all, will carry you to the sunny hills of the new Jerusalem, there to be where neither death, nor sorrow, nor sickness is; but where all is unclouded, eternal, and happy noon.

LECTURE XV.

THE WORLD'S FLEETING FASHION.

Paul's estimate of the duration and nature, and excellence of this present life, is briefly and justly expressed in these words :—

"*For the fashion of this world passeth away.*"
1 CORINTHIANS vii. 31.

"THE fashion of this world passeth away," is, strictly speaking, an inference, or rather the ground on which the Apostle constructs the truly practical prescription in the previous passage. "This I say, brethren, the time is short." What duty does he infer? That you should run from the world, and become an ascetic? No. That you should not, therefore, feel the least interest in the world, and become a Stoic? No. That you should plunge into all the dissipation and folly of the world, and become the Epicurean? No. But what is replete with good sense, "The time is short: therefore it remains, that they that have wives be as though they had none; and they that weep, as though they wept not; and they that rejoice, as though they rejoiced not; and they that buy, as though they possessed not; and they that use the world, as not abusing it." Why? "For the fashion of it passeth away." It is lawful to weep, or to rejoice; it is lawful to buy, and to possess; it is only sinful to be so absorbed in the blessings God has given you, that your heart becomes glued to them, and cannot lift its affections, or unfold its wings, or rise where it can have true communion in the presence of God and of the Lamb.

The language which the Apostle uses to describe the ground of this reasoning, is borrowed from the usages of the playhouse or the theatre in ancient times. The literal translation of the word rendered "fashion," is the shifting of the scenes in the playhouse, as one scenic representation succeeds another in rapid succession. The Apostle having witnessed this in the ancient theatre, applies it—for he draws illustrations of his doctrine from all sources—to the present world, and says, "the fashion of this world passeth away." The great master of dramatists, that most of us, as readers of the English tongue, must have read, says:—

"All the world's a stage,
The men and women merely players;
They have their exits and their entrances."

The phrases of the great dramatist are borrowed from, and built on the language of the inspired Apostle, "the fashion of this world passeth away;" literally, "the shifting scenes of this vast panorama, this great theatre, commonly called the world, are in rapid succession, the more brilliant extinguishing the less so, one now dimming by its splendour one that was yesterday, what entrances to-day ceasing to delight to-morrow; the whole world is a stage; the whole world is a theatre; the earth is but its stage; and all you see above, around, before you, are but the successive dramatic exhibitions of a grand spectacle, which is going with us, and with all that live, to the judgment-seat of God, or to the last ordeal, when the earth shall burn, and the elemen.s melt with fervent heat; and the theatre in which each has played his part more or less perfectly shall be lost in that place where there are no masks, no disguises, nothing to conceal the naked heart from the omniscient and penetrating eye of Almighty God."

It needs very little proof to convince you that "the fashion of the world passeth away." In every man's library, however limited; in every man's memory, however young; on every face over which have swept the lights and shadows of half a century; on every head on which sixty or seventy years have shed down their whitening snows; in every failing memory, and failing affection; in our loves or hates, in our sympathies, our joys, our sorrows, on all within, and on all without, he must be blind who cannot see, and deaf who cannot hear the ceaseless lesson, "the fashion of this world passeth away." We all feel, every day of our life, the future is ceaselessly rushing into the present; the present ceaselessly rushing into the past; till the whole past becomes the gigantic storehouse in which are treasured up youth and beauty, age and talent, riches and poverty; which no eloquence can recall, and no force can pluck back, from the bosom of the unrelenting past. Into its abyss all things seem ceaselessly to rush, like rivers to the sea; to be forgotten of us, but not forgotten of God.

But whilst we turn from the past, which is the storehouse of so much that is precious and beautiful; and whilst we cherish the thought, that only the fashion of the world is passing, that the good, the true, the great in the world, endures for ever; I proceed to illustrate the sentiment by showing that the world, in the various aspects, features, and manifestations, in which we see it, is constantly like a flood that rushes to the ocean, passing away. The world physical, the fashion of the world physical, is passing away. The mountains are rent by the lightning, or disintegrated by the frost; and scarcely one lifts its brow to the skies shaped as it was a few centuries ago. The rocks are transmuted into palaces, and these again are reduced into dust. Seas and shores, waves and sands, are constantly changing places; fountains, and springs, and rivers, are drying up, and the sands of the desert are daily engulphing the majestic monuments of the mighty Pharaohs. The surface of the earth is vastly altered from the days of Noah to those of Napoleon. Deserts lie where gardens once bloomed; and gardens bloom where deserts once spread their gigantic sand-wastes. Were an old monk to rise from beneath the flagstones of some mediæval cathedral, and were he placed in the midst of this great city, and made acquainted with all that is going on on the surface of this little patch of the earth that we call Great Britain, he would suppose that he had been translated into another orb, and come in contact with a new, a strange, and an unexplained world. The fashion of the world physical passeth away.

The fashion of the world material, as far as man has altered it, is also passing away. Babylon, once the lady of the kingdoms, diademed and throned, the mistress of the ancient world, is now reduced to a mound of molten bricks, dissolving in the rains, or plundered by the inhabitants around it. Persia is but the shadow of what it was when its legions shook the world. Tyre is now a rock, on which a few poor fishermen bleach their nets. Jerusalem, once the joy of the whole earth, is discrowned and dethroned; and her inhabitants are exiles—a nation without a land to live in, families without a home; a people that have no rule, no laws; and yet preserved, till they return again to Palestine. Athens is the merest shadow of what that proud capital was in the days of Pericles. Rome retains but its name; and it shows the force of a name when that miserable place, sinking if not sunk, so awes the nations by its very word. Thebes, and Palmyra, have all disappeared; and gorgeous Nineveh lies in the grave from which a Layard digs it up stone by stone, and fragment by fragment. A mysterious curse, created by sin, not part and parcel of the original creation, wastes down and wears out all the workmanship of man's hands; and time rushes along a resistless stream; and floating down its bosom, like driftwood, are palaces and hovels; are sceptres, and scythes, and crowns; and every voice that we hear, and every scene that we witness, only authenticate and impress the solemn aphorism, "The fashion of this world passeth away."

The fashion of the world social also passes away. What family is there that cannot attest it; what parish, what village, what city in the empire, that cannot speak of the ebb and flow, and the mutation of the things that are about it? To-day a home rings with the music of glad voices; to-morrow it is hung with the drapery of sadness. To-day a bride is given to a rejoicing husband; to-morrow orphans are desolate and widows weep. To-day a babe is born; to-morrow a grey-haired patriarch, the support and pillar of the house, is carried to his grave. Year after year as we go along we perceive companions, friends, relatives, brethren, weary with the march of life, drop down and disappear. The house that knows us to-day will soon know us no more; the houses that knew many yesterday know them no more for ever. New ties are formed; old ties are dissolved; and the life of the most illustrious noble in the land is but as the vapour that appeareth for a little time, gilded for an hour by the golden beams of the setting sun; but like the vapour that is the symbol of the lowliest life, to be dissolved and to disappear, and to attest what all see, "The fashion of this world passeth away."

The fashion of the world political also passeth away. Theories that were once thought essential to the very existence of the nation are abjured or exploded; parties that held the reins and ruled the fierce democracy have passed away, and their names are almost forgotten. Statesmen revered yesterday as destiny, whose word echoed against thrones, and whose nod awed the multitudes that looked up to them, are derided, despised, and undervalued. Institutions once thought fixed as the everlasting hills are tottering to their ruin. Nor is the future of the political world bright. What a seething chaos is the wide world at this moment; what ominous shadows; some tokens of approaching disaster; some, like birds of ill omen, begin to emerge from every point of the horizon, and to darken with their outspread wings the European sky. What a testimony comes from parliament and palace, from counting-house and sanctuary, from homes, and families, and nations, to this simple, short, but pregnant sentiment, "The fashion of this world passeth away."

All around us bears witness to the fact that the fashion of it passeth away. On a random spark depends the existence of the noblest edifice in the realm! Whether the charred and blackened walls of Covent Garden Theatre were witness of great sins, I do not discuss; nor can I pronounce that the proprietors and the performers were sinners above all men. But we may gather from its former ashes the lesson that none of us may have gathered from its first glory; we may learn on its grave what we could not learn from its meridian pride; and there, the spectator may see an impressive illustration of the words, "The fashion of this world passeth away." What wealth was laid out in its decorations! what artistic genius in covering it with all the pomp and splendour of the age! Literally and truly we could apply the words of the seer when he said, "And now the voice of harpers and musicians, and of pipers and trumpets, shall be heard no more in thee at all; and the light of a candle shall shine no more in thee at all; and the voice of the bridegroom and the bride shall be heard no more in thee at all." The scene of the burning theatre, described a year or two ago in the usual channels of information, was most illustrative of the fashion of the world passing away. If ever it was true, it was emphatically there, that the flames seem to have conspired together, and seized simultaneously upon all that was fair, beautiful, and attractive; and literally comedy passed into tragedy, without an interlude between; and men who laughed, and mocked, and derided all solemn thoughts, felt themselves in an instant upon the very verge of the grave and eternity. The sleeper started from his sleep, scarcely persuaded to flee; the maskers rushing from their revelry, their dancing literally turned into mourning. Why do I refer to that theatre on fire? It was a rehearsal on a very microscopic scale of that last and solemn drama described in solemn terms by inspiration itself. "But the day of the Lord will come as a thief in the night, in which the heavens shall pass away with a great noise, and the elements shall melt with fervent heat; the earth also and all the things that are on it shall be burned up. Nevertheless, we according to His promise look for a new heaven and a new earth, wherein dwelleth righteousness." Or, as Paul expresses it, "To you who are troubled, rest with us; when the Lord Jesus shall be revealed from heaven with His mighty angels, in flaming fire taking vengeance on them that know not God, and that obey not the gospel of our Lord Jesus Christ." I fear in that last day, of which all the conflagrations that have ever occurred are the dim and poor types, many a sleeper will be found then, crying up to the last moment, "Peace, peace; all things continue as they were from the beginning;" forgetting that the day of the Lord will come, and in an instant the heavens and the earth shall be on fire. But blessed thought, that we can cherish even in that dread prospect, "Whosoever," even at the eleventh hour, "shall call upon the name of the Lord shall be saved." And at that day, too, when this world's fashion shall pass away, the elements shall melt with fervent heat, all the things that are therein shall be burned up, all those masks, for such they really are, which we call crowns, and coronets, and mitres, and wealth, and riches, and imperial circumstance, shall all be consumed. All those disguises which make wicked men look like godly men, and sinners seem saints, shall be torn off. And what a cry and how piercing, will that be that rises from the ruins of a burning world; when men learn for the first time that they have saved a thousand things, but forgotten to seek to save their immortal souls, now lost, irrecoverably lost, for ever and for ever lost.

What new fabric has risen upon the ashes of that which has been consumed, we now know; and we know that on the ashes of this burned earth shall rise an orb far more beautiful, far more glorious, which shall endure for ever. The bright mirror that was shattered in Paradise shall be recast—the glorious temple that was unroofed by sin shall be restored; and on its altar shall be rekindled more than its ancient glory. All space will then be holy; all days will then be Sabbaths; all faces gladness; all sounds praise; and its every hill shall be a joyous Gerizim, a mount of blessing; from which streams of benedictions shall pour down upon a happy and a holy world. Sin shall flee away like a shadow; sorrow's springs and deep fountains shall be dried up; the curse shall be removed, the incubus under which the world now groans; error shall be torn up by the roots; and this strayed and prodigal world of ours, restored to the sisterhood of stars that never fell, shall awaken in the wide universe a congratulation such as was never heard on earth; for the orbs and morning stars shall sing together then as they never sang at creation's birth; "Let us rejoice and be merry; for this our sister earth was lost, and is found; was dead, and is alive; it is meet that we should rejoice and be merry."

But whilst we look at the fashion of this world passing away, there are some things that remain far more important to us than the recollections of the things that have passed away. The fashion of the world passeth away, but God's word abideth for ever. This book remains; no flames can consume it, no winds quench its bright light; no opposition subvert its influence, arrest its march, or destroy its divine authority; it remains like the throne of Him who inspired it; a directory to the ignorant, a pharmacopeia to the sick, a tree of life in the midst of the earth, whose fruit is for food, and whose leaves are for the healing of the nations. The fashion of this world passeth away, but your soul and my soul remain. It had a beginning; it can never know an end. What a magnificent being is he who knows that before him there stretches out an endless, inexhaustible eternity. When the body is gathered to the grave, the soul, disentangled of all its bands and bonds and imprisonment, shall rise and appear just as it is at the judgment-seat of Christ But what a solemn thought is it that this soul has capacity for endless woe, as well as capacity for endless joy. The soul as it now is, is dead in sin, lost, ruined, guilty. You have nothing to do to destroy yourselves but be still; you have something to believe, to accept, to apply for, to lay hold of, in order to be saved,—Christ Jesus, and him crucified. Have you ever entertained this question? have you ever soberly reflected on it? "What shall it profit a man if he gain all the glories, all the honours, all the riches of the world, and lose his own soul?" Have you ever reflected upon your own state in the sight of God? In other words, have you regarded Christianity as truth, as addressed to you? have you felt the responsibility involved by hearing the Gospel preached? Have you ever passed from the evanescent to that which is indeed eternal; and felt, that there is nothing in this world of such moment to you, as that immortal, precious soul which was wrecked in Paradise, and was retrieved only by the cross and through the blood of Christ Jesus?

If the fashion of this world passeth away, blessed thought! the Saviour still remains. He offers you to-day, pardon for the greatest sin, peace to the greatest sinner. Salvation is not going to a church or a chapel, or a service; or joining a denomination, or giving something or doing something; that is man's way, or the priest's way; salvation is God's way; all heaven gratis to that poor guilty one who will only honour God by accepting it. What a grand truth is that, the price of heaven is a Saviour's blood; and there is no monopoly of it; no exclusion of the worst; there is no debarring of the oldest; to each and to all I can proclaim this day, and if, instead of being surrounded, as this church lately was, by the ashes of a burned playhouse, we were surrounded by the flames of a burned and dissolving world, I can say to you, to each one apart, "Believe thou in the Lord Jesus Christ, and thou shalt be saved." And in doing so, I only echo the words of Him whom I preach, when He says, "Him that cometh unto me, I will in no wise cast out." "Come unto me, all ye that are weary and heavy laden, and I will give you rest." "Look unto me, and be ye saved, all ye ends of the earth; for I am God, and beside me there is no Saviour."

If the fashion of the world passeth away, let us remember our opportunities and means of grace still remain. We know not what home is next to blaze, or what estate is next to perish; and if the home be preserved from the fire, and the estate be preserved from the Amalekites, remember the inhabitant may be taken from the home, the proprietor may be snatched from his estate: and whose shall these things be, is one question of value; but what shall my soul be? is a question of intenser moment still. But now, this very day, there is no sin that may not be forgiven; there is no sinner that may not be accepted. This very day salvation is freely offered. "To-day is the day of salvation; this is the accepted time; to-day if ye will hear his voice, harden not your hearts, as in the provocation."

Let the frantic mummer, rushing from the devouring flame that consumed the scene of idle, stupid, and foolish merriment, be to us a lesson; and let us learn to flee from the wrath to come. And when around us shall be a dissolving world, over our heads will be the opening brightness of a glorious home, where Christ is, and all that have preceded us to glory.

Let us rejoice to know that when all these things shall be dissolved, there remains a rest for the people of God, a house not made with hands; a city that hath foundations, whose builder and whose maker is God. And let us remember, that there is something that survives all wreck. The good we do never perishes. What a blessed thought is that! The good we do, though not merit but the evidence of grace, never, never perishes. At that hour that comes to all, and that may come to the youngest, the happiest, and the brightest heart that beats on earth, it will be a recollection of intenser joy to have given a cup of cold water to some thirsty sufferer than to have electrified a crowded playhouse by your acting, or entranced a mighty audience by the sweetness of your minstrelsy. At that day it will be a happier recollection to have added one stone or rafter to a ragged school, than to have rebuilt Covent Garden Theatre, or to have raised all the palaces of London. At that day it will be a thought that will give more real joy to you to have fed some hungry orphan, or given a garment to some poor and desolate widow, than to have composed a grander drama than Shakespeare ever wrote. I condemn not his writings; I can appreciate and admire what is beautiful in poetry, or what is expressive in eloquence; but we may depend upon it, when memory becomes, as drowning men have said, preternaturally susceptible and exciting, and when the whole scenes of a lifetime seem, like the shifting scenes of a drama, to rush in rapid succession before us, the amusement we have afforded will give little joy; but the good we have done, the blessings we have bequeathed, the widows we have made to sing for joy, and the orphans we have clothed, and the impulse we have been the humble instrument of giving to the cause of Christ, will awaken in our hearts reminiscences that, while in no sense merit, will yet mingle with the joys and be responded to by a welcome at the very gates of glory. "I was in prison, and ye visited me; I was hungry, and ye fed me; I was a stranger, and ye took me in; I was naked, and ye clothed me;" and another verse shall be added, "Inasmuch as ye did it to the least of these my brethren, ye did it unto me." "Come, ye blessed of my Father, inherit the kingdom prepared for you from the foundation of the world."

Use this world as not abusing it; in the beautiful words of the Apostle, "Let them that weep, be as though they wept not; and they that rejoice, as though they rejoiced not." Consecrate the world to divine ends; do not canonize it, and make it an idol to worship. The distinction is broad and palpable. You may consecrate your genius, your learning, your spare time, but you must canonize nothing. Everything you have should be made an anointed servant of Christ; nothing that the world contains is fit to be an idol or a god for the human heart to worship. Set your affections on things that are above; these are weighty; these endure for ever; these are beyond the tides and the transformations of time; these cheer and comfort the heart that looks upon them and dwells amongst them. Thus looking up and thus living, the lights of time will grow dim as the lights of eternity grow brighter; and the more you have your heart in heaven, the less it will be injured by the losses and the less it will be thrilled by the excitements of a world, the fashion of which passeth away. Carry into all life's duties a sense of God, a sense of true and living Christianity; and if you do so, the church will see you far oftener than the playhouse; the Bible will be read far more than the drama.

LECTURE XVI.

THE SLEEPING CHURCH.

"*They all slumbered and slept.*"—MATT. xxv. 5.

AFTER giving the prescription in the 24th chapter, "Therefore be ye also ready; for in such an hour as ye think not the Son of man cometh;" our Lord illustrates it by this most instructive parable. The portion of it which I select for special meditation is, "All of them slumbered and slept." Instead of watching—the duty enjoined in the previous chapter, and the duty which the parable is spoken to illustrate in this chapter—they all of them, mark you, Christian and unchristian, the foolish five and the wise five, slumbered and slept; five of them slept so soundly that they lost the glorious and golden opportunity, and the other five only awoke or were awakened with difficulty, and trimmed their lamps, and, according to the custom of eastern marriages, went out in the dark with their lamps burning, to accompany the bridegroom to the festal scenes which were on such occasions to take place. I will try here to illustrate the nature of the sleep which these virgins slept. It is sinful, perilous; and unless awakened from by some great interposition, it issues still in the sleep of death.

The Spirit not only enjoins watchfulness, but guards against sleeping. "Let us not sleep as do others; they that sleep sleep in the night." Constantly we are warned against sleeping, not with the eyelids, for that is nature; but with the heart, the conscience, the intellect, for that would be sin. There are three sorts of sleep spoken of in the Bible: there is the sleep which nature needs,—

"Tired nature's soft restorer, balmy sleep,"

which is natural and necessary. If many of our stirring men of business in the city slept a little more in that sense, and woke a little less, they would not be less healthy and prosperous on that account. There is another sleep which the Bible often speaks of; "They that sleep in Christ;" "Them that sleep in Christ will he bring with him." This refers to the dead dust that is laid aside in the grave, the wardrobe of the earth, folded like a robe which the wearer, the soul, has cast off, that disentangled it may ascend into heaven; watched over by the sleepless eye of Him that slumbereth not nor sleepeth, until the roll of the resurrection trumpet sends its vibrations through the homes of the living and the graves of the dead, and that mortal robe put on immortality, and that corruptible garment incorruptibility. There is, lastly, the sleep here spoken of; that sleep which is fraught with peril; that inner insensibility which ruined the five foolish virgins, and from the opiate power of which the five wise virgins were snatched as if by a miracle. Sleep, the figure employed, denotes the cessation from work. When a man is asleep, and sleeps soundly and sweetly, the whole body is at rest; but the mind is never at rest. If we could recollect in the morning the dreams of the night, we should find that while the body has been sleeping, the mind has been a thousand miles away, either on the ocean's bosom, or visiting bright scenes, or holding converse with near and dear, yet distant relatives. But the body does rest, at least certain organs of it. While man rests the loom stands still, the busy mill-wheel ceases to revolve upon its axis; as far as he, the sleeper, is concerned the fields may remain uncultivated, and all work be completely suspended. When Christians sleep—I mean in the third and sinful sense of the word—all missionary and aggressive energy has ceased, or is completely withdrawn; the minister sleeps in the pulpit, the hearer slumbers in the pew. Neither literally closes the eyes, but the mind is off upon the wings of the wind into dreamland; and while the hearer seems to be thoroughly awake, he is literally and truly asleep. As long as man is asleep in that moral sense in which the word is employed here he does no good, and he gets no good, and he cares for no good. When people sleep they cease to feel an interest, in so far as they do sleep, in the things that interest them day by day in this present world. When one falls asleep, the senses all retreat from the shores of the senses to which they rise, like the rising tides in early morn, and they shelter themselves in the caves, and bays, and quiet retreats of the inner man, that by this withdrawal they may look forth again upon the world freshened and strengthened, and fit for their work. But during sleep you have no interest in and take no part in that which occupies you during the day. A house may fall, fires may blaze in the next street, an earthquake may rock the building, and the floods may rise and overwhelm thousands; but you do not hear the crash, you do not see the advancing waters; you feel no interest in these things, because you are sound asleep. Whenever a Christian falls asleep, he takes no interest in those things that ought to stir the heart and absorb the energies of a Christian man. Souls may perish at his threshold; the ignorant may be unenlightened; the heathen may be unvisited; he cares as little for them as they care for him. Scenes may transpire across the very street in which he lives of moral dramatic interest that heaven and hell are agitated by; but he is sound asleep, and he feels no concern about the matter. Ever as you find a person who takes no interest in the spread of religion, who gives no guinea to a Bible Society, or Missionary Society, or to a Ragged School, or to a school of any sort, nor feels the least interest in the subject; if he be not a Christian, he is simply dead; but if he be a Christian, he is one of the five virgins that were wise in one sense, but suffered themselves to fall sound asleep when they ought to have watched. When one is asleep there is a cessation, so far as we can act, of personal safety. This is a beautiful provision of God, a most beneficent one; that just in proportion as you feel no interest in others in consequence of your being asleep, in the same proportion there is no guarantee of safety for yourself. When a man is asleep he is so unprotected that the assassin may approach him; fire may blaze in the rafters of his house; the earthquake may level his house to the ground; the sound sleeper enjoys his sleep as if he had impunity from fire, and flood, and earthquake, and lightning. Samson slept so sweetly that Delilah was enabled to cut off his hair; and with the loss of his hair was the departure of his strength. Sisera too slept so sweetly that a nail was driven into his temple, and he slept the sleep of death.

A Christian falling asleep, in the moral sense of that word, not only fails to take an interest in those subjects already referred to; he also lays himself open to Satan, who, like a ravenous lion, goes about seeking whom he may devour; or to evil passions, that, like serpents, twine round his heart and sting him to the quick; or he falls so sound asleep upon the pillow of a fancied security, that some great moral catastrophe ends his sleep in that sleep from which there is no awakening. The most useless life is the most defenceless state. In sleep there is also waste and decay. If a man were to sleep long enough, he would die of inanition. We do not eat and drink when we are asleep; we simply rest. Apply this to sleeping Christians, to the virgins that slept. They raise no cry for bread, "Evermore give us this living bread;" they have no sense of hunger; they utter no cry, "Give us this living water, that we may thirst no more;" they do not feel the need of a Bible, a Saviour, salvation; they are sound asleep, they feel no want, and they offer no prayer, and if they sleep long enough, it will end necessarily in the sleep of death. Such are the perils of spiritual sleep, as illustrated and suggested by the very expressive figure employed by our blessed Lord when he says these virgins slumbered and slept.

What is the cause of this moral or spiritual sleep? The first is either entertaining doctrines that are positively false, or turning to a wrong account doctrines that are in themselves true. For instance, if a man makes up his mind that it does not matter what one believes, of course he falls comfortably asleep; and feels no trouble at all about the subject of religion. If he believes that everybody will be saved—good, bad, and indifferent—of course he falls soundly asleep, and cares nothing about his soul. If, on the other hand, he holds true doctrines, but perverts them; for instance, if he believes in the doctrine of election, but makes it a sort of reason why he should care for nothing, and think about nothing, but be sure that if he is to be saved he will be saved, and if he is to be lost he will be lost; he feels no anxiety on the subject; he has got a view of election that enables him to fall asleep. Thus the belief of false doctrines, or the misapprehension of doctrines that are positively true, may lead to that sleep from which there is no awakening. A second cause of this sleepiness is taking too great and absorbing an interest in any of the pursuits or things of this world. Our danger lies less in crossing the line which forms the margin of forbidden things, and more in being absorbed altogether in things most lawful, but in their excess provocative of a sleep from which we may never be aroused. The things of the world, be it science, or literature, or music; be it any of those amusements, enjoyments, and employments which in themselves are intrinsically right, prosecuted to excess create this stupor in reference to religious things. Every one knows that there is something that he likes exceedingly; and that if he were to give license to his liking it would become a consuming and exclusive passion. Whatever one allows to dominate within, the danger is, that that will carry us away, and involve us in sleep, or stupor, in reference to eternal things. There is another reason: too much worldly prosperity. I really pity that man who is so rich that he has not to work, and so prosperous that all things seem to favour him, and no cross winds ever touch him; I pity him from the heart, for the inevitable tendency is to send him sound asleep in reference to God, a judgment-seat, and an eternity to come. Not only does outward prosperity cause this sleep, but even health has this tendency. Who are the most spiritually-minded men? Generally speaking, those who have had the greatest losses and crosses, whose estates have been taken from them, whose wealth has taken wings, who have drunk deep of the cup of sickness and suffering.

Let me mention some dissuasives from sleeping. You are redeemed with precious blood. How can a man cease to feel who accepts that grand fact, and feels its infinite value? Every picture of a Christian in the Bible is that of a racer. Will the racer win the race if he fall asleep on the course? Will the soldier gain the victory who falls asleep in the ranks? Is it possible that the wrestler will succeed, who becomes the victim of stupor and insensibility? Awake, says God, thou that sleepest, and Christ will give thee life. Another reason why you should not sleep is that which these virgins forgot, namely, "The Bridegroom cometh." Does a bride sleep when the bridegroom comes to meet her in the sanctuary? If Christians be, according to that beautiful figure, the bride, as they are, "The bride hath made herself ready;" and if Christ, the Bridegroom, comes from heaven; and the very figure, a bridegroom coming to his bride, should not occasion terror, but the very reverse; if then, "Behold the Bridegroom cometh," be the cry, if the signs of nature intimate it, if the convulsions of the nations foreshow it, if men's hearts failing them for fear of the things that are coming on all parts of the earth show it; surely, surely, the cry, "The Bridegroom cometh," is a reason why we should not only not sleep, but why we should be found where we should like him to find us. Some of you perhaps go to theatres. I do not here pronounce upon the subject. Is the theatre the place where you would like to meet death, or Christ the Bridegroom to find you? Were the Lord to come, would you like him to find you in the theatre, or in that I suppose sister institution the opera, admiring some accomplished *artiste*, fascinated by some grand music, charmed by some beautiful danseuse? Your presence may not be crime, it may not be sin; I do not here feel it necessary to pronounce. But somehow I fancy I should not like to be found in the theatre or in the opera-house when the Bridegroom comes. One day that Bridegroom will come; and if he do not come, death will come. If I were a member of parliament, I should be very willing to be found on my legs advocating the cause of my country and the good of human-kind; or if I were a tradesman, I should not fear to be found behind the counter selling the best goods at an honest price to every customer; if I were a sailor, I should be quite happy to be found fulfilling my duties on the deck; if a soldier on the field of battle, awful as that is;—each of these would be the post of duty. Wherever duty carries me, wherever I am engaged in a lawful exercise, or enjoyment if you will, there I should not object to be found when the Bridegroom cometh. But there are places—it may be my ignorance—it may be my peculiar taste—somehow where I must say I should not like to be found, when the cry, startling and impressive, shall ring from heaven and descend to earth, and open every grave, and summon the living and the dead before the great white throne, "Behold, the Bridegroom cometh."

LECTURE XVII.

READY.

In the prospect of the things coming on the earth the Redeemer says,

'*Be ye also ready; for in such an hour as ye think not the Son of man cometh.*"—MATTHEW xxiv. 44.

THE subject before us is the speed and suddenness of the Saviour's second advent. Why are men so reluctant to believe the possibility of the fulfilment of the words? "In such an hour as ye think not the Son of man cometh;" no one can say with absolute certainty when; but every one this day may be as he is commanded, "ready." Why do so many evade or ignore the Saviour's words? It is the excessive love of the world in their hearts. The heart of one is in his bank; the heart of another is in his home; a mother may make idols of her children; a merchant may make a god of his gold, a sanctuary of his bank, a bible of his cheque-book. Another heart is in the world's pleasures; in the opera, the play-house; and without discussing arguments, objections, and allegations, I ask, as in my previous lecture, would you like to die at the opera? would you like to be found there when Christ comes? I do not here condemn the one or the other; I leave the subject simply as a matter of feeling. Alas! all our hearts are imbedded too deeply in the world. The heart may be in the world of literature, or in politics, it may be in science, or in eating and drinking, in marrying and giving in marriage, in grinding at the mill or in labouring in the field; it matters not what the thing is, if it so absorbs our thoughts and so concentrates and fixes our sympathies that we cannot look intensely above, or look wistfully forward, or for one moment leave the thick atmosphere which we have chosen so ceaselessly and so excessively to breathe. The reason then why so many are not ready is just this; that they are absorbed in the world's thick clay, their hearts are weighed down by its pressure; and so much are they in it and of it that they send up no shooting thoughts to the sky; they have no room within for Christ, no time to spare for prayer, no moments in their closet they can consecrate to reading the sacred volume, and meditating upon the things that pertain to their everlasting peace; their whole inquiry in the morning is, "What shall I eat?" and their whole question in the evening is, "Where shall we get gain and spend next day?" They are so utterly taken up with the things of this world, that for all practical purposes it is the same to them as if there were no God, no such thing as an eternity, no judgment-seat, no Saviour soon to burst on the world with the speed and the splendour of a lightning-flash, and in an hour when men think not. Such cannot be said to be in any sense ready for the coming of our blessed Lord as admit the truth of all this, but procrastinate what they admit to be a duty from to-day till to-morrow. There are few who do not admit the importance of religion, and the duty of being ready for so startling an event as the coming of the Son of man; and they mean to be ready; but they wish first to settle this little law-suit, and to get over that difficulty about which he is so much troubled; and settle that other matter; or they want to have another month at the opera, or at the play-house; they wish to have a little more of the world, its enjoyments, its honours, its dignities; and then they mean to make ready for the coming of the Lord. All this is pure delusion. God's command is, "Be ye ready;" if obedience be duty, it lies in the present. All duties are in the present, never in the future. If it be duty, it is now your duty. But if God says, "Be ye ready to-day;" and you practically answer, "I mean to be ready to-morrow;" disguise it as you like, that is saying to God, I will not. But have you instances in the Bible that are at all encouraging in this your idea? Take the case of Felix; he put off a solemn duty to a convenient season; but there is no record that the convenient season ever came. By a law, and a most solemn and a grave law it is, he that procrastinates to-day will more easily procrastinate to-morrow; till standing on the very brink of the grave he will procrastinate and procrastinate still. "Be ye ready" belongs to "now, the accepted time;" and your adjourning the duty is simply refusing obedience to the commandment of God.

Let me make the subject plainer, by answering the question, first, what we are to be ready for, and secondly, why we are to be ready.

What are we then to be ready for? To be ready to leave all that is about us and all that belongs to us, however cherished, or deeply beloved, when Christ shall say from heaven, "Come up higher." I do not ask you to fling away your wealth, or to give up one innocent enjoyment; I do not ask you to leave your duties, or to renounce your business, or to go into a convent, or mechanically to separate from a world from which moral separation alone is a duty, but I do ask you to hold all the wealth that you have so loosely that you can without a very severe struggle let it go when the time comes for this action; and to hold all your nearest and dearest relationships upon earth so subordinate to the grand relationship, that eternity will perpetuate and seal what is in you when the Elder Brother comes, and you will be able to leave father, and mother, and sister, and brother, and home, and children, and to count them all but loss in comparison of the glory and the excellency of Him who cometh in an hour when men think not. In other words, it is to be ready to leave this world with all its cares, its troubles, and anxieties, for a better. Is there in this world very much to attract you? Have not some of its brightest spots in the past become disenchanted of much of their beauty by the loss of those whose presence made them so lovely? Is there a fireside that hath not a vacant chair? Is there a flock or family in which there is not one dead lamb? Can you take a retrospect of the past, and not see much that reminds you, this world neither is nor is fitted to be the rest of the people of God? Should we not, therefore, sit to it so loosely, and be mixed up with it so lightly, that when the message comes from the skies, borne by Him who comes in an hour when we expect Him not, "Come up here," you shall be ready, not reluctantly but gladly, to say, "Blessed Lord, we come, we come." But to be ready is more than this; it is also to be willing to be rid of many things that we now long to be rid of, of many things that now burden us, and that every Christian more or less feebly desires to be rid of. There is the burden of sin that weighs so heavy on the conscience; there is the burden of sorrow that lies like a cold shadow upon the heart; there is the burden of sickness that sinks many an aged or frail frame to the earth; there is the burden of appetites, desires, and passions, of which we are all more or less conscious; there is the burden of disquiet, discontent, dissatisfaction, and yearning for something better, brighter, nobler, than we have tasted yet. Are we not only ready to be rid of this, but do we now cry, "O Lamb of God, who takest away the sins of the world, take away its burdens also, we beseech thee." It is, also, to be ready to stand at the judgment-seat of Christ. It is not only to be ready to leave this world by having a loose and light hold of it; it is not only to be willing and anxious to be disburdened of much that crushes us to the earth; but it is also to be ready to stand at the judgment-seat of Christ. "We must all appear at the judgment-seat of Christ." Now how do you expect to appear? What will be your answer when you stand before the great white throne, and when you are asked why sentence of endless exile should not be pronounced upon you? Have you the answer in the depths of your heart, on your tongue and on your lips, ever ready to be uttered the instant it is inquired for, "He that knew no sin became sin for me, and bare its curse, and therefore I ought not to bear it; He stood in my stead, obeyed the law for me, fulfilled all righteousness, and deserved heaven as my Elder Brother; and therefore I am entitled to it." That answer is conclusive and complete; and were you the worst and the wickedest of criminals, if in the hour of death and at the day of judgment you can plead that glorious sacrifice, that perfect righteousness, let the hour be when you think not and where you think not, all is well with you; the bride hath made herself ready, you are prepared for the kingdom of heaven. Be ye then ready; as a ship is ready to set sail—her canvas in order, her tackling right, every sailor at his post—-ready as an eagle to stretch her wings and soar to her eyry; ready to depart like the venerable Simeon of old, having seen God's salvation.

What is the reason why we should be ready; what necessity is there for being ready? First, it is Christ's command; surely that is enough. What he commands is duty; instant duty; the highest and the most obligatory duty. If He had not given the reason, it is enough that He has given the command; and as Christians grow in grace the more simply they accept Christ's command, and the less they inquire the reason why. And He, in the next place, who commands us to be ready, is also competent to say what that readiness consists in. If, therefore, I am commanded to be ready, I open the book that contains the words of Him who commands me, in order to understand what that readiness is. It is not what we think, nor what the minister prescribes, nor what custom says; but what Christ has inspired in his own holy word. Here then is the explanation of it. "What must I do to be saved?" that is, "How shall I be ready?" The answer is, "Believe in the Lord Jesus Christ, and thou shalt be saved." "He that believeth on the Son of God hath life; he that believeth not shall not see life, but the wrath of God abideth on him." "This is life eternal; to know thee, the only true God, and Jesus Christ whom thou hast sent." This is readiness; it is to be found in Christ, not having our own righteousness, "but his." The whole system of the Gospel is a remedial economy. The church is not a home for the perfect, but a dispensary for the sick; the words of the Bible are not laws for the strong, but prescriptions for the feeble and the dying; and hence in the Bible we are oftener told how to be healed, and so made happy and healthy, than commanded to do this or do that, to avoid this or to avoid that. We are patients in a vast hospital—invalids, seeking to recover strength, in the sunshine and the sweet air of heaven. But let me add, He who thus commands us to be ready, and who has power to say wherein readiness consists, has promised to make us ready. "He works within us," we are told, "both to will and to do of his good pleasure." We are saved by grace. Salvation is not something we give to God, but something God gives to us; not something we do for Him, but something He has done for us. He creates within us the hunger that He satisfies, the thirst that He removes, the yearning that He answers; for He is the author first and the finisher next of our faith. One of the processes that He employs for making Christians meet for being transplanted from this world to the next, when the Saviour comes at the great transplanting hour, is affliction. The wind that shakes the oak and loosens its roots, when it is to be transplanted into a better soil and a balmier air, is a beneficent though a bitter one. The affliction that weans us from the world, that wins us to a better; the gap made to-day in our home and filled to-morrow with Christ, is meant to lead us to look and long for that blessed home in which there will be no gaps; every furnace in which we are placed detaches merely the alloy, that the fine gold may come out purer, and brighter, and more beautiful.

Let us try to answer briefly the question, why is it so important to be ready? We are going on an errand such as we never went on before; and what is that errand? It is to see the Son of God. We now see Him by faith; we shall then see Him as He is. And when He comes at that day, all the splendour of the lightning, all the brilliancy of the noonday sun, all the brightness of the stars, all the glory of the firmament, shall be merged in his brightness as rain-drops are lost in the ocean, as the glow-worm's light is obscured by the noonday sun. We shall see such a sight as we never saw before. If one prepares for the visit of an earthly sovereign, or makes ready to appear in her royal court, is it not reasonable that we should make ready for an interview the grandest, most solemn, and overwhelming that eye ever saw? It will be no trivial meeting, no gala day, no mere splendid procession; but an interview with Him whom having not seen we love, and in whom, though now we see Him not, yet believing we rejoice with joy unspeakable and full of glory. Such readiness will not interfere with the duties of this world. Did you ever meet with a man who could say honestly from the heart that his religion interfered with his duties to his sovereign, his master, or his home, his business, or his country? If a man ever said so, he either deceived you or he deceived himself; he who makes religion a pretext for neglecting the duties that he owes to his superiors is either a hypocrite or a fool. If a person were to tell me, I was bound to be at my house of business at such an hour, but I was so busy distributing tracts that I was two hours behind; I would at once tell him, The tracts you ought to leave to others to distribute who have the time to spare; you have no right to rob your employer of his time, under the plea and pretext of promoting the kingdom of God. Nothing upon earth, however sacred, can justify the violation of the plain and obvious duties that we owe as servants to masters, employed to those that are our employers; and therefore the deeper your Christian feeling, the more entire your readiness for heaven; and the more you have your heart where Christ is, you will not be the less dutiful, obedient and laborious, in the sphere in which God by his providence has placed you. On the contrary, men will say, Christianity makes the noblest servants of God, the most honest and industrious servants of man; and shows that it is a pure, an ennobling, and an elevating, and an inspiring power, not only for the world that is to come, but for the world that now is.

And at that day, clad in a Saviour's righteousness, washed in a Saviour's blood, resting on Him as your hope, anchored to Him as the great rest amid the storms and tempests of this present world; whenever He shall come, wherever He may find you; if you are what his grace can make you, ready, justified, adopted, sanctified, believing, hoping, loving, living; then, as you shall stand on the margin of the everlasting rest and at the gates of glory, not an angel will dare to exclude you, not a saint that has preceded you will dare to find fault, not an attribute of God will oppose you; on the contrary, all heaven will ring with the joyous shout, "Open the everlasting gates; let Christ, the King of glory, and these his attendants enter." And when some one shall ask, "Who are these that are clad in white robes, and whence came they?" the answer given will be, "These are they who have washed their robes and made them white in the blood of the Lamb; therefore are they before the throne of God, and serve Him day and night without ceasing."

LECTURE XVIII.

COME YE BLESSED.

Here is presented a scene of unparalleled magnificence and interest. The court is the universe; the sentenced are immortal men; Christ is the judge, and two eternities the issues.

" *When the Son of man shall come in his glory, and all the holy angels with him, then shall he sit upon the throne of his glory: and before him shall be gathered all nations: and he shall separate them one from another, as a shepherd divideth his sheep from the goats,*" *&c.*—MATTHEW XXV. 31–40.

THIS solemn scene is only the historic fulfilment of what is given as prophecy in the prophet Daniel; when he tells us in chapter vii. 13, "I saw in the night visions, and, behold, one like the Son of man came with the clouds of heaven, and came to the Ancient of days, and they brought him near before him. And there was given him dominion, and glory, and a kingdom, that all people, nations, and languages, should serve him: his dominion is an everlasting dominion, which shall not pass away, and his kingdom that which shall not be destroyed." This same Son of man, thus predicted by the prophet, thus proclaimed by the evangelist, is none else than He—oh, marvellous change—who sat upon the well of Jacob, and conversed with the woman of Samaria; who walked the streets of Jerusalem; who hung over it, and wept tears that were the awful premonitory tokens of its approaching doom; who was despised and rejected of men; who was emphatically a man of sorrows. What will the sceptic say, what will the philosopher feel, when He they despised, and mocked, and scorned, and scoffed at, shall appear the throned King, the arbiter of inexhaustible destinies; whose word shall fix for ever, an eternity of woe that flesh and blood will never exhaust, or a destiny of glory and of beauty which eye hath not seen, and man's heart hath not conceived.

When this great scene shall appear; this closing act of the stirring drama of time; when that last act in that dread drama shall arrive, we are often tempted to ask where will the scene of its manifestation be? It will be on that very earth, on which a cross stood, that a great white throne shall also be raised; and on that very place, in all probability, where the Saviour cried, in words so instinct with sympathy and compassion that after ages have not yet adequately entertained and felt them, "O, Jerusalem, Jerusalem, how often would I have gathered thee as a hen gathereth her chickens under her wings, and ye would not;" there, in all probability, where they mocked, and despised, and scorned Him, will He appear throned in majesty, cherubim and seraphim standing before Him ready to execute his behests. Pilate, at whose bar He stood, shall stand at that bar; and Scribe and Pharisee, that cried in scorn, "He saved others, and himself he cannot save," shall then see that the Saviour is now the Judge; and every eye shall see Him, and all the tribes of the earth shall mourn; and what an awful fact! thousands of millions will pray, shedding tears of blood, that the very rocks would crush them, and the everlasting hills would bury them, if only it would conceal them from the reality of what is the most awful expression in God's word, "the wrath of the Lamb."

There is added here, as if to fill up the grand picture, "All his holy angels shall be with him." What a magnificent scene will that be! Earth itself shall be the gigantic amphitheatre, tier rising above tier; each seeing, what none can escape, the spectacle of the Great Judge upon the great white throne. Before Him shall be angels innumerable, bowing like white statues in their stillness as they listen waiting to execute his least or his mightiest behests. And before Him shall be archangel and angel, ready to move east, west, north, south, as the great thought-bearers and missive-bearers of the Son of God. The angels, that chanted his birth over that lowly manger, shall be present in the glory of his second advent; the angels that ministered to Him in Gethsemane, when He sweated great drops of blood, shall be there to grace the pomp and splendour of his retinue: "mighty angels," in the words of Paul, "innumerable angels," in the words of John; in the Apocalypse, ten thousand times ten thousand and thousands of angels, admiring the magnificence of the scene; wondering, as they have done for eighteen hundred years, that one who is the King of glory should ever have been such a sufferer; and wondering still more that human nature could have ever in one instance been so sunk, so wicked, and so ruined, that it rejected and despised Him, and would have none of Him.

Another touch in this great picture is, "He shall sit upon the throne of his glory." Now He sits upon the throne of his grace; now the worst are welcome to Him (and here are the riches of the Gospel); there is no sin so heinous that there is no atoning blood equal to wash it all away; there is no sinner so old or inveterate in his wickedness that there is not for him this day complete and perfect forgiveness. This day He cries from a throne of grace, "Spare that barren fig-tree only for another year." But when He shall sit upon the throne of his glory all is changed. Then the awful words, scarcely felt when uttered from the pulpit, shall ring with piercing reverberations in the depths of every lost sinner's conscience, "The harvest is past, the summer is ended, and we are not saved; and there remaineth but a terrible looking for of judgment, and fiery indignation, which shall consume the enemy." At that day a lost spirit would give all that Australia contains for one hour of the privileges we now enjoy; grace is then merged in glory, probation is gone into judgment; and the throne of grace, to which all are welcome now, will be the throne of judgment to which many will be driven then. Oh, happy, happy are they who now love, believe in, and live to, and for Him, who is the Prince of the kings of the earth, the mighty Saviour, the perfect and precious sacrifice.

"And before him shall be gathered all nations." Some students and interpreters of prophecy, who take extreme and untenable views, think that the judgment here is only to be upon the heathen and the gentiles; and that the "all nations," that no doubt may be translated "all the gentiles," denotes only the heathen that never heard of Christ. They argue, how could a Christian say, "When saw we thee hungry? when saw we thee naked?" when every Christian is taught that what he does in Christ's name will be received as done to and for Christ himself? They think that those that are thus spoken to are heathen, that never heard the Gospel, but to whom in some way the grace of the Gospel has been applied. I dare not say so. At the same time, I never would assert that all the heathen will be lost. I feel that there is no salvation but in Christ, yet God may, by ways inscrutable to us, so reveal that name to many a heathen that he shall be saved in it, and by it, even when he has never heard it; but this is mere conjecture; our duty remains obligatory and plain, "Go, and preach the Gospel to every creature." It seems to me, that the "all nations" here does not mean the pagans, or even, exclusively, the gentiles. Refer back to the first commission, and what do we find? "Go, and teach all nations;" or, as another evangelist, Mark, gives it, "Go, and preach the Gospel to every creature;" or, as it is given by St. Luke, "That repentance, and remission of sins, should be preached in his name among all nations, beginning at Jerusalem;" showing here that Jerusalem is the first of the nations; and, therefore, that all nations which are gathered before the dread judgment tribunal does not mean exclusively gentiles, still less pagans; but the same "all nations" to whom He told them to preach the Gospel, the same "all nations," whose beginning was at Jerusalem; and, finally, the same "all nations" of whom he speaks in this very chapter, "This gospel of the kingdom shall be preached in all the world for a witness unto all nations, and then shall the end come."

I, therefore, take "all nations" to mean Jew and Gentile, converted and unconverted, civilized and savage. What a gathering will be there! what a sublime congregation shall be assembled there! the king and the beggar, the prince and the peasant, the rich and the poor; and not one of them able to carry to the judgment-seat aught save his responsibility and immortality. The robes of priests, the purple of kings, the wealth of the richest, the honours and dignities of the greatest, are such trash that they must all lay them down upon this side of the grave; and from the mightiest sovereign of the mightiest empire upon earth down to the meanest serf or subject in that empire, all shall appear, with nothing but the recollection of what they have done, the deep, and in many cases withering, sense of what they are; and in the hearts of many that awful looking for of judgment and foreboding of fiery indignation, which shall consume the adversary. That great trumpet voice shall be heard. Whether this be literal or not, we gather that some loud and piercing sound shall one still night, when men think not, break upon the agitated air; and the instant its reverberations ring through the homes of the living, and the habitations of the dead, the green turf will heave under some mysterious force beneath it; and marble monuments will crack; and the ocean itself will fling up its long sepulchred dead; and the Pharaohs will come forth from their stony pyramids, and great men, and celebrated men, from their resting-places in abbeys and cathedrals, under ancient brasses and monuments of bronze; and brushing off the last traces of the dark and solitary sepulchre, they will look up and see thousands startled by the terrible spectacle—Him whom they pierced, once crucified, crowned now the Lord and King of all.

When they shall gather round Him a mighty multitude, in that valley of decision, "He shall separate them one from another, as a shepherd divideth his sheep from the goats." One word, the word that made all those shining stars,—that mighty host in the sky, the mere sentinels and outposts of which we see upon the plains of infinitude—that made the earth, and clothed it with all its beauty; shall cleave like a sharp two-edged sword through the innumerable masses that are gathered round the white throne, and shall split the whole into one eternally separated twain; so that at that day there shall be seen, and felt to be, but two great groups; sinners by nature, and left so, rushing like an awful torrent into that sea of wrath which has no bottom, and no shore; and saints by grace, ascending to that panorama of beauty, and of glory, and of blessedness, which has no horizon and no end. On which side shall we be? I am not sketching a dramatic picture, or reading a piece of poetry from Milton's 'Paradise Lost,' I am telling, in the simplest and severest words, words that sink utterly beneath the vastness of the theme, that great and solemn ordeal through which we must pass. All distinctions of church, chapel, system, caste, colour, complexion, wealth, poverty, greatness, or meanness, are gone; and felt to be, what God grant we may see and feel them more to be now, fugitive, evanescent, superficial. There are only two questions of infinite moment; are we sinners, as Adam left us, or saints, as the second Adam has made us? If this question were unanswerable, I should shrink from stating it; if any were now not welcome, I should dread to speak of it; if hell were an inevitable necessity, I should scarcely refer to it; but when I know that the glory of the dispensation in which we are is this, that there is for all, without exception, an open heaven, and an eternal home, and a way to it; and that if any perish they perish suicides; when I state this, I can afford to speak of the state of the lost in terms not equal to, but approaching to the occasion; for it is our own fault, and our own fault only, if we perish. There is no decree, or curse, or predestination, crushing any man to hell against his will. If there were, I should pity but not blame; I should not trouble any with the terrible and inevitable prospect before it occurs.

But it is because there is instant forgiveness for every human being, if he will only accept of it, that I can talk of a heaven so beautiful, and speak of a ruin so terrible.

When this great division shall have taken place, Jesus will set His own upon His right hand; a shelter, a sequestered refuge, a sunny scene, into which no storm can penetrate, no flame rise, no avenger enter. To that blessed group upon his right He will say, "Come," "Come." This is the olden sound. "Come unto me, all ye that are weary." "Him that cometh unto me I will in no wise cast out." This is the olden sound that we heard in the chimes of Sabbath bells, in sermons, from the lips of missionaries, at communion tables, in the Bible; "Come unto me and I will give you rest." Now it is, "Come, ye sad;" then it will be, "Come, ye rejoicing." Now it is, "Come, ye poor;" then it will be, "Come, ye unspeakably rich." Now it is, "Come, ye soldiers of the cross, with the weapons of warfare in your hands;" then it will be, "Come, ye conquerors of Emmanuel, with palms of victory, the evidence that you have conquered." Now it is, "Come, ye martyrs from your beds of sufferings;" then it will be, "Come, ye martyrs, put on your coronation robes, make ready for the bridal of the Lamb. Now is honour, and glory, and salvation to our God and to his Christ." Come, ye Rachels weeping for your children, who will not be comforted; come, and weep no more. Come, ye sorrowful and mourning ones, whose nearest, and dearest, and best beloved have been struck down in India, or in the Crimea, by Delhi, or Sebastopol, and left on your home one dark shadow, a shadow the more terrible that it is not only on your fireside, but on your hearts. Come, and meet, and mingle with, and recognize—for recognition is as certain as immortality and responsibility—those seprated for a season, now to part with them no more. Come, Adam and Eve, from your graves beneath the shadow of the walls of Paradise; come, Abraham and Sarah, from your cave of burial under the oaks of Mamre. Come, Paul and Peter, from your resting-places, not where tradition has laid you, but where I have stored and kept your consecrated dust. Come, Knox, who never feared the face of clay; come, Luther, from your lonely grave in Wittemberg Cathedral; come, Melancthon, and Calvin also; come, all ye that have faithfully lived, however obscurely; and all ye that have died in Me, wheresoever, and in whatsoever state in reference to this world; come, Baxter, and Howe, and Ridley, and Latimer, and Cranmer; come, Chalmers, from thy resting-place in Edinburgh; and come, Edward Irving, your errors renounced, your sins forgiven, from beneath Glasgow's magnificent cathedral; come, and inherit the kingdom, the oldest and the youngest, prepared for you from the foundation of the world. When they come, what will they enter on? Not something untried, untasted, and unknown; it will be the perpetuation of what they have enjoyed upon earth; for what is the happy state of the saved? The culmination of a glory commenced in grace. What is heaven? The flower of grace. What is the happiness of the blessed? Happiness without mixture, or alloy of any sort or kind. There will be change of place, but not change of direction; they will receive in heaven not another, but a wider horizon. "Come;" that is, advance still; "he that is just, let him be just still." What is their character? "Come ye blessed of my Father." You may have been cursed by popes, cursed by councils, as all the great reformers were; you may have been cursed by the wicked, cursed by the ungodly; but what does that matter? The man that is blessed of

God can afford to smile at, and pity men that cuıse him. Did you not often think, ye blessed of my Father, that God had cursed you, or forgotten, or forsaken you? But what you thought cursings were simply disguised blessings; the afflictions that fell upon you almost like bolts from heaven no sooner touched you than they were transmuted into infinite and endless mercies. The cloud that casts its cold and its freezing shadow over your home broke into innumerable blessings. Those things that pained you when they touched your flesh no sooner approached the chancel of the soul, the immortal spirit, than they became the very soil on which character grew up, and ripened into happiness and heaven.

There is not a line of suffering visible upon your road that has not had parallel with it a line of glory, of happiness, and joy. When you thought you were cursed, you were really blessed; what you dreamt in your ignorance were calamities were the very credentials of the people of God; and if God had not so dealt with you, you had never been in that happy group to whom he speaks those thrilling words, "Come, ye blessed." Do you see a mother with an infant in her arms? The infant in its ignorance puts forth its hands to touch the flame of the candle, as if it were a bright and beautiful plaything. The mother draws back its hand, or puts away the candle; much to the child's disappointment, but much to the child's happiness and comfort. So God deals with children of a larger growth. We in our ignorance would seize the flaming thing that would burn to the quick; he in his compassion puts it away, and bids the heart be still; and what you know not now he tells you you shall know hereafter. Then, "Come, ye blessed of my Father." But for what? Oh, beautiful! oh, magnificent address, "Inherit!" If he had said, "Receive," it would have looked as if it were something new, as if it were a gift that has no connection with us, and we no connection with it. If he had said, "Come, and purchase," we should have found, like the virgins that slept, that we had neither oil nor money wherewith to purchase. But he says, "Inherit." A son inherits the titles and the property of his father, not because he is virtuous and good, but because he is the son. Inheritance is relationship, is birthright; and the very phrase, "Come, ye blessed of my Father, inherit," shows there is in us no desert, no right, no merit; it is because He made us sons by his grace, by regenerating us by his Spirit; "for to as many as received him, to them gave he power to become the sons of God; and he hath sent into our hearts the spirit of adoption, enabling us to say, Abba, Father;" showing us, therefore, that as the first chime in the church below is by grace, the anthem peal of the church above will still be by grace. Not one stone in paradise regained on which shall not be engraven that name which is above every name; not one gem that shall flash its light, and find a place in the diadem of the Prince of the kings of the earth that has not his name on it; not one flower that shall not have the Rose of Sharon for its perfume; not one song of which the key note, the harmony, the end, and the burden shall not be, "Unto him that loved us, and washed us from our sins in his own blood, be glory, and honour, and thanksgiving, and praise." Ye who are seeking to get to heaven by your good deeds are on the wrong road altogether; ye who are attempting to expiate your sins by your sufferings are pursuing a disastrously mistaken process. There is no way to heaven but one; and that way is the old beaten way, Christ the way, the truth, and the life. There is in the armies of our country, when encamped upon the field of battle, what is called the password; and if you had been in the Crimea, and moving where all was suspicion, and all was necessarily precaution, and knew not the password, you would either have been seized as a spy, or shot as an enemy. Christ's name is the password of the universe; the instant that you mention it angels and archangels will bow before the magnificent utterance, and all heaven shall bid the man right welcome who can say, "I know in whom I have believed; and that he is able to keep what I have committed to him against that day." But you are to inherit what? Some paltry spot, some little acre, some sequestered nook? No. "Inherit the kingdom." All the sacredness of priests shall be yours, and all the dignity of kings; yours shall be all the splendour of a throne without its cares; all the beauty of a diadem without the aches in the head that wears it; all the happiness, and more than the happiness ever dreamed of on earth, and none of the alloy that invariably mixes with the purest. When all the pomp and splendour of terrestrial kingdoms shall have passed away like a vision; when all the brightness of this world shall be quenched, that empire shall only begin its expanding progress, its never retreating march, its ever widening circle; your happiness and your horizon expanding with the years of eternity, till men marvel that in this world of ours sin ever had such a grasp as to dim the sheen, or dilute the splendour, or diminish the attraction of things divine, unseen, and eternal.

This kingdom, we are told, is "prepared for you." Prepared by whom? Here is the answer, "I go to prepare a place for you." Then every spot of it is prepared by the hand that was nailed to the cross for us; it shall not be a strange land, it will have a home-like aspect, a place where the Elder Brother has long been its preoccupant for us. And what gives it to many a truly home-like aspect is that some of you have your children there, mothers, sisters, and wives there, some the nearest and the dearest there, till this world is becoming the foreigner's land, and yon world is growing daily into all the beauty and the gentleness of a happy home; "a kingdom prepared for you from the foundation of the world." And oh! what a kingdom! Its soil ever fresh with flowers, the very stars in its canopy the scriptures of the sky; all sounds harmony, all sights light; the wide universe about you the temple whose builder and whose maker is God.

It is the rest that remaineth for the people of God, in which is the realization of their brightest hope, their grandest anticipation: the presence of God and of the Lamb.

Are you on your way to that kingdom? Have you the kingly spirit? Have you the priest-like character? Are you pleading the only password? Are you blessed of the Father with all spiritual blessings in heavenly places? How worthless is posthumous fame! When one reads of statesmen, and poets, and painters, all hoping that after they are dead they will be praised, what a miserable hope! It is like wishing to have loaves upon one's tombstone, when one sleeps in death beneath. But there is a posthumous renown that will indeed be noble—one word uttered from the lips of Jesus, "Come, ye blessed;" one "Inasmuch as ye did it unto one of the least of these my brethren, ye did it unto me," will sound sweeter than the shout of loyal millions.

There, are those everlasting gardens,
Where angels walk and seraphs are the wardens;
Where every flower, brought safe through death's dark portal,
Becomes immortal.

LECTURE XIX.

DEPART YE CURSED.

The other side of this picture presents a very awful scene

" *Then shall he say also unto them on the left hand, Depart from me, ye cursed, into everlasting fire, prepared for the devil and his angels: for I was an hungred, and ye gave me no meat: I was thirsty, and ye gave me no drink: I was a stranger, and ye took me not in: naked, and ye clothed me not: sick, and in prison, and ye visited me not. Then shall they also answer him, saying, Lord, when saw we thee an hungred, or athirst, or a stranger, or naked, or sick, or in prison, and did not minister unto thee? Then shall he answer them, saying, Verily I say unto you, Inasmuch as ye did it not to one of the least of these, ye did it not to me. And these shall go away into everlasting punishment: but the righteous into life eternal.*"—MATTHEW xxv. 41–46.

AFTER our Lord's address to those upon his right hand, "Come, ye blessed of my Father, inherit the kingdom prepared for you from the foundation of the world;" he turns round and addresses those upon his left, and pronounces the only awful curse recorded in the Gospel. Evidently at this point he lays aside the priestly office, leaves the altar and ascends the throne, and as King of the universe, He pronounces righteous and inexhaustible retributions. His own hear the olden voice, " Come, ye blessed," and continue that ceaseless approximation to the infinitely distant centre, each step a new ledge of happiness and joy; their happiness growing as the years of eternity accumulate. To those on his left He addresses words of which we cannot but speak with deep and awful solemnity; words desolating, withering, scathing, too terrible to be conceived,—too awful to be trifled with, "Depart, ye cursed;" an inexhaustible centrifugal impulse, ever retreating from the fountain of all light, and life, and joy, each step in the terrible descent aggravating their woe, and increasing their misery, and no step ever touching the bottom of that unsounded sea of sorrow. "Depart," and they depart for ever, and for ever, and for ever. In his presence is fulness of joy, and the redeemed are ever nearing and enjoying it; in his absence is fulness of misery, and the lost in hell are ever drinking of it; the guilty are ever seeking to be rid of recollection of God and themselves; the righteous ever thirsting for God, and eve gratified as they thirst, neither receiving a new direction for what is the condition of God's people now? Ever coming to Christ. What is the condition of those that are not Christ's people? Ever departing from Him. What is the great conflict of a worldly, thoughtless, ungodly man? To get rid of God. He says in all his employments and all his enjoyments, "Let not God's eye see me; let not God's presence be with me." It is one of the best tests we can apply to any work we are engaged in, " Could I bear God here?" That ledger that will not bear the inspection of God; that counting-house that will not endure the look of God; that transaction in business which you endeavour to hide or which you wish to hide from God; that deed, whatever it may be to flesh and blood, which will not bear the searching eye of God; all this is evidence of wrong. It may be the commencement of that worm that never dies, and of that fire that is never quenched.

The character of those thus addressed is "cursed." There is no condemnation to them that are in Christ. There is nothing but condemnation to them that are out of Christ. The law of old was, "Cursed is every one that continueth not in all things that are written in the law." To the curse of a broken law is added now the still more fearful curse of a rejected, or a neglected Gospel. But the contrast here is remarkable. When He speaks to the saved He says, "Ye blessed of my Father." When he speaks to the lost, He says, "Ye cursed," but not "of my Father." In the case of the one class their blessing is traced to its origin, God; in that of the other, the curse is a retribution on character provoked by themselves. All of good that begins on earth and culminates in glory is from God; all of pain, of sin, of tears of sorrow, and of suffering, that are experienced on earth and aggravated in hell are not from God. In life's sunny places I see my Father; in life's dark and dreary places I see my sin. Ever as I gaze on storm, earthquake, tribulation, bereavements, losses, and crosses, I see the evidences of what sin has done; but ever as I gaze upon what is beautiful, and bright, and happy, and holy, I see pervading all, giving tone, colouring, and shape to all, the loving kindness and the grace of our Father. The curse is from sin; the blessing is entirely from God. This distinction runs through the whole of the New Testament Scripture. In the epistle to the Romans we have a very remarkable illustration of it, "What if God, willing to show his wrath, and to make his power known, endured with much long suffering the vessels of wrath fitted to destruction;" "vessels of wrath fitted to destruction;" but it is not said by whom. He adds in the next verse, "And that he might make known the riches of his glory on the vessels of mercy, which he had afore prepared unto glory." God is the author and the origin. If one reads the Bible not in the light of creed, or confession of faith, or of Calvin, or Arminius, but in the light of itself only, he will see that all that is good is directly from God; all that is evil is entirely and exclusively from the creature; and whilst the glory of all that is good redounds to God, the discredit and the dishonour of all that is evil rest with, and upon the creature, and nowhere else. There is contrast, not only between "blessed of my Father," and "cursed," but also between "inherit a kingdom," and "depart into fire." The two contrasting points are "a kingdom" and "fire;" the one the glorious receptacle of the blessed; the other, sin its fuel, sinners its sufferers, eternity its inexhaustible length; the lake of fire prepared for the devil and his angels. There is also contrast in "a kingdom prepared *for you*," and "everlasting fire," (prepared not for you, but) "prepared for the devil and his angels." In other words, God made not hell for any human being; it was never meant for an immortal soul, it was never kindled by Deity for the torture of any one of his creatures; and if any lost spirit finds itself in hell, it sees it has forced itself into a doom which God never meant for it. It is hell prepared for fallen angels that kept not their first estate; for whom no atoning blood was shed, for whom no Saviour died; prepared for them because they were never to be redeemed, and not for man, who, awful recollection in the realms of the lost, will feel the fire that is never quenched, the worm that never dies, to be this most corroding recollection, God's decree did not damn me; predestination did not damn me; God's word did not damn me; I am a suicide self slain here, because I would not go elsewhere. I can conceive no thought more terrible than to know that we have rushed in a direction the very opposite of what was opened to us; rushed against remonstrances, against providential warnings, against the calls of God's word, against the solemn testimony of his Gospel, and have perished. The lost in hell will ever say, ever feel, "We did it all ourselves, and nobody did it for us;" the saved in glory will ever feel and ever sing, "We earned none of it; grace did it all, from the first pulse of the new heart on earth, to the first beat of the new heart in glory."

The awful record is added as the fulfilment of the curse, "These shall go away into everlasting punishment." What a dead march will that be; what an awful funeral procession will start on its downward career from that great white throne; what a wail and *miserere* from myriads! I wonder if the saved will witness it. One cannot help thinking that in such a case, as they behold the awful spectacle, tears will be shed by the redeemed, as they touch the margin of the better land.

It is so awful that any one of God's creatures should have been so infatuated, so criminally opposed to the blessed Gospel, should have so rejected, despised, and neglected it, that they have prepared for themselves so dreadful, so terrible a doom. Is this awful doom a reality? It is. Are souls lost? The answer of Scripture is, they are. Is there such a thing as departure into everlasting hell? The answer is, "These *shall* go away." In the words of Robert Hall, "What, if it were possible to conceive such a thing,—what will be the funeral obsequies of a lost soul? Would it be sufficient to cover the heavens with crape, or to clothe the earth with mourning? or were the whole of nature to become animate and vocal, would it be possible for her to utter a groan too deep, or a cry too piercing to express the magnitude of such a catastrophe?" And in the still more impressive words of one mightier than Robert Hall, "What shall it profit a man if he gain the whole world, and lose his own soul?"

The sorrow of the lost will be something beyond all that we can conceive. We need not a material fire to make the sufferings of the lost terrible enough. All have felt incidentally the sense of remorse; it is one of the most excruciating feelings that the human heart can be pierced by. Conceive that feeling intensified to an infinite degree; conceive that remorse to be not only for what you have done, but for what you have lost, neglected, despised, and trodden under foot. Conceive the society all around you to be intensely and unspeakably polluted and evil; conceive all the vile passions of the corrupt and diseased human heart, crawling out like scorpions from their nests in all directions; conceive over all the thick gloom of an impenetrable curse; memory raking out of its embers every past wickedness, and as its leaves are turned over in the light of that lurid flame, revealing what conscience ever moans and grieves over and rebukes. Add to the awful tragedy no hope for ever and for ever of any deliverance; and I need not material fire to constitute a torture which it is best to be silent on, for human words but mock, and human sensibilities shrink when they attempt to depict and to delineate it. This leads me, therefore, to the last subject—the duration of such curse, or the eternity of future retribution, denied in the most emphatic terms by some most able and argumentative writers; it is this: the horror of the prospect has appeared to flesh and blood so intensely awful that they have tried to escape from the terrible foreboding, by showing that the tortures of the lost are not only mitigated by hope, but are transient in their nature, and eventually must terminate. In other words, just as some preachers try to frighten people into heaven by depicting the terrors of hell, which is not the Gospel; these preachers are leading people into ruin by showing that hell is not so terrible after all; and that if you have, they would say, the misfortune to stumble into it in your search after a holier and a happier place, you need not be alarmed; the hour of deliverance from it will soon be at hand. Now, it seems to me, if these preachers would only show that the road to heaven is so plain that a wayfaring man cannot err therein; that the gates of glory are so wide open that all, and thousands upon thousands more, may enter; that every voice from heaven and every cry upon earth bids you welcome; and that your ruin can be created by none in heaven, and in hell, and on earth, but by yourself; if that be true, surely it is the profitable way to show how easy it is to get to heaven, and how impossible it is for any man to be lost who lays hold with all his heart upon Christ, the hope set before him. But to show that the theory advanced by these men is false, I refer you to Scripture itself. I feel no pleasure in showing it; my wish is to believe that the torments of the lost are not eternal; that hell is not so terrible; for I must say, it is the one difficulty I have encountered in studying this holy book, that there should be one spot in God's magnificent universe where tears will be ceaselessly shed, where the wild and the piercing wail of sorrow will rise disturbing the harmony of songs that are perpetual; and where there shall be ceaseless sinning, and therefore ceaseless suffering. I say, that is just the thought that has always struck me as the most difficult; and my wish would be to prove that our interpretation is not correct.

But I am a Protestant; the Bible is my rule of faith; what I wish, what flesh and blood would like, or what is most sentimental, or what is most delightful, are not the determining elements of my creed; "to the law and to the testimony," I must bow before that oracle. "Thus saith the Lord" settles all difficulties and substantiates all truth. Throughout the whole New Testament two distinct states are constantly referred to. "Many shall come from the east and west, and shall sit down with Abraham, and Isaac, and Jacob, in the kingdom of heaven. But the children of the kingdom shall be cast out into outer darkness: there shall be weeping and gnashing of teeth." I read in another passage, "The Son of man shall send forth his angels, and they shall gather out of his kingdom all things that offend, and them which do iniquity; and shall cast them into a furnace of fire: there shall be wailing and gnashing of teeth." I read again, "Enter thou into the joy of thy Lord; but cast the unprofitable servant into outer darkness." Similar to these words are, "Come, ye blessed;" and "Depart, ye cursed." These two states constantly come out together; the time that measures the duration of the one invariably determines the duration of the other. If "everlasting," as applied to the punishment of the lost, means a limited period, I cannot see how you can escape the logical inference, that "everlasting," as applied to the case of the blessed, must be limited also; the same word—nothing less and nothing more—is attached to the one that is attached to the other; and you cannot pour cooling and refreshing floods into the midst of the lost without emptying that glorious fountain from which the saved in heaven shall drink ever-refreshing streams. If there be a limit in the duration of the penalty of the lost, I cannot see how you can come to the conclusion that there is no limit to the duration of the happiness of the blessed. The same phraseology, the same adjective, the same strong and expressive words, are applied. If possible, words of yet greater emphasis, denoting, if possible, intenser duration, are applied to the sufferings of the lost, than to the happiness of the blessed. "Everlasting contempt;" "everlasting punishment;" "everlasting destruction from the presence of the Lord;" "eternal damnation;" "eternal fire;" "the blackness of darkness for ever;" "the smoke of their torment ascendeth up for ever and ever;" "unto ages of ages of ages." The argument of those that take the opposite view is, that the word "everlasting" is used occasionally in a limited sense. I answer, it is. But be it observed, it is modified by the subject to which it is applied. We read of "the everlasting hills;" that is the hills that last as long as the earth itself lasts: they are not to be moved. But I take even that application in its strict and literal sense, holding, as I do, that the earth is never to be annihilated, but to be one of the most beautiful orbs amid all the stars and constellations of the universe; and that its hills and valleys shall never be destroyed, or cease to be. The word "everlasting," as applied, for instance, to the Mosaic covenant, is used in a limited sense, but does that prove that it must always be used in a limited sense? If so, then "the everlasting God" must mean a God that does not live for ever. If we find that "everlasting" is employed in nine cases out of ten in its strict sense, and that incidentally and by a figure it is employed in a limited sense,—we do well, I think, to use it and understand it as the spirit of God does, and not to make the universal bow to the incidental, but the incidental rather yield to the universal. But it has been thought by others that the souls of the lost are to be annihilated; and that ceaseless suffering is not to be the conscious experience of any sentient and immortal being. One might almost wish that in such cases this could be so; but will the words warrant it? What is the opposite of everlasting life? The answer is "Everlasting," not cessation of, "punishment." But punishment implies consciousness of the infliction. And besides, "everlasting life" in Scripture does not mean simply an everlasting being, or the perpetuation of the present life; but it means life on a loftier level, a higher, nobler, better state of existence. The correlative of everlasting being would be everlasting annihilation; but the proper correlative of everlasting happiness is not annihilation, but everlasting punishment. The phrase, we allege, "everlasting punishment," denotes conscious, sentient feeling, and not cessation to be; or what some allege, the annihilation of the soul, if capable of annihilation, altogether.

But the argument employed by Professor Maurice and others is, that this is inconsistent with the goodness of God; that such punishment is inconsistent with the goodness of God. In the first place, we must recollect that God is not the Lucretian deity, all love, all goodness; but that he is holy, just, faithful, true; and if the escape from such suffering should be incompatible with his justice, it is in vain to plead that such punishment conflicts with his goodness. We do not know what may be incompatible with God's goodness. In this land, the highest goodness is exhibited by the sovereign, when a great criminal is visited with condign punishment; and it may be an essential display of the highest goodness of Deity that those who have rejected so great a Saviour should be the recipients of so inexhaustible a curse. It has been argued again that this everlasting punishment is contrary to the justice of God, in so far they say, as it is unjust to inflict an everlasting punishment for an incidental and a temporary evil. Does our experience justify or contradict this? Do we not find in society, that one false step taken at twenty, will project a shadow over a life that extends to eighty? Do we not find in the providential government of God, that one sin committed—it might be in thoughtlessness—casts a destructive and a ruinous influence over all the years of your life that follow? If it be unjust to inflict enduring punishment upon a whole lifetime of sin, and therefore it may militate against the justice of God, it must be unjust to let a whole lifetime in this world suffer because of one incidental offence against the law of God. But may it not be that there is in sin something that we have never fathomed, and do not yet know? If nothing short of the blood of incarnate God could expiate sin, must there not be in sin a virus that we never can estimate, an intensity of evil of which we have no adequate conception? Judging of the demerit of sin by the stupendous interposition that was necessary to deliver from it, there may be in sin that immensity of evil that needs an eternity of suffering: not for its expiation, for that is impossible, but to express the just and terrible retribution that necessarily belongs to so great an evil. Others have argued in another way: is there not a hope in the rolling epochs of eternity to come, that the glorious Gospel will be proclaimed, even in the regions of the damned; and that one word, "Come," will be heard there, after centuries have rolled away, and sufferings adequate to the offence, as they suppose, have been endured? There is no intimation in the whole Bible that any covenant rainbow shall spread itself upon the concave that hangs over the lost; there is not one whisper from Genesis to Revelation that the angel of the everlasting Gospel, on his flight of mercy and beneficence, shall ever preach to the damned one hope of mercy, one prospect of forgiveness. If the Gospel will be preached to the lost, what mean these words: "My Spirit will not strive with man any more?" What mean these words; "I must work the work of him that sent me: the night cometh when no man can work?" What mean these words: "What thy hand findeth to do, do it with all thy might: for there is no work nor device in the grave, whither thou art hasting?" What do the words imply, "He that shall blaspheme against the Holy Ghost hath never forgiveness?" What is the meaning of "He that despised Moses' law died under two or three witnesses. Of how much sorer punishment, suppose ye, shall he be thought worthy who hath trodden under foot the Son of God, and counted the blood of the covenant, wherewith he was sanctified, an unholy thing?" "We are in them that perish," says the apostle, "the savour of death." "If the righteous scarcely be saved, where shall the sinner and the ungodly appear?" In fact, if a lost spirit can be saved by the Gospel from hell, then what would follow? That the Gospel must be preached with greater power, grace must be bestowed in greater richness, on the lost in hell, than ever was exhibited to those that were candidates for heaven in the church upon earth.

But it has been said by others, that all suffering must necessarily exhaust itself; and that therefore the sufferings of the lost must come to an end. The illustration they would suggest is this :—a person commits a crime; he is imprisoned, or banished for seven years; if he spend the seven years in exile, he has suffered the penalty, and he goes free. But suppose during the seven years he has committed worse crimes: then another seven years will be added; the law requiring that ever as he sins, or commits crime, ever will the punishment strike. It is so of necessity with the lost. They are ever suffering, because they are ever sinning. Sin is cumulative in its nature, suffering cumulative, as the consequence of that sin. I can see no hint that the Gospel will be preached to the lost; that annihilation will end the sorrows and the agonies of the condemned. I can discover no hint that suffering is expiatory in any sense. If any sufferings could expiate sin, the Son of God had not died a sacrifice for our sins upon the cross. If the sufferings of a creature would have been accepted as the expiation of the creature's sins, God's truth is concerned in this, for he has said, "The soul that sins shall die:" but the soul that sins does not die for ever, and God thus proves unfaithful to his threats; my confidence in his promises is shaken, and I cannot be sure that the soul that believes shall live for ever and ever. Unless, "Depart, ye cursed, into everlasting fire," be a literal reality, I cannot see how, "Come, ye blessed, inherit the kingdom prepared for you," is a literal reality. If the first be a myth, an exaggerated and alarming shout, the second can be nothing else; you cannot do away with the certainty of a penal hell without sweeping away with it the prospect of a paternal heaven; the same words that describe the one, changing what ought to be changed, describe the other. I must therefore conclude, that as heaven is an everlasting kingdom, hell is an everlasting fire; as the one shall have no end, and endure no admission of sin, or sorrow, or tears; the other wil. experience no end, and taste no admission of happiness, hope, joy, or peace.

O tremendous scene! A splendid palace sinking into the consuming flame; a magnificent ship full sail sinking in the all-devouring sea; the noblest cathedral struck by the lightnings of heaven, and shivered into splinters; a whole city engulphed by an earthquake; are feeble, feeble, feeblo illustrations of that last terrible catastrophe which ends the reign of sin upon earth, and commences the sufferings of them that have rejected the only Saviour. But while I state this, because God's word says it, let me again remind all, hell is not for you; you cannot be driven there, you may go there; you cannot be impelled there against your wish, you go there willingly. What are you now living in? Are you doing every day in your counting house, on the Exchange, in Parliament, in your families, in the world, in society, in the sanctuary, what your conscience tells you is inexcusably criminal? You are paving your road to ruin. Are you every day hesitating about the acceptance of that Saviour as the only sacrifice for your sins, and trusting to something else? You are on the downward course. But if you can say from the heart, My whole trust for a judgment-seat is nothing I have done, nothing I have suffered, nothing I have said; but only what Christ has suffered for me, and done for me; and if you can say that with thousands of drawbacks, with the memory of many thoughts I would unthink, many deeds I would undo, many words I would recall; with much in my nature and experience every day that is sinful, and wrong; yet I can say from the very heart, that my struggles and efforts are against all that is evil, and my prayers are daily offered that the Spirit of

God would make me conquer over all; and my conclusion every night is this, my trust—"the blood of Jesus Christ cleanseth from all sin; then fear not, you are on the road to heaven; angels will welcome you; Christ gives you eternal life; and He that has begun in your hearts the least work of grace, oh magnificent hope! will not leave you till he has consummated it in the mightiest and most lasting work of glory.

LECTURE XX.

THE GLORY-FILLED EARTH.

The son of Jesse breathed his last prayer in these glorious words,—

"*Let the whole earth be filled with his glory. Amen and Amen.*"—Psalm lxxii. 19.

This is the prayer of David, the son of Jesse, in which he prays that the whole earth,—no village, hamlet, capital, country, continent, or island excluded, or exempt,—may be filled with the glory of God—a glory that involves in its bosom the highest happiness and the most lasting pleasures to all.

Once this prayer was an impossibility. Adam could not have prayed in Paradise, "Let the whole earth be filled with thy glory;" for he must have praised his Maker that the whole earth already was filled with his glory; he saw it lying like a soft and shining atmosphere over all space; every bush in that beautiful Eden burning like Horeb's bush; every mountain glowing with the splendours without the transience of Mount Tabor; and in all whispers of the wind—in all chimes of the waves—in all murmuring of brooks—and in the voice of God at early morn and dewy eve he heard the most delicious music. On every acre and on every footpath of that beautiful and sequestered spot he recognized the footprints and the trail of the glory of his God and Father as he passed by. He praised him that the earth was filled with his glory; he could not pray that that might be which was already come. But since that day—I appeal to the hearts that falter in their beating, to the eye, the ear, and all the senses, to the annals of nations, to the history of the world—a great deterioriation has passed upon our earth; deep shadows are now mingled with its brightest sun-streaks; and the lingering and flickering bits of sunshine alone remain to remind us what a beautiful Paradise has passed away; yet presenting tokens and prophecies also that a yet more beautiful Paradise is one day to dawn. In our present experience there is scarce a line of glory upon our world that a line of suffering or a shadow of sorrow does not run parallel with.

Yet, fallen as our world is, one can see traces of what it once was. An architect visiting Jerusalem guessed from the fragment of an arch what must have been the measure of its span, and the resting-place of its piers. From seeing the fragments of this ruined world, we may form a rude conjecture what a magnificent thing it once was; and even in its darkest places one can notice many things that prove if it hath fallen it is not utterly forsaken. Are there not some days in the loveliest summers that seem rays of glory just come forth from the gates of Paradise, to give us a transient glimpse of a faded glory? Even in the deepest winters the laurel, and the bay tree, and the holly, and the group of evergreens, seem to say, "We will not yield as others have; we will keep the path open between the summer that has left us and the summer that is to come, thus ministering to man's heart hope in the deepest depth of nature's decay; and with other vestiges leaving on the bosom of our world memorials that if fallen it is not altogether forsaken. But the mere natural glory that breaks upon our world in fragments is shaded by the departure of that moral glory which once overspread the whole heaven and earth as with the very presence of God. If in Adam's day all was harmony without, it was only responsive to a deeper harmony within. If man saw all the tokens of perfect peace above, around, and beneath, he appreciated and felt the peace the more because of the perfect repose and quiet that was within. But since the fall, these sombre shadows have covered up not only the outer glory, but they have also projected themselves into the very heart of man; and in his inmost soul he feels that more has gone wrong with it than even with the world outside. He needs to pray, whether he looks within or without, with intenser fervour, O Lord, let the departed glory return; let Ichabod be erased from the surface of our globe; let the days of Eden come round again; let the tide of sin and sorrow ebb, and let the whole earth be covered with the glory of God. But do we not read in the Psalms even in this dispensation, and in the world as it is, "The heavens declare the glory of God, and the firmament showeth forth his handiwork?" If then the heavens declare the glory of God, is it so shaded as has been alleged? Few, indeed, can study the heavens without seeing a glorious apocalypse of God's glory; no one can read the last discoveries of astronomy without being struck with the evidence of the magnificence of that Being who sits enthroned amid the shining hosts that are encamped on the plains of infinitude. Were we to see a starry frosty night once in our life, it would be an apocalypse such as we should never forget. It is the commonness of the spectacle that dims its beauty, or rather deadens our sense of it. But if it be so beautiful now what must it have been ere that mist between us and the sky had exhaled from earth! If while we see nature through a glass darkly there be so much to admire, what must have been the splendour of the spectacle when we saw it face to face! It is, however, necessary to explain what is the glory of God. A human or finite being receives glory when something is added to him that he had not; an infinite being receives glory just in the ratio in which He is made known. The more we know of man the more we detect the evidences of the fall, and the less we admire him; the more we know of God, the intenser is our admiration. To glorify a creature we must add to him dignities that he has not; to glorify Deity we have simply to make known more of what He actually is. If you wish to see God's glory, or rather to read a record of it, let us refer to that passage where Moses prays, "I beseech thee, O Lord, show me thy glory." What was the answer? The Lord descended in the cloud, and proclaimed the name, which he there regards as synonymous with the glory of God. "The Lord, the Lord God, merciful and gracious, long-suffering, abundant in goodness and truth, keeping mercy for thousands, forgiving iniquity, transgression, and sin." That is the glory of God.

In this revelation of God's glory there is an answer to every doubt and difficulty of a perplexed sinner. Does some one say, I am poor, guilty, and ruined, and have nothing of good in me, and am myself nothing in God's sight? His name is the Lord Jehovah, who can create a good thing out of a bad thing, and anything out of nothing; and, therefore, is able to transform the greatest sinner into the greatest saint. But if you should answer, My heart is so hard, my feelings, appetites, and passions, so deranged, that I have no hope whatever; his name is the Lord God, the omnipotent God; nothing is too hard for Omnipotence to achieve. But you say I am a sinner, a miserable sinner; sinner in thought, sinner in word, sinner in deed. I answer, you only want to see another ray of this bright glory pass before you to give you peace; for if you be a sinner, what is the next beam of his glory? He is merciful. What is mercy? If there were no sin there could be no mercy. Mercy is love through the prism of a Saviour's mediation refracted into all the beautiful colours of the covenant rainbow. God is good to angels, He is love to the unfallen, He is mercy to sinners. And therefore, if you be a sinner, a chief sinner, an inveterate sinner, let a ray of glory shoot through your heart; and you have a God who is mercy—the very thing you need. Ah, you reply, that is very true; but that does not comfort my soul. I have nothing to give for it, and, therefore, there is no hope for me. What is the next ray of his glory? He is gracious. What is grace? Literally good given gratis. What was the prayer of John Wickliffe, the morning star of the Reformation? "Good Lord, save me gratis." God saves only gratis. If you were to pay anything, there is no mercy for you; if you promise anything by way of equivalent, there is no mercy for you; if you offer to endure anything as expiation, there is no mercy for you. You must take mercy in all its amplitude, without promise, pledge, or anything on your part but grace, just as God gives it you. But you answer, This may be all very true; but I have sinned so long, I have sinned against light, against conscience, against law, against love. If I had been your judge, you had been crushed long ago; if the most tender-hearted man had been your judge, you would have been destroyed; but let a ray of this glory sweep through your troubled spirit, and what does it show? That whilst He is merciful and gracious He is also long-suffering. How glorious is this attribute! He suffers long, and is not easily provoked; delighting in mercy. But if you should say, Ah, this is very true, very comforting; but it does not meet all my case; for so many have drawn upon his mercy, so many have got it gratis, such multitudes have tasted of his long-suffering, that I fear it is exhausted long ago. If God were a cistern, his mercy would have been exhausted; but we are told He is a fountain, and a living fountain, inexhaustible, and springing up to everlasting life for ever and ever. But the ray of his glory that meets your case is that while He is long-suffering, He is also abundant in goodness and truth. But if you should say, So many generations have drawn upon Him, from the world's gray fathers that trod the deserts of Palestine and the pavements of Egypt; the prophets, and evangelists, and apostles, and martyrs, and reformers, and the long procession of sufferers, have all, generation after generation, drawn upon his goodness, drank of his mercy, sought it gratis, and enjoyed it in all its fulness, that I fear it is impossible that God can have supplied so long a world of rebels so countless, and all his mercy is surely dried up long, long ago. The answer is, He keeps mercy for thousands of generations. But you add, perhaps, Well, all this is very delightful; but I have been guilty of sins of thought, sins of word, sins of deed, all kinds and degrees of sin. I have no doubt of it; and I am sure you are far more guilty than you think, and far more so than you feel; but here is another ray of God's glory; He forgives iniquity; that is the first sort of sin; transgression, that is the second sort; and sin, that is the third sort. In other words, He forgives sins of thought, sins of word, sins of deed.

What then is the prayer of David? That this glory may overflow the world like an illuminated ocean; that wherever the sunshine penetrates, God's glory may penetrate also; till every star that you see in the firmament suggests the bright and the morning star; till every rose that you smell the fragrance of reminds you of the Rose of Sharon; till every stream reminds you of the river of living water, and every tree reminds you of the tree of life; and all sounds, and all sights, and all scenes, set forth the glory of Him whose highest glory is exhibited when He stoops from Heaven to forgive the greatest sin, and thus the experience of a few will become the possession of all mankind. Such, then, are the component parts of that which is here called the glory of God.

Now let us ascertain why David prayed thus; and why we too should offer up this prayer. First of all he thus prayed what we are bound to pray also, because there are countless places in our world on which this rich glory does not shine. Are there not pagan tribes that never heard of a Saviour's name? Are there not jungles in India into which neither nature's sunshine nor the glory of the Sun of Righteousness have ever penetrated? Are there not deserts whose bosoms have never been trodden by the feet of them that bring glad tidings of great joy? Is there not many an ocean on which the mariner, as he wrestles with the wind and the wave, sings no hymn, prays no prayer, reads no Bible; nor sees in the ocean one single gleam of the glory of God? If so, is it not our duty, is it not our instinct, to pray, "O Lord, let the whole earth be filled with thy glory?" But there are not only places which have not been visited by this glory, but there are places that resist it when it seeks admission. The crescent still protests against the cross; and the Mahometan looks upon the steady approach of the glory spoken of as a bitter national calamity. In China, the stupid and degraded superstition of Confucius has raised its formidable walls to throw back the influx of the light and glory of God. In India, the inveterate superstitions of a thousand years resist and oppose the entrance of the glory of God. And not only in these countries do we find resisting forces, but in Russia we see all the superstition of Rome without its terrible consistency; in Italy and Austria, the fogs that rise from the marshes of a dark and miserable apostasy. But, alas! we need not go abroad for proofs of great crime, or dark places; read the judicial proceedings of our country; come with me not across the ocean, but across the partition or brick wall that separates St. Giles from St. James; and you will find people from whose hearts and homes everything like the light and love of God seems to have ebbed away, and to have left nothing but wreck and ruin, capable of terrible mischief; and incapable, without transforming grace, of doing any good.

Let me tell you too that those magnificent palatial residences in the west are never safe when revolution and discontent are brewing in the miserable dens of the east. Let me remind you that when the foundation rocks, the apex of the pyramid will be very precarious indeed. And if you wish to do the utmost to make your own condition more secure, you will do more to make the masses more enlightened, more contented; more acquainted with the glory, more impressed with a sense of the goodness, the mercy, and the loving-kindness of God. If you feel the great degradation in which thousands are plunged; if you agree with me in conclusions which facts, the most stern and irresistible of all arguments, establish—that vast masses, in every British city, are the victims of the most withering and blasting influences in this world, and aliens and strangers to the bright hopes and blessed prospect of the Gospel of Christ; if you feel that God has blessed you, that he has given you light and the knowledge of your duty as well as the enjoyment of rich privileges—you will not rest satisfied till the whole earth is filled with the glory of God.

When David prays that God's glory may thus cover the earth, he prays that every individual may feel and taste of its influence, that no heart may beat that is not in unison with God; that every pulse in human nature from the humblest even to the highest, may be love to God; that every district may be covered with this glory—that there may be no lane, nor court, nor alley, into which the sunshine of heaven does not penetrate, and none into which the light of the Sun of Righteousness does not shine. No interest that we feel in the distant must make us overlook the near; we must not carry corn to the ends of the earth, whilst many are starving from want at our own doors and upon our own thresholds; we must not be so taken up with the romance of a converted world, that we forget the very plain but very dutiful necessity of a converted individual under the shadow of our own residence. Whilst we pray for each individual, and for each district of our country, we at the same time still pray that the whole earth may be covered with the glory of God, that every continent may bask in it—that every capital may reflect it from its spires, that the hum of great cities may have it for its key-note; that all the nations of the earth, inspired by love, illuminated by truth, may constitute together, one worshipping, united, and happy church; until the nations rise to a state of peace, of happiness, and rest, that will multiply with the multiplying years and ages yet to roll; and David shall no longer say, "Let the whole earth be filled with his glory;" but shall sing, "The whole earth is filled with thy glory."

There are many and strong reasons why we ought more and more to pray this prayer. The first reason is sympathy with man simply as a sufferer; if you want to be humane, and to do the slightest good to man as an individual, you pray and try to practise this prayer. The highest happiness of man is involved in the greatest glory of God. Christianity feeds the roots of all social development. Where is it that nations have reached a culminating grandeur? Where Christianity has struck deepest its roots. And, therefore, when you pray that the whole earth may be filled with God's glory, you pray that there may be the most substantial temporal happiness to your fellows; and that our country under the influence of the Gospel may, as a country, rise to its greatest pitch of happiness, peace, and enjoyment. But you pray this prayer still more because of the preciousness of each individual soul. After all, this is the great argument for trying to do good. To make man happy and contented here is right; but to show him a way that leads to a better world when this world departs, and to show him that his soul, which had a beginning, but never can have an end, depends for its happiness upon the blood of sprinkling, and its interest in the sacrifice of Jesus; to teach man that, and to tell him how he can be saved; and to go to the beds of the sick and the pillows of the dying, and to tell them that there is a God, our Father, and that he may be happy here and happier hereafter; I say, the man that does so is entitled to your greatest sympathy, and the cause in which he is employed to most munificent and liberal support. We pray this prayer because we believe that the Gospel, which is the glory of God, is adapted to every order of the human race, to every want, and every necessity; that there is nothing in it local, nothing exclusive, nothing national; but that to the people in the purlieus of St. Giles's, and to the people on the plains of India, the same Gospel may be carried with the same results, because embosomed in the same sure promise: "My word shall not return to me void." And we pray this prayer specially, because it is God's own promise that it shall be fulfilled. He himself says to Moses, "As I live, saith the Lord, the whole earth shall be filled with the glory of the Lord;" and David, recollecting God's promise, which is the guarantee of the successful prayer, says, "Let the whole earth be filled with God's glory."

David beautifully adds, "The prayers of David are ended." When are they ended? When the whole earth is filled with God's glory. And what then shall be our case? At present we say with stammering lips and hesitating hearts, "Our Father which art in heaven, hallowed be thy name; thy kingdom come; thy will be done;" all having the under-thought that God's kingdom is not come, that God's will is not done. But in that day, when the prayers of David the son of Jesse shall be ended, we shall no more pray the Lord's prayer as we do now; then we shall say, "Our Father which art in heaven, hallowed is thy name; thy kingdom is come; thy will is done in earth as it is in heaven; our bread is given us, and our sins are forgiven us; we are led into no temptation, we are delivered from all evil; and as it began in thy name, Father, it will end with thy name, Father, again; for thine is the kingdom, and the power, and the glory, for ever and ever. Amen."

END OF THE FIRST SERIES.